# THE FLYING COW

## EXPLORING THE PSYCHIC
## WORLD OF BRAZIL

*By the same author*

If This Be Magic
The Indefinite Boundary
The Cycles of Heaven (with Scott Hill)
This House is Haunted
The Geller Effect (with Uri Geller)
A Question of Memory (with David Berglas)
The Haunted Pub Guide
The Evil Eye
MindForce
Twin Telepathy
New Clothes for Old Souls
Chico Xavier: Medium of the Century

# THE FLYING COW

## EXPLORING THE PSYCHIC
## WORLD OF BRAZIL

Guy Lyon Playfair

The Flying Cow

Second edition,
revised and enlarged

Exploring the Psychic World of Brazil

Published and printed in the United States of America and the United Kingdom by
White Crow Books; an imprint of White Crow Productions Ltd.

For information, contact White Crow Books at
P. O. Box 1013
Guildford
GU1 9EJ
United Kingdom
or e-mail info@whitecrowbooks.com.

Cover Designed by Butterflyeffect
Interior production by essentialworks.co.uk
Interior design by Perseus Design

Paperback ISBN 978-1-907661-94-5
eBook ISBN 978-1-907661-95-2

Non Fiction / Body, Mind & Spirit / Parapsychology

www.whitecrowbooks.com

*To Hernani Guimarães Andrade*

*1913 - 2003*

# Contents

# INTRODUCTION

THE telephone rang in my São Paulo apartment one day in 1974. The caller told me she had just arrived in Brazil and had been given my number by a friend of a friend. She was interested, she said, in psychic phenomena.

'What can I do for you?' I asked. I had a deadline to meet for a long and boring commercial translation job.

'I'd like to see a materialization,' she replied. 'Tonight, if possible.'

'So would I,' I said. 'But the last one I heard about was ten years ago and 350 miles away, and was probably faked.'

'Oh. Perhaps a psychic operation, then? You know, those people who do operations with their bare hands ...'

I knew. But the only psychic surgeon I could recommend in São Paulo was on holiday.

'Well, maybe just a levitation or something?' the eager voice went on. 'Or one of those poltergeists?' I began to feel like the manager of a toyshop that has suddenly run out of toys. I excused myself, gave my caller some other phone numbers to try, and went back to my translation. I needed the money to finance my own researches into all these things, which I had been doing since my arrival in São Paulo the previous year.

Would this have happened anywhere else but in Brazil? Is there any major city in the world where a visitor would expect to come across examples of almost every known type of psychic phenomenon within minutes of stepping off a jet? I doubt it.

For Brazil is surely the world's Most Psychic Nation as well as one of the largest. (Fifth in both area and population). Imagine a country stretching from Edinburgh to the Sahara desert and from Lisbon to Istanbul with a population fast approaching 200 million, according to its 2010 census. In a land of such a size, strange things are bound to happen and so they do, being generally accepted as normal rather than 'paranormal'. Almost anything is possible. Brazilians like to tell the story of the man who comes home one day and tells his wife he has just seen a cow flying across the road. Her immediate reaction is not to question his sanity, but merely to ask : '*Ah, é?* (oh, really?) What colour was it?'

So it was hardly surprising for Brazil to be visited by another TV crew, solitary reporter or just curious tourist looking for some of the action they had heard about from friends of friends or read about in the books of such experts in the stranger side-effects of Brazilian Spiritism as Pedro McGregor, David St. Clair, Isa Gray, John G. Fuller and Anne Dooley.[1]

What was surprising is that so little else had been written about psychic phenomena in Brazil and the Spiritist context in which many of them tend to occur. It should be an ideal country for research, for there seem to be too many phenomena and too few researchers. Indeed, until more than half way through the twentieth century, there were almost no serious researchers at all in this field. The first Brazilian to make a sustained attempt to study his country's psychic scene on a scientific basis, and to collect a vast amount of first-hand evidence for it, was Hernani Guimarães Andrade, an engineer and senior civil servant in the São Paulo state government who in 1963 founded the *Instituto Brasileiro de Pesquisas Psicobiofísicas* (Brazilian Institute for Psychobiophysical Research, or IBPP) of which a good deal more anon.

Perhaps I should first explain what had led my caller to think I might be able to provide some psychic entertainment on demand. What had I done to get such a reputation? Let me sketch in some background.

I arrived in Rio de Janeiro in 1961 as an English teacher hired by the British Council, although I had no experience of teaching English or indeed anything else. After a couple of years I was offered an extension of my contract, a passage home, or the price of a passage home. So luckily I took the money and stayed, determined to do what I really wanted to do, which was write. I started in the traditional way on the local paper, the Brazil Herald, then moved up to Brazilian Business, the monthly journal of the American Chamber of Commerce for Brazil, also managing to do some moonlighting for Time, the Associated Press, The Economist, and several other outlets for my (hopefully) emerging talent.

I then spent four years working full time in the press department of the U.S. Agency for International Development (USAID). For seven or eight years I was able to earn my living and generally enjoy myself. Then, in 1971, the press office at USAID was abolished and I became redundant. By then, my Portuguese was good enough to do translations and interpreting at news conferences, and before long I was doing very nicely as a freelance. I seemed set for a comfortable life in Rio.

All this time I had never taken more than a passing interest in stories I occasionally heard about flying saucers (and flying cows), psychic surgeons and so on. I had been quite impressed by a ceremony I had attended in which a young woman was initiated into one of the many Afro-Brazilian cults, but somehow I never explored the subject any further.

Then one day in 1972, Larry Carr dropped in for a chat. He was a Hollywood actor who had come to Rio to make a film some eight years previously and decided to stay on. I had met him while doing some script translation for the film, and was intrigued by his accounts of the local Spiritist scene, which he had clearly taken the trouble to study at first hand, and had even become a member of a Spiritist group headed by Pedro McGregor, which I also joined more out of curiosity than any kind of religious conviction.

So when Larry asked me if I would like to meet a psychic surgeon, I thought 'why not?', and in Part 2 I describe what I saw when I did meet him. It was after that meeting, and my visits to Pedro's group, that I felt all this psychic stuff should at least be investigated. If it was all illusory, if not totally false, it might at least make a fun story, perhaps a background 'mailer' for the Associated Press.

Before long I was satisfied, as I will describe, that it was not all illusion or fakery. I read everything I could find on psychical research in Brazil, which did not take very long, and I soon came to the conclusion that there were more things going on around me than were dreamt of in Horatio's philosophy, or anybody else's. I needed some first-hand evidence, though, and I asked Pedro if he knew of anybody in Brazil who was doing the kind of work that was done in Britain by the Society for Psychical Research.

Yes, Pedro said, there was a man in São Paulo named Andrade who was doing this, and thought I ought to meet him. He didn't have an address for him, though, and I had no idea how to contact someone with a fairly common surname in a city of several million people. Then I happened to pick up a book in a bookshop and saw his name on the back cover as 'editorial consultant'. So, I thought, the publisher must know how to get in touch with him.

On an impulse, I hopped on a bus, and as I rolled along the 250-mile motorway to São Paulo that USAID had helped to build, the idea slipped into my head that I was going to move there. Arriving early one Monday morning, I headed at once for the publishing house, where a friendly secretary promptly put through a call to Andrade's office, and told him that a British writer from Rio would like to meet him.

Half an hour later, I was in his office, and an hour later I left feeling that we were old friends. Hernani said I would be welcome to work with his institute, the IBPP. He could not offer me any payment, since he financed the institute out of his modest salary as a civil servant, but I would be free to write about anything I might find in his files. It was an offer I could not possibly refuse, and I accepted it without hesitation.

But I still had to earn a living somehow. So leaving Hernani's office with the promise that I would be back, I got in touch with a translation agency a friend in Rio had mentioned to me. The owner was glad to see me, as he was getting more orders than he could handle, and promised me plenty of work at rates far higher than I had been getting in Rio. Then I looked up an old friend from my teaching days who now had his own language school, and offered me a spare bed in his basement while I looked for a flat to rent. So in one day I had been offered a well-paid job, a place to stay, and a chance to do research with the IBPP. That was the day my life changed.

Now for a word on the Spiritist background with which most of the contents of this book are connected in some way or other. The words Spiritist or Spiritualist may conjure up visions of funny old ladies peering at crystal balls, communing with Native American guides, and talking a lot of trivial rubbish.

The position in Brazil is somewhat different. There are at least three major Brazilian religious cults in which belief in spirits and their active participation in our earth lives is implicit. I am mainly concerned here with the largest of these, which is known as Kardecism, or Christian Spiritism according to its codifier, the Frenchman who wrote under the pseudonym Allan Kardec (1804-69).

Spiritism, which has been well entrenched in Brazil since the end of the nineteenth century, is not quite the same as Spiritualism. A Spiritualist according to Kardec, 'believes that there is in him something more than matter,' whereas a Spiritist accepts communication with the spirits of the departed on a regular basis. A Spiritist is automatically a Spiritualist, but the reverse may not be true. Many Spiritualists of Kardec's time did not believe in reincarnation, for instance. This is a fundamental corner-stone of Spiritism, and Kardec was one of the first to popularize the concept of it in Europe while his follower Gabriel Delanne (1857-1926) was the first to collect evidence for it.

Spiritism, as presented in Kardec's *The Spirits' Book* (1857) is a science and a philosophy as well as a religion. It is the only religion that can claim to be based on scientifically demonstrated and repeatable facts rather than on unverifiable traditions, occult revelations or subjective mysticism. Kardec was no mystic or pagan, but a stolid and rather pompous schoolmaster who was educated in Switzerland. He insisted that he did not invent or found Spiritism himself; his books contain instructions purportedly dictated by to him the spirits themselves via a couple of Parisian mediums, and Kardec refused either personal credit or payment for them. His role was merely that of 'codifier'.

He defined the purpose of Spiritism as follows: 'To make a coherent whole of what has hitherto been scattered; to explain, in clear and precise terms, what has hitherto been wrapped up in the language of allegory; to eliminate the products of superstition and ignorance from human belief, leaving only what is real and actual.' [2]

It was intended to complement and complete existing religions rather than replace them, and Spiritists fully accept Kardec's view that the faith he codified was no more than Christianity restored to what it was at the time of its founding - a dynamic and militant creed unencumbered by priests, dogmas and inquisitions; a practical way of life aiming to help us evolve towards our ultimate destiny of pure spirit and communion with the source of all creation.

However, Brazilian Spiritists are very much concerned with the here and now. Their welfare activities are out of all proportion to their official numbers. They build, staff and run huge hospitals, orphanages, asylums and job-training centres that are among the finest in the country. At one time it was officially estimated that Spiritists ran no less than 36% of all social-assistance establishments in Brazil, though since 1962 the annual government census has not listed social work by religions.

The other two major Brazilian cults that are based on acceptance of the spirit world and regular communication with it are Umbanda and Candomblé. The former is a wholly Brazilian blend of traditional African practices with certain superficial features of the Roman Catholic Church, while the latter is a purely African cult brought over by slaves and faithfully preserved, especially in the city of Salvador in the state of Bahia. Each of these is sometimes mistaken for *macumba*, a word with no generally accepted definition normally used to denote black magic, for which the correct word is *quimbanda*.

Tourists and journalists are usually welcome at Candomblé or Umbanda meetings, and these colourful cults have received far more attention outside Brazil than the less spectacular Kardecist meetings, which are usually held in simple unadorned rooms in rented buildings or private homes. It is not true to suggest that Brazil is one vast voodoo arena, with exotic rites at every street corner and African drumming filling the tropical nights along with the smell of incense. Nor is it true (as has been suggested to me by non-Brazilians) that assorted Spiritist beliefs are merely a hangover from the country's backward colonial past, confined to rural regions and fast dying out in the big cities.

Take São Paulo. This is the largest industrial centre in South America, where well over half of Brazil's gross national product is generated. It is a city largely made by immigrants, and a family with a German, Italian, Japanese or Lebanese surname is to be found on every block. Yet no less than one quarter of all Spiritists recorded in a recent government census come from either the state or the city of São Paulo, and the faster the city grows (it is said to be the fastest-growing in the world) the stronger the Spiritist movement seems to become.

The São Paulo State Spiritist Federation (FEESP) was founded in 1939 by a group headed by a colonel in the military police. Its impressive headquarters is a large eight-storey building a few blocks from the city's main banking district. It was built entirely by voluntary and unpaid labour using donated materials and is staffed by 200 unpaid volunteers, providing free assistance to a daily average of more than 1,000 people. Like Rio de Janeiro's gigantic Tupyara Spiritist centre, it must be one of the largest mass psychotherapy clinics in the world. It has a whole roomful of files of patients who have been cured of what non-Spiritists might call psychological or psychosomatic disorders.

The Federation also runs the Casa Transitória, a complex of buildings also put up by volunteer labour on a 50,000-square metre piece of former swampland on the outskirts of São Paulo. It specializes in assistance to members of needy families, and offers boys and girls from the slum areas training in a number of skills and trades. Over the years it has helped hundreds of thousands, perhaps millions.

Another impressive example of Spiritism in action is the Casa André Luiz in Guarulhos, a few miles from São Paulo, where 1,400 retarded children are cared for with love and devotion they would be unlikely to find elsewhere. 'We haven't got a welfare state like you have in England,' a Brazilian Spiritist told me once. 'So we have to provide one as best we can.'

'What kind of people are the Spiritists?' a visitor once asked me. He seemed to think that they must all be slightly peculiar, if not actually mad.

'They're just like anyone else,' I replied. 'Only perhaps slightly better, on the whole.' I mentioned a few names of prominent Spiritists I had met in São Paulo.

There was José Freitas Nobre, a lawyer and federal deputy for the opposition MDB party, who polled the second largest number of votes in his state in the 1974 elections. In the same year he launched the *Fôlha Espirita*, one of several hundred Brazilian periodicals devoted to the propagation of Spiritism.

There was Rafael A. Ranieri, a former city mayor and senior police officer who was elected state deputy for São Paulo. We shall hear more of his extra-mural activities later.

There was Jarbas Marinho, a successful civil engineer who specialised in supermarket construction, and who would dash weekly from his drawing board to give classes in magnetic healing at the Federation, for which he did much of the structural engineering work - for free, of course. He was also a council member of the IBPP, and a regular delegate to international parapsychology congresses.

There was Elsie Dubugras, a retired airline company employee who became Brazil's most active Spiritist journalist. As editor of the popular monthly *Planeta*, she was still working until shortly before her death at the age of one hundred.

There were so many Spiritist doctors in São Paulo that they had their own association, whose members offered their patients spiritual guidance and healing along with conventional treatment, only charging a fee for the latter.

Other Spiritists I knew in São Paulo included psychologists, psychiatrists, teachers, government officials, in fact members of just about any walk of life. I was interested to discover that many of them became

Spiritists because of personal experience of what they considered evidence for the existence of a non-physical world, agreeing with Kardec that 'phenomena which are inexplicable by any known laws are occurring all over the world, and revealing the action of a free and intelligent will as their cause.'

As I was soon to find out, they were certainly occurring in Brazil, and this book is about some of them.

The first edition of The Flying Cow was published in 1975, followed a year later by The Indefinite Boundary. For this edition I have combined the two, omitting material that did not relate to my own experiences and adding some new cases that were investigated by my IBPP colleagues after I had left Brazil and returned to England. I have also omitted material that has now been published separately: my account of the career of Brazil's best known medium Francisco Candido ('Chico') Xavier, and three of the best cases from the IBPP files. [3,4]

Although Chico deserves, and now has, a book to himself, no survey of the Brazilian psychic scene can be considered complete without mention of this remarkable medium who, on his death in 2002 at the age of 91 was described by no less than President Fernando Henrique Cardoso, as 'a great spiritual leader who touched the hearts of all Brazilians, who over the years have learned to respect his deep commitment to the well-being of his neighbours.' In 2010 the Brazilian post office issued a special stamp to mark the centenary of his birth, and two million cinemagoers paid to see the feature film based on his life, entitled simply *Chico Xavier*, within a month of its release. He had, in short, become a national hero who had even been nominated for a Nobel Peace Prize, no mean feat for the barely educated son of a lottery ticket seller who had dropped out of school at fourteen and done various menial jobs before obtaining regular employment with the Ministry of Agriculture, where he stayed until his retirement in 1961. How had he done it?

The answer is simple – he was a medium, and an exceptionally gifted one. While still in his teens, he began to write poems, which he always insisted were not his own work but were dictated to him by some of the best known Brazilian and Portuguese poets. He became an overnight literary sensation in 1932 with the publication of a selection of these in *Parnaso de Além-Túmulo* (Parnassus from Beyond the Grave), and over the next seven decades went on to produce a total of more than 450 books, all of them by 'spirit authors'. They included novels, both contemporary and historical, stories for children, a history of Brazil, works on Spiritist doctrine, a couple of scientific treatises and a steady flow of poems. With sales nearing the 50 million mark in his lifetime, Chico could have been a rich man. Yet he never accepted payment for anything he wrote, donating all his royalties to an estimated two thousand charitable projects and living on his modest government pension.

He also brought comfort to many who had lost loved ones prematurely in the form of messages allegedly from the deceased, who would give not only their full names and those of their relatives, but detailed accounts of their cause of death and assurances that they had survived it. One such message became legal history, when a statement from the victim of an accidental shooting was accepted as evidence in court and led to the acquittal of the accused. A follow-up survey of forty-five such communications revealed that they contained not a single statement that was untrue.

When Chico died, some 120,000 people filed past his coffin, and the governor of his home state of Minas Gerais declared three days of mourning. He was indeed a medium like no other.

In Part One I describe three cases from the past involving three very different mediums: Francisco Lins Peixoto ('Peixotinho'), Carlos Mirabelli and Otília Diogo who between them provide evidence that ranges from the probably genuine to the almost certainly fraudulent.

Part Two deals with the controversial subject of 'psychic surgery', that is, operations performed by people with no medical qualifications at all in conditions that would make any conventional surgeon shudder.

Part Three is mainly concerned with the most colourful of all psi phenomena, poltergeists, and with cases suggestive of reincarnation, both of which Brazil seems to get more than its fair share of.

'Tell me, thou unknown power...' Macbeth ordered, when he found himself mixed up in an interesting case involving precognition, materialisation and a few other inexplicable phenomena.

'Seek to know no more,' the witches told him.

I am glad I decided not to take their advice.

# ACKNOWLEDGEMENTS

I am most grateful for the help given me, in some form or other, by:

Joaquim Alves, Commandant Edgard Armond, John Baines, Theodore Besterman, Newton Boechat, Larry Carr, Michael Collins, Eric J. Dingwall, Elsie Dubugras, Fenelon Alves Feitosa, John G. Fuller, Dr Ary Lex, Pedro McGregor, Dr José Hortencio de Medeiros, Cesar Augusto Mirabelli, Regene Mirabelli, Jocelyn Playfair, Dr John Playfair, Rafael Americo Ranieri, Rolando Rammaciotti, Rubens Romanelli, Edivaldo Oliveira Silva, Fanny Sobral, David St.Clair, and Chico Xavier.

A special word of thanks to my colleagues in the IBPP: Ricardo and Sergio Andrade, Virginia Bressan, Suzuko Hashizume, Jarbas and Carmen Marinho, Apolo and Neyde Oliva, Ney and Maria Julia Peres and Agenor Pegado.

A very special word of thanks to Hernani Guimarães Andrade, without whose encouragement and full cooperation this book could never have been conceived, let alone written. Not forgetting Ernest Hecht, but for whom it might never have been published and publicised as only he and Vicky Stace knew how. And finally, thanks to Jon Beecher of White Crow Books for rescuing it from out-of-print oblivion.

G.L.P. 2011

# PART I

# 1

## PEIXOTINHO

O
F all psychical phenomena, materialization must be the hardest for most of us to believe. Telepathy and clairvoyance have now become generally accepted even by much of the scientific community (about a century behind psychical researchers); reincarnation is beginning to look highly plausible, as we shall see in a later chapter; and poltergeists undoubtedly exist, as we shall also see later. But materialization? Spirits of dead people appearing to the living, speaking to them, letting themselves be touched and examined, giving them presents as well as medical treatment and discourses on the life hereafter? For the average rational human, this is too much.

Not that there is a lack of evidence. As with so many other varieties of psychical experience, one of the chief problems for modern sceptics is that they must overlook, reject, or simply remain in ignorance of whole shelves of evidence regarding every one of these varieties.

At one end of our shelf devoted to materialization, we have the detailed testimony of Sir William Crookes, who has left us most carefully worded descriptions of his experiments with several mediums, using such phrases as 'absolute proof' with regard to full-form materializations.[1]

At the other end of our shelf we have the theories of Hernani Guimarães Andrade, who has never witnessed a materialization, but is satisfied that they have taken place on very rare occasions, and has gone to the trouble of working out a scientific hypothesis regarding their mechanisms.

How nice it would be if we had evidence for materialization collected by somebody whose professional duties include the gathering of evidence of all kinds. A police officer, for instance. Turning again to the Brazilian section of our shelf, this is just what we find.

The book is called *Luminous Materialisations* and its author is Dr Rafael A. Ranieri, whom I mentioned in my Introduction. In 1973 he became one of São Paulo's senior police commissioners after a lifetime in the state force. He was a qualified lawyer, and was also the first Spiritist to be elected mayor of his home town of Guaratingueta, a hundred miles east of São Paulo and adjoining the town of Aparecida, one of Brazil's leading Catholic pilgrimage sites. He became so popular during his term that the town had no hesitation in choosing another Spiritist to succeed him.

His book is subtitled 'Testimony of a Police Commissioner' and is dedicated to a former Colonel-in-Chief of the state force. 'This is the declaration of somebody who understands the arts of deceit and illusion,' Ranieri states in his matter-of-fact introduction, which is as clear and uncompromising as a report of a traffic accident. 'Constant suspicion is the police officer's best working instrument and his most powerful weapon.'[2]

Brought up as a Catholic, Ranieri first became interested in Spiritism, as is so often the case in Brazil, because of a severe personal tragedy. In his case it was the sudden death of his daughter Helena, at the age of two. This was in 1945, and three years later, after a series of inexplicable phenomena had taken place in his home, mostly noises made by an invisible agent, he attended his first Spiritist session at the invitation of a friend.

The group's medium was Francisco Lins Peixoto, known to all as 'Peixotinho', who is now regarded as one of the purest and most irreproachable mediums of all time by Brazilian Spiritists. Almost nothing is known of his personal life, except that he was a non-commissioned officer in the Brazilian army, father of a large family, and a physical effects medium who devoted all available spare time to the Spiritist cause. He was regarded as one of the most developed and 'evangelized' of mediums, winning the approval of Chico Xavier, which in Brazil amounts to a kind of Order of Merit, the highest honour a medium can hope for.

Ranieri's first contact with Peixotinho took place in a hotel room in Pedro Leopoldo in February, 1948. As he, the medium and three other friends were settling down for the night, the medium began to suffer from one of his regular attacks of asthma, lying on his back and groaning.

He asked his friends to pray for him, that the spirits should come and help him. They did so, and:

'We all saw the light green luminous band placed over his chest. The medium's bed was between two others; Jair Soares on one side and Inacio da Silva on the other watched the phenomenon from a distance of about fifty to sixty centimetres. I was about two to two and a half metres away. We had arrived at dusk and we had not been separated for a moment, so that there had been no time for any preparation on the part of the medium.'

The day of the formal meeting arrived, and Peixotinho told his friends not to drink, smoke or eat meat beforehand. (Few Brazilian Spiritists do any of these things anyway.) Ranieri had known the medium for only two or three days, and had not discussed any of his personal problems with him. He had not mentioned his dead daughter. Yet at his very first formal session, Ranieri was treated to a succession of luminous materializations, including that of Helena, who handed her father a flower still wet with dew and spoke a few words of greeting.

'It was really her,' Ranieri states with his usual economy of words, 'with no doubt at all.'

At the same session, at least ten stones of varying sizes were thrown violently around the room, each one falling at the feet of the person whose name had been called out by a disembodied voice. The room was dark at the time and Ranieri reckoned that flinging so many stones around without hitting anybody would have been impossible under normal conditions.

At his next session, he was able to witness the materialization of one of the best-known spirits on the Brazilian scene; Sheila, said to be a German nurse who died in Berlin at the end of World War II. Her arrival was preceded by flashes of coloured lightning, after which her luminous figure simply appeared out of the darkness, 'clothed in light', carrying in her hands what looked like a pale green stone, which she used to treat a woman present who was suffering from a liver condition. The stone was described as a transmitter of radioactivity as yet unknown on earth.

Ranieri noted that light was radiated by Sheila as if from the fibres of her clothing, enabling the half dozen people in the room to see each other clearly (including the medium who, as usual, was sound asleep on a bed). He was satisfied that such an effect could not have been simulated in the small room without elaborate electrical equipment, which was not to be found. It is only fair to point out that at this early

3

stage Ranieri was still new to the world of psychic (psi) phenomena, and only later was he to take more detailed notes of what he saw. As I know from my own experience, first contact with such phenomena can be somewhat overwhelming, and it takes time before one can settle down to an objective frame of mind.

Shortly after these sessions, Ranieri returned to Rio de Janeiro, where he was living at the time, and brought Peixotinho along to the small Spiritist centre he ran himself. Here, as he points out, he had the chance to check everything personally without ever finding evidence of fraud. 'If there had been, I would have been the first to know.'

One Saturday evening, a session was held to remove the appendix of a (named) woman who was obviously in considerable pain. For this, the same mysterious pale green strip that Ranieri had seen applied to Peixotinho in the hotel bedroom was brought along. When placed on the woman's body, her appendix became visible on it, as was witnessed by her sister, a fourth-year medical student.

On the following Thursday, the woman came back to the centre to give a talk, speaking in a loud voice and walking normally. Something extraordinary had clearly taken place inside her.

'It is possible that we had been deceived,' Ranieri writes, 'but can a simple mystification eliminate pains and appendices? If so, we should regard mystification as a profoundly therapeutic action!'

Yet another intriguing piece of equipment turned up at another session, brought along by a friendly spirit doctor. It looked like a deep dish of a gelatinous substance, and again it was pale green in colour and transparent. When it was placed on the patient's body it proved to be a kind of portable X-ray machine, for all present could clearly see through it into the inside of the lady's body.

'It was like looking at fish in an aquarium,' as Ranieri describes it. 'There was the heart beating away, the living lungs, and the blood flowing along the veins and arteries.' The spirit then proceeded to plunge his hands into the bowl and pull out some dark matter, which was immediately thrown into the air and dematerialized.

Chico Xavier has described a similar piece of equipment, and it reminds me of an interesting effect that I have often observed myself during psychic surgery, to be described in later chapters, when a kind of cavity appears on the skin into which the medium plunges the hands. It is not possible to make such a cavity remain in position without pressure by the hands, yet I have often seen them when no hands were touching them. The effect is exactly as if something invisible were pressing down on the skin, causing a conical depression deep enough to contain liquid.

As far as materializations of human beings are concerned, and I am only mentioning here a small fraction of Ranieri's witnessed cases, either these things do happen or they do not. If they do not, I can only say that Ranieri was regularly deceived over a period of several years for no apparent reason and to nobody's profit. After meeting him and reading his accounts of a bewildering procession of visible discarnates that floated in and out of his sessions, making speeches, painting pictures, handing out gifts, doing operations, even dancing and playing tambourines, I am left with the feeling so well expressed by Sir Oliver Lodge with regard to the findings of Crookes: 'It is almost as difficult to resist the testimony as it is to accept the things testified.'[3]

Ranieri includes five photographs of allegedly materialized spirits in his book, each of which is endorsed with a hand-written statement by Chico Xavier. The name of the photographer and full technical details are given. The photographer makes the interesting observation that although he took each picture as the result of spoken orders by the spirit, he saw nothing unusual by the light of his flash at the time, and only found the spirit forms when he developed his film. The pictures are sharp and clear, but like all other such pictures they cannot easily be distinguished from simple fakes. I cannot resist the testimony of either Chico or Dr Ranieri, yet I cannot easily accept the photographs to which they testify. I am inclined to think that still photos of spirits will never be convincing.

Ranieri's chronicles are most convincing in their minor details. If we accept the 'bundle of sticks' theory, according to which one incident, like one stick, may be weak whereas a lot of them together can be strong, then it must be admitted that the bundle of evidence that Ranieri has compiled assumes considerable strength.

There was the time when the materialized Sheila handed out what felt like flowers to each of the thirty men and women present. Later, when the lights were turned on, it was found that each man held a red carnation while all the women had white ones, although there was no segregation of the sexes in the seating plan.

There was the occasion when a spirit took hold of a 78 r.p.m. record and folded it neatly into a roll, like a giant pancake, while Ranieri himself was holding on to it. At Ranieri's request, the spirit obligingly unfolded the disc again and then refolded it, repeating the whole performance with a second record. A photograph of the two twisted records is included in his book. They certainly look like two twisted records.

Ranieri is also convincing when he is describing something he is clearly at a loss to explain. Here, the police training comes out and he simply states what he saw with his own eyes. Once, on entering the cabin where Peixotinho was in trance, he found the medium's body to be luminous all over, as if lit from within. Although wearing pyjamas, he was radiating light 'like a firefly', illuminating the cabin after the manner of soft moonlight. Ranieri and six other persons took the medium's hand and examined the effect before the light gradually faded.

On several occasions, luminous letters would appear in mid-air, spelling out answers to questions. This is a form of communication new to me; it seems the spirits are able to produce ethereal neon signs, and even write their names by this method.

If Ranieri was subject to hallucinations, which I have no reason to suggest, they were certainly durable ones. There was, for instance, the night he was handed a stone-like object by a spirit, who told him it was radium and worth a fortune. As he held it, the stone became hotter until it was too hot to hold, and Ranieri's hand hurt for the next eight days.

Then there was the case of the luminous candy. A member of the group had brought some along to see if spirits had sweet teeth. They had, and like the friendly souls they were, they offered something in return. A spirit told Ranieri to hand out a piece of candy to each person present, which he did. Next, the spirit went up to him and shone his pale green light on his own piece, which immediately became luminous. On being told to go ahead and eat it, Ranieri put his candy in his mouth and began to chew it, whereupon an explosion of green light took place in his mouth. He found he could produce the same effect by rubbing bits of broken candy in his hands or crushing them on the floor under his shoe. Soon little green explosions were taking place all over the room as everybody experimented with the magic candy.

The spirit of the investigator stirred inside Ranieri, who asked the amiable entity to illuminate a few more pieces of candy so that he could take them home. The entity duly did so, saying the effect would last for twenty-four hours. The following day, Ranieri examined his gift from the spirits in a darkened room in his own house. 'I can affirm upon my word of honour,' he says, 'that the irrefutable and veridical phenomenon took place in all its grandeur and simplicity.' The same greenish light and the same little explosions were repeated, far away from the medium. This, he decided, was solid evidence of the powers of the spirit world.

The spirits seemed to enjoy playing around with their mysterious source of green light. One evening they announced that they were going to saturate the room with radioactivity, adding reassuringly that they would also throw in an element to counterbalance the prejudicial action of radium. A few moments later, all were surprised to find that by rubbing their clothing or their hair they suddenly became luminous, producing the same effect they had seen earlier on the body of the sleeping Peixotinho.

One cannot help feeling admiration for Peixotinho, the medium who made all this fun possible for others, while he himself remained sound asleep in deep trance throughout every session (quite often, by the way, not in an enclosed cabin but in full view of all). Once, Ranieri went to wake him and was startled to see a globe of red light the size of an orange hovering about a yard over the medium's head. As Ranieri began to make passes over Peixotinho's body to ease him out of the trance state, the light began to move around in front of him. He took both the medium's hands in his own, making sure the light was not connected to him in any way, and the mysterious fireball promptly passed in between his outstretched arms and around his back. At that point the lights were switched on, and the fireball slowly extinguished itself, seeming to back into a glass-fronted cupboard.

'How can one leave a session like that without feeling edified?' Ranieri asks.

The spirits attracted by the remarkable mediumship of Peixotinho seemed anxious to prove their reality in a variety of ways. One of the most convincing to Ranieri was their fondness for making moulds of their hands or feet in paraffin wax. This is a technique whereby the spirits supposedly leave their impressions on soft wax from which a plaster cast is made later.

At some of his sessions, Ranieri would bring some paraffin to the boil and leave it bubbling over a flame throughout the evening, so that, as he puts it, anybody who put their bare hand or foot in it had better be a spirit! Beside the drum of wax there would be another full of cold water.

He includes photographs of no less than seventeen wax models of hands and two of feet in his book. Two pictures show a pair of hands clasped tightly together. The feet, plus two of the hands, he identifies as those of his dead daughter, because of the position of two of the fingers that seemed to be joined together, as hers had appeared in life.

The moulds were made, he explains, by the spirit plunging hand or foot into the scalding wax, then into the water to cool and harden the wax covering. Next, the hand or foot was dematerialized, leaving a perfect hollow mould into which plaster was poured afterwards. A detail of the finger of one adult hand mould shows a clearly marked print.

Readers are warned that attempts to fake this effect might be very painful.

Other spirit visitors to Ranieri's sessions would leave behind evidence in the form of portrait sketches. Ten of these are reproduced in his book, one being an excellent likeness of Allan Kardec.

One spirit who stopped by one evening was Ranieri's old friend Jean-Jacques Rousseau (1712-1778), this time through the mediumship not of Peixotinho but of a regular member of the group named Amaury Santos. It was a private session, with only Ranieri and the medium present. To the soothing sounds of Gounod's *Ave Maria*, Santos went into trance, then suddenly sat bolt upright and began to speak in French.

After a lengthy discourse he switched to Portuguese, explaining that he had used his native tongue merely to establish his identity, and that he was perfectly capable of speaking Portuguese through this particular medium.

'Remember that speech you made at the Mineiro high school in Belo Horizonte?' the voice asked. 'Well, it was I who helped you write it. I've been with you ever since you were a kid with long hair who hated to go to the barber!' Ranieri notes that when young he did indeed have long hair and had an aversion to having it cut, and that moreover even before being interested in Spiritism he had seemed to be haunted by the ideas of Rousseau. Once, a school friend had interrupted him in the course of some impassioned outburst with the words: 'Oh, come off it! That's one of Rousseau's ideas and it's been demolished ages ago!' 'Who's Rousseau?' Ranieri had asked. 'I've never heard of him!' But on several subsequent occasions, people kept telling him that he sounded like Rousseau when he spoke.

'This fellow kept getting between my brain and my tongue!' And now here he was in person, or rather coming through the person of Amaury Santos. He and Ranieri, he explained, had been friends in Greece, Rome, India and Babylon.

'The world crumbles, but the spirit marches on,' was Rousseau's final message to his old pal on earth.

One of Ranieri's most interesting experiences took place mostly outside the séance room. It concerned a girl named Ifigenia França, who might well be called the Reluctant Medium, for she both rejected Spiritism altogether and refused to believe in her own mediumship.

Her story began when her father turned up at a centre in Belo Horizonte, which Ranieri was attending, to say that his daughter was in a desperate condition, suffering all kinds of horrible attacks that left her face and body grotesquely distorted, and that doctors had given her six months to live.

The man was a Catholic who admitted that Spiritism was wholly repugnant to him. He was convinced that Spiritist 'cures' were the work of the devil seeking to seduce human souls. (This attitude is still to be found in some diehard Catholic circles even today). But for his daughter's sake he would try anything, although if the local priest found out that he had been to a Spiritist centre, he would surely have him excommunicated.

As so often happens in Brazil, a Catholic was turning to Spiritism as a last resort, after neither his own faith nor his local doctor could do any more for him. Spiritists are quite used to such situations, and however persecuted they may have been by the Catholic Church (and to some extent still are) they make no distinction between the faiths of people needing help.

Ranieri and the group's medium accordingly went along to the França home, where they found Ifigenia, then aged nineteen, lying in a twisted and rigid heap on her bed. 'She was a veritable monstrosity,' Ranieri recalls.

The medium began to give her some passes, and Ranieri, who knew his Kardec, noticed that Ifigenia would groan and tremble as the medium's hands passed over her body, although they never touched her. Aha, Ranieri thought to himself, here we have a case of exteriorization. This is nowadays usually known as OOBE; out-of-body experience. The passes seemed to have some effect, for the patient straightened herself out and sat up on the bed, though still apparently in trance. Ranieri also gave her some passes, and at last she woke up and seemed fairly normal, so they left her and went away. Some days later, however, she had another attack; her father again went round to the Spiritist centre for help, and since the regular medium was not there at the time, Ranieri went alone to see the patient.

While giving her passes, he noticed that even with his hands nine inches from her body, she would react as if she were being touched. He concluded that he had a case of possession in front of him, one in which the 'perispir-it' body had been pushed out by an invading entity. Ranieri therefore set about making contact with the invader, talking normally to it, and getting an immediate response. Ifigenia then began to speak in a clear voice, de-scribing or rather reliving a previous existence in England.

Ranieri managed to get her out of trance by placing her hand on her head and calling out her name. She woke up with no memory of what she had been saying, and seemed completely normal. Ranieri then as-sured her father that his daughter's problem was not a medical one, and that she could be cured by some prolonged treatment at his Spir-itist centre. The desperate father agreed at once.

At the centre, they were able to observe the young medium more close-ly, finding that she could produce some astonishing phenomena while in trance. She could write lengthy messages in the dark, without her hand run-ning off the paper, putting all the accents in the right places and separating the words correctly. She could tell at once what object was in somebody's pocket or was being held behind her back. She could give descriptions of what was happening in another place, even apparently in another world.

She could give vivid accounts of no less than four of her previous incarnations, repeating passages to order on different days without al-tering any detail. She even reproduced symptoms of tuberculosis, from which she had suffered in a previous life, spitting out blood that made Ranieri's stomach turn over.

Most interesting of all, though, was the way she would cry out in obvious pain when a needle was brought to within nine to eighteen inches of her body, as if she were really feeling it touch her skin. She would also react, although in trance, when people came close to her, the distance varying from day to day from two feet to five yards.

She also developed X-ray vision, describing the internal disorders of a person placed in front of her, and prescribing treatment. While in trance, her own body would become freezing cold, though her head would heat up alarmingly. In fact, she seemed capable of producing al-most every phenomenon known to Spiritist mediumship.

Interested as they were in all this, Ranieri and his colleagues took care of the immediate problem, that of curing a case of possession. This they did along conventional Kardecist lines, with repeated passes and conversations with the invading entity.

Ifigenia França made a total recovery, got married, had a baby and lived happily ever after. She refused, however, to have anything more to do with Spiritism.

I'm not going to any more meetings,' she announced after her cure. 'All that happens is that I go to sleep and only wake up when it's all over. It may be great fun for you, but it certainly isn't for me!'

'She could have been another Chico Xavier,' Ranieri laments.

A medium, says Ranieri, is an open door to the invisible world. What comes through the door depends to a large extent upon the personality of the medium, and it is quite wrong to suppose that the spirit world consists entirely of angelic beings devoted to our welfare. There are plenty of evil spirits around, also others who seem to have nothing better to do than fool about and amuse themselves at our expense by such elementary (to them) parlour tricks as lifting up tables and throwing things around the room. This would seem to be the level of spirit most often to be found at some of the more widely-publicized séances, and those who find spirit communications trivial, as many are, should blame the mediums and not the spirits.

The more advanced the medium, the better the phenomena are likely to be, though not necessarily the most spectacular. Spiritists regard phenomena as merely a means by which the spirits offer proof of their existence. Once any given Spiritist group feels it is in touch with a good team of constructive spirits, it no longer has any need of such entertainment, and can get on with its more serious work of spiritual regeneration and raising the level of one's personal life in addition to helping others to do the same.

The São Paulo State Spiritist Federation, for instance, is today a highly respectable institution that is far too busy with its extensive programme of education and social welfare to have any time for physical effects séances. In its early days, however, as one of its founders (another senior police officer, incidentally) has assured me personally, such sessions used to be held at the Federation headquarters, though members now feel they have grown out of that stage.

Ranieri emphasizes the fact that mediums themselves are not likely to know much about mediumship, since the best of them are out cold all the time they are at work. The long-suffering Peixotinho once told him that his greatest ambition was to be able to watch a materialization séance, but mediums as far advanced as he was must be content with a life of total self-sacrifice. This may explain why there are so few of them around.

Therefore, Ranieri points out, one should not pay too much attention to what ex-mediums, who have lost their powers, may say about themselves. Confessions of fraud have been known since the earliest days of Spiritualism, but assuming the medium concerned to have possessed genuine powers at one stage, how would he or she know what had gone on during trance, except from the testimony of those present? As far as the serious researcher is concerned, mediums are often of little assistance. The spirits themselves, however, have given their own views on the question of materialization, notably in a passage from *Words from Emmanuel*, one of Chico Xavier's books which came out in 1954, in which his chief guide (Emmanuel) explains that well-directed curiosity is the beginning of all knowledge, and that even well-developed spirits may indulge now and then in a little of what he calls 'vibratory descent', if they feel it will do any good.

Materializing is simply a matter of condensation, Emmanuel points out, or of 'reconverting fluidic values and making visible the subtle and intangible'. After all, he observes, the world itself is one vast long-term materialization phenomenon, much of it having previously existed only in human minds! As to how it is done, another of Chico's books, *Missionaries of the Light* (1945), gives all the necessary details. It is clear that materialization, though not particularly difficult, calls for some fairly elaborate preparation on the other plane, and the better class of spirits obviously do not go through the lengthy process unless there is some valid reason why they should.

Peixotinho died in June, 1966, his reputation as one of Brazil's most honourable and dedicated mediums intact until the end. Since he never sought any kind of publicity, little has been written about him in Brazil, and none as far as I am aware elsewhere until now. Fortunately, some of the members of the Spiritist groups in Belo Horizonte, Pedro Leopoldo and Rio de Janeiro where he produced his best effects were still alive in 1973, and I was fortunate enough to secure strong corroboration for Ranieri's evidence from two of the best known: the distinguished Brazilian professor of linguistics Rubens Romanelli, and Newton Boechat, a very prominent name in Brazilian Spiritism as speaker and writer in addition to being a man of great intelligence and apparent honesty. Romanelli attended only one session with Peixotinho, held in 1948 at the home of a regular member of the Ranieri group named Jair Soares, in the city of Belo Horizonte. Ranieri himself was not present on this occasion, but among the six or seven others named as being at the session he describes were a local doctor and a professor of engineering from the local university.

Romanelli, who was passing through Belo Horizonte at the time, was taken to the séance somewhat against his will. He had never heard of Peixotinho and was not particularly interested in tales of alleged materialization. A friend insisted on taking him along, however, and he duly went to the Soares home one evening to undergo what he describes as 'the most impressive experience of my life'.

Choosing his words carefully, as befits his position as a leading authority on the history of Indo-European languages, the Professor now describes what he saw: 'I was somewhat sceptical regarding these phenomena, for I had already attended some materialization sessions that had left me totally unconvinced.

'There were two rooms separated by a partition which had been removed for the occasion. Peixotinho lay down on a couch, wearing pyjamas, while we sat in a semicircle in the other room. It was completely dark; somebody put a record on the player, and we said an initial prayer.

'I kept my eyes open, looking in the direction of Peixotinho, but saw nothing. The darkness was total, but all of a sudden I noticed a whitish milky mist gradually forming a little to the right of where he was. As this cloud began to condense, the room became lighter, and as the cloud grew both upwards and downwards, it gradually began to take a shape that was visibly that of a human being.

'Within, I suppose, about ten minutes, we were face to face with the figure of a very beautiful woman. The tresses of her hair fell over her bust; she had fair hair and blue eyes, and she came walking slowly towards us. I could hear her steps sounding on the floor, they were the footsteps of somebody of flesh and blood, which convinced me it was a materialized being. She stopped about three metres away from us and greeted us with the words: "My beloved brothers in our Lord, Jesus Christ!"

'As she spoke, we noticed a strong German accent; she seemed to be speaking Portuguese with some difficulty. So this would be Sheila, a spirit that often materialized through Peixotinho. I wasn't satisfied that she had merely greeted us verbally; I wanted her to shake hands so that we could really feel we were faced with a materialized being.

'She held out her hand, and I took it, feeling the resistance of a carnal body, the warmth of a human hand. She repeated the same gesture with the others present. I noticed that her eyes were lacking in brilliance, and asked why.

'She explained that this was quite normal during materialization because it was not possible to reproduce the gleam of human eyes. I also noticed a dark patch between her right arm and her thorax, and she explained that since the medium was suffering from a cold, it was not possible for her to materialize fully. She said this was proof that she really was a spirit, and told me to pick up the cover of a record album and pass it between her arm and her thorax, which I did without difficulty, finding that there was no physical connection between her arm and her thorax. The arm gave the impression of being loose.

'She explained that her arm was not loose. There was no physical connection to our eyes, but there was a spiritual dynamism that eluded the physical eye, and this dynamism enabled the arm to be articulated. This was proof that we were in the presence of a materialized spirit.'

Next, after a brief conversation, the spirit announced that she was going to give some treatment to Jair Soares' wife, who was suffering from cancer of the uterus, for which Romanelli states she had been examined and X-rayed. Sheila told her to lie down and began to give her longitudinal passes.

'What impressed me most was that as she did so, sparks began to fly from her fingers, as bright as those of a voltaic arc, lighting up the room as if under very strong lightning. The light was blinding ...'

'Later,' Romanelli continues, 'I learned that the patient was examined again by doctors after her treatment by the spirit, with both X-rays and biopsy revealing no trace of cancer,' (This was in 1948, and the woman died early in 1972.) Romanelli next asked the spirit for some information on how the materialization effect was produced. Psychical researchers may be wondering at this stage why he did not ask all sorts of other questions as well, but they must remember that Brazilian Spiritists are on the whole not in the least concerned with inflicting their beliefs on others, and we are lucky that Romanelli asked any questions at all, remembered the answers he was given, and was prepared to discuss them later.

'She made a comparison that struck me as quite convincing,' he continues. 'She reminded us of the experiment we used to make in the physics and chemistry labs at school, where you scatter iron filings on a piece of paper with an electromagnet underneath, and when you switch on the current, the filings take the form of the so-called field of the magnet.

'She said the same thing took place in the case of materializations. The spirit makes use of matter, orienting the ectoplasm exteriorized by the medium, and using it to mould the form and structure through which it materializes itself. In the case of death, or dematerialization, the elements are reabsorbed so that the structure is totally dissolved.

'I was struck by the fact that at this point the room was not dark at all; we could see each other quite clearly, and as the spirit dematerialized it gradually became darker until once again we were in complete darkness.' In addition to Sheila, Dr Romanelli was able to make the acquaintance of another regular spirit member of the Peixotinho group, a jovial fellow called José Grosso, a northeasterner who was fond of playing innocent little jokes on people and generally having fun. On this occasion, Grosso did not materialize fully, confining himself to what Spiritists call an 'ectoplasmic throat', or the minimum human anatomy required to produce audible sounds.

'Grosso, of whom I had never heard, announced that he was preparing a surprise for me. He asked me to say something from the Gospels, anything I liked. I said something or other, I forget what, but the spirit said it was too long, and asked me for a shorter phrase. So I said "I am the light of the world", and he replied "Yes, that's good, that'll do. Wait a minute!"

'So I waited for something to happen, and then he told me to go to the back of the room, which I did. Then I saw a luminous focal point coming towards me, taking shape as it came. When it was about one metre away I could see it was a panel suspended in mid-air, the kind you see hanging outside commercial stores, and on it was written "I am the light of the world. Jesus."' A few other phenomena took place, including the manifestation of a voice that seemed to dart around the room while it was speaking, but the appearance of Sheila and José Grosso were enough to convince Romanelli of the reality of spirit materialization. He pointed out that Peixotinho had been plainly visible to all present for much of the evening, the windows had been tightly closed, and the group was made up of a small number of close personal friends.

He summed up the effect the session had on him at the time in a single word that means overwhelmed, amazed or fascinated:

'Deslumbrado!'[4]

Newton Boechat's testimony, a small portion of which has been published, is of particular interest in that he attended a great many sessions with Peixotinho, managing to keep calm while the most amazing things were going on, asking questions and remembering the replies.

He begins by defining some terms and questioning the correctness of the word 'materialization' in this context: 'In my view, the word is not right,' he says, referring to an appearance made by Dr Bezerra de Menezes (who died in 1900) at a Rio de Janeiro session held in 1957.

'It was a "densification" in concrete light, for the spirit body was lit from head to foot, with no trace of shadows. The whole body was entirely radiant, like an alabaster statue suddenly illuminated from within, so that the light overflowed beyond the limits of the perispirit and lit up the whole room.

'He stayed with us, concretized in brilliant light, for eight to ten minutes. He spoke for a few moments about earthly life, touching some sick people with a baton he carried, at the end of which there was a blue light. The room became so light that I could easily have seen to read the small print of a newspaper, if I had wanted to. He spoke very clearly, on the subject of immortality and the opportunities we have for renovation.'

The appearance of Dr Bezerra had been preceded by a small light the size of an orange which had zigzagged round the room and then disappeared. This seems to be one of the two ways spirits announce their impending condensation down to our plane. The other, which Boechat also witnessed, is the lightning effect already described by Dr Ranieri. Boechat saw this at a session at which Sheila appeared, though he points out that her way of appearing was not always the same.

'I was sitting on a chair close to the cabin where the medium was asleep. Then the typical flashes of lightning began, Peixotinho having already exteriorized abundant ectoplasm. The flashes began intermittently, on and off, then stabilized themselves and became normal. Suddenly we saw a female entity with long tresses - I couldn't say it was Sheila, as she was entirely black from top to bottom, her blackness contrasting with what light there was in the room.' (By light here, he means that although the session had begun in total darkness, the lightning flashes had become almost continuous, keeping the room illuminated.)

'She left the medium's side and went over to a mirror, where she seemed to be making herself up as if to improve her appearance. When she came out of the cabin it was as if coal had been transformed into diamonds; she was gleaming all over. That was when we could see it was Sheila. It was like seeing a photograph before and after development. I didn't know why this was done and never found out.' (In retrospect, I am sure that what Boechat means here is the difference between a negative and positive photograph.) On another occasion, at which Chico Xavier was present, Boechat noticed that Sheila, who had appeared in all her usual radiance, seemed to go opaque as she walked past a row of four or five people sitting together.

'We asked Chico Xavier why this happened, and he said she was passing by some businessmen whose thoughts at that moment had not been turned towards spiritual matters, and that Sheila had felt restrained by the vibratory magnetic impact of their mental irradiations. When she moved closer to people more concerned with spiritual matters, or to people who were suffering, she began to glow again.' How often at healing sessions have I heard exhortations to 'fix the thoughts on Jesus', especially while a difficult operation was in progress? Can our silent minds really be capable of causing turmoil on the spirit plane? Evidence seems to indicate that they can.

'It shows,' says Boechat, referring to this incident, 'that you cannot overlook the moral factor in psychical research.' He is not the first person to make this often overlooked point; the advice given by Sir William Barrett over fifty years ago is worth repeating here:

'Too many investigators forget that the mental atmosphere they bring is almost as important as the part played by the medium; it does not occur to them that their cooperation is necessary. No advance in any branch of science would have been possible if the investigator set out not to elicit truth, but with the determination to expose what he considered was fraud. Moreover, in psychical research a medium is a sensitive instrument that reacts to its environment; a sitter who is suspicious, or who plays the fool, may entirely inhibit the production of any phenomena.'[5]

On another occasion, Barrett wrote: 'Psychical researchers need sympathy with their subject, whereas scientific workers do not', and his own remarkable success in both fields suggests that he knew what he was talking about.[6]

I hardly need mention the obvious corollary; that too much sympathy with the subject may turn one into an uncritical apologist for the cause, ignoring inconvenient evidence for the sake of proving one's ardently desired hypothesis. I am well aware of this dichotomy that must face all researchers in all fields, and since none of us is perfect I would rather err on the side of credulousness, albeit as little as possible. This is at least a positive attitude, whereas scepticism is not.

But let us get back to Newton Boechat, who has plenty more to say. First, here he is describing the evening he had his throat treated by the spirit nurse, Sheila ...

'She took me by the hand into the cabin and told me to lie down. She was not totally materialized, perhaps to save the medium's energy or possibly because she did not need to be. As she was talking to me, I could see she was only materialized as far as her bust.

'She stretched out her right hand, and something like an insecticide spray appeared mysteriously. She pumped it once or twice into my throat, and instantly I felt freezing cold inside. Before this, she had stuffed some cotton wool into my tonsils, and this became extremely hot, upon which she took it out. The heat was outside and the cold inside, rather like when you rub yourself with vapour-rub; it's hot at the time but feels cold afterwards.

'Sheila was mobile and vital. She would nod her head back and forth, throwing her hair back. She was very beautiful; she reminded me of Jean Harlow. She said my throat would get better, and it did. I had an operation scheduled, and cancelled it. Now, I can drink cold drinks with no trouble.'

Next, Boechat describes some of Sheila's medical appliances, of which we have already had tantalizing glimpses from Dr Ranieri and Dr Romanelli. The portable X-ray device he recalls as being in the shape of a yam leaf, with a surface like stainless steel and slightly flexible. Sheila brought one along and placed it on a sick person's stomach.

'Through this substance, we could see the organs and the glands working, in their natural colours, moving as observed in ordinary research. Sometimes, the apparatus would go opaque, and then light up again. It was less bright in colour than Ranieri describes it, perhaps because on this occasion the medium was suffering from a cold and had less power.' On another occasion, Boechat recalls that Sheila used an invisible instrument for a long treatment session that lasted nearly an hour. It sounded like a lighter, being flicked on repeatedly, but nothing was seen of it.

Yet another piece of equipment, which resembled a lipstick capsule, was brought along by Sheila at a session held in a Pedro Leopoldo bedroom (not the one described by Ranieri), with Peixotinho asleep on a single bed in full view of his companions. Sheila put the thing on his stomach, explaining that it contained energies withdrawn from what she called the psychosphere of our planet to help the medium avoid attacks of bronchitis while work was going on.

Peixotinho suffered much of his life from asthma, and would occasionally start to cough during trance. This would invariably interrupt proceedings. On one such occasion, Boechat was watching a materialized hand writing on a piece of paper under the light of a glowing ball 15 to 20 centimetres in diameter; as the medium began to cough, the hand shot back into the cabin as if on the end of a piece of elastic.

Boechat noted a number of details that check with what many other witnesses of various forms of séance have reported. On numerous occasions the room would be impregnated with an intoxicating perfume, while the temperature would often drop sharply. In Rio de Janeiro, where room temperature even at night can be as high as 90 degrees (F), Boechat had the impression of being in the mountain climate of Petropolis, at least twenty degrees cooler. This may be an exaggeration; since there is so little variation in Rio temperatures, people there tend to feel even slight changes very acutely. One or two degrees difference can make them complain of the heat, or the cold, as the case may be. Boechat also had the honour of having a spiritual signboard made for him by the ever playful José Grosso. He asked how this was done, but Grosso merely laughed. 'He said he would show me when I came over to his side!' Boechat recalls.

Finally, after so much discussion of materialization, or as he prefers to call it, 'structuring in light', Newton Boechat has a further surprise in store.

Would you believe *dematerialization of the medium*?

Breaking my strict rule of not using third-hand material, I will simply let Boechat tell this story in his own words as he learned it from friends at the centre run by Jair Soares, a prominent member of the Ranieri circle. The medium in question was not Peixotinho this time, but Fabio Machado, who enjoyed an equally high reputation in Spiritist circles and who often helped materialize the same spirits as those of the Peixotinho sessions.

'Somebody had placed a cloth over the illuminated dial of the record player rather carelessly, and while a spirit was materialized it fell off. The spirit immediately vanished and the voice broke off, while the medium began to groan. Two or three people rushed over to see what they could do to help. As they were giving him passes, they felt his body and noticed that he was dematerialized from the waist down. His pyjamas were still there, but there was simply no continuation of the body ...

'Then the voice of the entity José Grosso announced that Fabio was indeed dematerialized from the waist down, and that the resources for his reintegration were pulverized in the room, or stretched out as if in sustaining threads, dissociated from the physical body. They would, he said, try to reharmonize the room, calm the minds of those present and make an adaptation - a fitting together of millions of millions of cells in the model, the dynamic structure or perispiritual body of the medium.

'The operation lasted about 50 to 60 minutes, and Fabio was totally restored to the power of his body. But a very curious thing happened; this was before the days of plastic surgery (in Brazil), and everyone knew that Fabio had a gash on his right thigh in a childhood accident, and that the scar had remained fully visible. Well, in the materialization of his body, the scar completely disappeared, as if some skilful plastic surgeon had just rooted it out while reaccommodating the cells around the lines of force of the dynamic body.'

This story is well known and widely believed in Brazilian Spiritist circles, and may account for many mediums' insistence upon working in complete darkness. One appreciates their point of view.[7]

One of the many things I learned while working with the IBPP is that no case should ever be closed. New evidence can always turn up, as it did after The Flying Cow was published, and I was going around Britain promoting it on radio and television. One of my readers was Dr John Beloff of Edinburgh University, a distinguished parapsychologist and active member of the Society for Psychical Research of whose journal he was to become editor. He kindly invited me to lunch when I passed through the Scottish capital, and gave me a courteous but thorough grilling on some of the strange things I had described in the book. He was especially fascinated by my account of the materialisations produced by Peixotinho, and by the testimony of Prof. Romanelli, then working at UNESCO in Paris. Beloff decided to contact Romanelli and see how he felt nearly thirty years after his encounter with the medium.

Romanelli replied promptly at some length and in near perfect English, reaffirming his earlier account of his 1948 session. After summarising the phenomena described above, he concluded uncompromisingly:

'I have an absolute conviction that the phenomenon we witnessed was real. I felt precisely conscious at the time it occurred, and according to testimony from each present during the sitting, what I saw and heard was equally seen and heard by all of them. I should like to add that there is not one proof that the medium Peixotinho has ever been caught in fraud.'[8]

Peixotinho like Chico Xavier and Fabio Machado, is an example of what we might call the Classic Brazilian Medium; one whose entire life is devoted to the cause of propagating Spiritism without seeking or accepting any kind of financial reward.

Not all mediums in Brazil, however, have managed to withstand pressures and remain unaffected by success and popularity, and in the following two chapters we take a look at couple of mediums who were very well known in their time. It might be unfair say that we are passing from the sublime to the ridiculous, but we can certainly say that we are passing from the sublime to the rather less sublime ...

So, with a suitably operatic flourish from the orchestra, enter Mirabelli.

# 2

## MIRABELLI!!

I F everything they say about Carmine Mirabelli is true, he was without doubt the most spectacular physical effects medium in history. If anything they say about him is true, he should not be omitted from any survey of the psychic scene in Brazil, and since hearing some of the things they were still saying about him more than twenty years after his death, I find it difficult to think of his name without a pair of exclamation marks after it. For Mirabelli was surely the medium to end all mediums. You name it, and he is said to have done it; automatic writing in over thirty languages living or dead, speaking in numerous foreign tongues, materializing objects and people, transporting anything from a bunch of flowers to large pieces of furniture (including levitation of himself even when strapped to a chair), producing impressions of spirit hands in trays of flour or wax inside locked drawers, dematerializing anything in sight, himself included...

He could, they say, contact dead relatives of friends and paint portraits of them. He could sing and play the piano or violin with considerable skill while in trance, although he had no musical talent or training. He could write a message of several pages in a few minutes while chatting away at the same time in another language. He did, in fact, just about everything that any other medium has ever done, doing so for something like forty years. Moreover, he normally did his thing in broad daylight or in a well-lit room in front of anything up to 500 witnesses. He seemed to have no objections to having his house searched or to being handcuffed and tied to a chair, or to being investigated (up to a point) by all and sundry.

Fortunately for posterity, many of his feats were witnessed by a great many people, some of whom were still able to recall them for me in detail more than twenty years after his death. Two of his closest friends published a great deal of material on him, based on minutes of meetings at the various centres where he held forth. These were Miguel Karl, a businessman of German descent who spent a year in India with Swami Yogananda Saraswati; and Eurico de Goes (pronounced *goyce*), a highly literate and intelligent man who became organizer and director of São Paulo's first municipal public library.

De Goes, one of Brazil's first serious psychical researchers, had a special reason for attaching himself to Mirabelli. His attractive wife had died young, and he was forever trying to make contact with her. Though he never managed a complete materialization, he satisfied himself that she really had contacted him through Mirabelli's mediumship on a number of occasions, in the course of which he witnessed and described more than a hundred materializations of other entities. Some of these lasted over an hour, allowing themselves to be examined by doctors and prodded all over. Mirabelli was, de Goes concluded, a 'veritable laboratory' for the researcher, and though he was not researched anything like as thoroughly as he should have been, we must be grateful to his faithful Boswell for the great trouble he took to record his hero's feats. There is a large amount of literature on Mirabelli, but little of it apart from de Goes's well-written 471-page tome is of any value to modern researchers. Much of the information in this chapter is based on it, except where otherwise specified.[1]

Mirabelli was in his lifetime, and remains today, a highly controversial figure, and since his death the legend has expanded in all directions. Many stories told about him are almost certainly untrue or gross exaggerations, yet even when these have been discounted (as many were before the writing of this chapter), there remains a residue of evidence that suggests he deserves his place here.

Carmine Mirabelli (who later called himself Carlos to avoid confusion with the Brazilian female name Carmen) was born in 1889 in the town of Botucatu, some 160 miles from São Paulo. His father was a well-to-do Protestant pastor from Italy, whom de Goes generously describes as 'a man with the kindest heart although imbued with Lutheran doctrines', and amongst his many illustrious ancestors were said to be a president of the Italian royal court, an army general and a parliamentary deputy.

He was educated in his home town and at a primary school in the nearby town of Itu, where he showed a precocious intellect, although like many sons of immigrants he never quite mastered either his ancestors' or his adopted country's language. He learned some English and possibly also some German, but certainly became no skilled linguist.

He showed an early ability after leaving school for making money, in a deal involving a large consignment of gas mantles from Germany, and throughout his life he never had to rely on his mediumship to earn a good living, mostly by buying and selling land. He undoubtedly charged for his services on some occasions, one of his own leaflets clearly stating his very large fee for personal consultations, but it is also quite certain that he gave a lot of money away and was a generous and kind-hearted person.

His mediumship seems to have hit him (literally) while he was in his early twenties, working in the Clark shoe store in São Paulo. According to often repeated (and equally often denied) legend, boxes of shoes would fly off their shelves, while the young salesman would be seized by bouts of chills, visions, depression, neurasthenia and assorted other fits. Obviously, he had to leave, and it is said that when he did, some of the shoe boxes went out into the street after him.

The general opinion was that young Carmine had gone crazy, and he was duly committed to the Juquery asylum for the insane, where he was closely observed by two doctors, Felipe Aché and Franco da Rocha, after whom the asylum is now named.

'He is not a normal man,' Dr Aché declared, 'but nor is he sick.' Referring to the strange things that were beginning to happen whenever Mirabelli was around, he decided they were 'the result of the radiation of nervous forces that we all have, but that Sr. Mirabelli has in extraordinary excess'.

Dr Franco da Rocha later described what kind of a show Mirabelli could put on even at this early stage of his career: 'He placed a skull on top of a glass, and at my request it began to revolve, so that at a given moment both skull and glass fell over on the table. I replaced the objects in their former positions, and the phenomenon was repeated. I did so yet again, and the same thing happened. Nor was that all; as I held the skull I felt something strange in my hands, something fluid, as if a globular liquid were touching my palm. When I concentrated my attention further, I saw something similar to an irradiation pass over the skull, as when you rapidly expose a mirror to luminous rays.'

After a stay of only 19 days, Mirabelli was let out of Juquery asylum and went to live in the seaside town of Santos. Here, he became the representative of a homeopathic medicine company and opened his own charitable organization, the São Luiz House of Charity. Miguel Karl records that this was kept going for 14 years at a total cost to its founder of 751,000 milreis, during which time donations amounted to only 12,628 milreis. Photographs of the centre show that it was well attended by hordes of both rich and poor in search of physical or psychical diagnoses. For such an organization to last so long is quite a feat in Brazil, where Spiritist centres can appear and disappear almost overnight.

Eurico de Goes knew Mirabelli well for over 20 years, after they first met by chance in a São Paulo hotel in 1916. He describes him as a typical Italian, excitable, impulsive and impatient; but also tolerant and warm-hearted, a lover of good food, animals and opera. He led a somewhat Bohemian life, being especially fond of going for long drives at night in the countryside. He was a big spender, who would think nothing of buying ten suits or a dozen pairs of shoes at a time, only to give most of them away.

Yet despite his flamboyance and evident vanity, two qualities notably lacking in orthodox Brazilian Spiritists, Mirabelli fully embraced the Spiritist cause, founding and running a number of centres in São Paulo and Rio de Janeiro. One of these was nominally headed by a distinguished public health official, Dr Thadeu de Medeiros. Though one of the main purposes of these various centres seems to have been to promote Mirabelli himself, many who attended them were converted to Spiritism as a result. Modern Spiritists in Brazil certainly do not approve of Mirabelli or his methods, but they grant that he was an effective evangelist.

Throughout his career as a medium, Mirabelli was regularly witnessed by doctors and scientists, several of whose names are attached to the minutes of meetings reprinted by de Goes. He was also watched at work by a popular conjuror, Carlos Gardonne Ramos, who stated that 'it is entirely impossible for these (phenomena) to be achieved by sleight of hand'.

Foreign observers who saw him in action at least once at various stages of his life included Bruno Heckmann and Johann Reichenbach from Berlin, Italian chemist Tito Guarnieri, envoys May Walker and Theodore Besterman from the American and British societies for psychical research respectively, and most important of all, the eminent Leipzig philosopher and SPR president (1926-27) Hans Driesch.

May Walker described 'the best telekinesis I have ever seen' after a comparatively mild session in which rose petals floated from the ceiling, bottles jumped up and down on a table, and a fan began to 'wriggle about, as if alive' in her hand, while her hat went round in circles on her head. She was convinced that some of the phenomena were real.[2]

Mr Besterman attended at least five sessions in August 1934, during which (according to the minutes, which de Goes reports him as having signed) flowers materialized, bottles on a table jumped around, one even hopping onto the floor, a picture left the wall to float in mid-air and land abruptly on someone's head, a chair slid along the floor for about ten feet, the front-door key drifted out of its lock, and Mirabelli came up with a learned written discourse in French, writing nearly 1800 words in 53 minutes.

All of which led Mr Besterman to declare (again according to de Goes, who quotes him in English) that he found 'Mr Mirabelli's phenomena of the greatest interest... Many of them were unique of their kind.' Later, however, he changed his mind, as we shall see shortly.

Eurico de Goes writes that phenomena like those mentioned above came to be mere routine, though now and then Mirabelli would introduce such novelties as asking witnesses to indicate an unripe orange growing in the garden, then to go and pick it and find a rare coin embedded inside.

On one occasion a businessman friend asked for advice about a letter he had just sent to New York. Mirabelli told him exactly how his business deal was going, and when the reply came he sat down and dashed off translations in Portuguese, French, German and Hebrew without even looking at the original in English.

For a special session in 1933 held at nine in the morning, Mirabelli was handcuffed, his feet bound, and then asked to repeat phenomena he had produced at a previous meeting under artificial light. He promptly obliged; freshly plucked flowers floated in through a locked and sealed window, a religious statue weighing eight kilos drifted in after them, made the rounds of the room and drifted out again, while Mirabelli began to talk in Arabic to one of the investigators, who identified the voice as that of his mother who had died in Beirut 28 years previously. He became a Spiritist on the spot.

A tray of flour was placed inside a drawer, which was locked and sealed, and after 15 minutes three loud raps were heard. Opening the drawer, witnesses saw the clear impression of a human hand on the flour.

The lid of a water cooler took off and landed among the audience, and when one man went over to examine the cooler, it exploded in his face, soaking him with water.

Finally, it was time to read the minutes of the previous meeting, at which point the group secretary, the son of a German, found he had left his spectacles at home.

'Wait, son, I'll bring them right away from the room in your house where you left them,' came a voice speaking German, adding: 'I am your father and your protector.' The spectacles promptly appeared in the secretary's hands.

Mirabelli seemed to run a kind of lost property office for his friends. While driving from São Paulo down to Santos with him one day, Eurico de Goes remembered he had left his umbrella behind. As they arrived at the medium's house, it promptly dropped from the ceiling. Other property recovered via Mirabelli's unfathomable talents included a stolen gold crucifix, a fur wrap somebody had left on a bus, and several lost or stolen documents.

Some of his antics seemed no more than harmless jokes staged to prove the reality of such phenomena. When British poet and diplomat Sir Douglas Ainslie turned up for a session in a private São Paulo house in 1928, the first thing he saw on the hall table was the travelling clock he had left inside a suitcase in his hotel room. During the evening, the lady of the house mislaid her spectacles, which were later found in the home of one of the guests.

Many phenomena seemed entirely pointless; objects simply flying around the room or moving from one shelf to another, sometimes hitting people in the process and even hurting them quite badly. De Goes was once struck on the arm by a stone, while Mirabelli himself had a large picture smashed over his head, glass and all, at a public meeting held in a centre that was not one of his own.

Mirabelli himself would claim that inferior spirits were responsible for this sort of thing, using his powers like a magnet or focal point for their pranks. This is a theory sometimes advanced today to account for poltergeist phenomena in general, and the theory of 'like attracts like' with regard to mediums and the spirits they attract can account for much of the evidence provided elsewhere in this book.

Sometimes the atmosphere was thoroughly gruesome. At one session, a human hand materialized, and Mirabelli announced that he saw the skeleton of a lady who had been buried minus her head. This, he explained, had been removed for study as she had been mentally disturbed before her death. He named the exact plot in São Paulo's Araçá cemetery where she had been buried, and said that her remains had been secretly removed and were being kept at her son's house. At the following session, after the family in question had indeed found the box of remains to be missing from the grave, a terrible smell of decomposed corpse filled the room, as bones began to materialize one after the other and fall on people's heads.

De Goes managed to keep control over his feelings, and his stomach, to note what appeared. There were, he meticulously recorded, 'humeri, radii, ulnas, carpuses, a metacarpus, fingers, ribs, parts of the vertebral column, femurs, tibias, tarsi, metatarsi, anklebones and hair'.

It was, he recalled, like something out of Edgar Allan Poe.

Other Mirabellian feats read more like science fiction. One evening, after a long and tiring session, he asked for the lights to be switched off, and then with two men holding him firmly by the arms he began to glow all over, lighting up the whole room. Another time he levitated into the air while handcuffed, whereupon there was a sound of falling handcuffs as he disappeared altogether, reappearing in his nearby office which was locked from the outside, where startled witnesses burst in to find him stretched out on a chaise longue and chanting away in Latin.

But the most incredible Mirabelli feat of all one that must strain anybody's frontiers of belief concerns the occasion when he went with a group of friends to São Paulo's Luz railway station to catch the train to São Vicente, about 50 miles away. On the platform, he simply vanished and after fifteen minutes his worried friends managed to get through by telephone to the house they were heading for in São Vicente. Mirabelli, they were told, had been there for about fifteen minutes.

I cannot substantiate this story, but I am surprised at the number of people I have met who believe it. Eurico de Goes includes it in his book as if it were quite a normal thing for Mirabelli to do, and it should be mentioned that de Goes claimed to have investigated a number of mediums other than Mirabelli, and been impressed by none of them. He was constantly on the lookout for fraud, he says, and records that whenever he was a guest at the medium's home he would always check everything personally before going to bed, searching the whole house to find an unlocked or unbarred window.

De Goes had nothing to gain except ridicule for his championing of a well-known and controversial medium; for during the twenties and thirties there was a great deal of hostility in the press towards anything remotely psychic or occult, and Mirabelli bore the full brunt of it, though de Goes claims that no Brazilian who actually troubled to witness him ever said or wrote a word against him. Even some Catholic priests, often hostile then as now towards any form of Spiritism, could be won over by the medium's charm and apparent sincerity of purpose. A certain Father José Maria de Castro wrote in Mirabelli's private scrapbook: 'Mirabelli is a man of faith whom the chiefs of the church in Brazil cannot condemn without knowing him.'

Condemned he was, all the same, and he somehow survived no less than fifteen court appearances, all for allegedly illegal practice of medicine or witchcraft, the former usually consisting of doing no more than 'magnetize' a bottle of water.

Although he could apparently produce accurate diagnoses of diseases while in trance, Mirabelli does not seem to have gone in for curing after the fashion of the American trance medium Edgar Cayce, or the Brazilian psychic surgeons mentioned later in this book. There was one occasion when he claimed to have received the spirit of a former sufferer from tuberculosis, and in front of witnesses he put on a realistic demonstration of a pulmonary haemorrhage, spitting half a litre of very real-looking blood all over the floor, fully recovering in half an hour.

Dr Thadeu de Medeiros testified that Mirabelli once spotted signs of incipient cardiac lesion and renal disturbance in a patient of his, which helped him considerably in effecting a cure. He also correctly diagnosed a serious condition in the solar plexus of another patient Dr Medeiros had already examined, coming to the same independent conclusion.

But on the whole, having Mirabelli around the surgery seems to have been more liability than asset; bottles of expensive or even dangerous medicines were liable to leap out of glass-fronted cabinets and fly across the room. 'Phenomena like this were frequently observed,' the doctor noted. We can understand why he seems to have made little use of his medium friend's services.

Mirabelli's clinical methods during such healing as he did were, as we might expect, unusual. A prominent society lady calling on him in 1933 reported feeling something invisible touching her near the heart. Oh yes, Mirabelli assured her at once, that would be Dr Oswaldo Cruz (highly respected in Brazil as a pioneer of tropical medicine).

'He's saying that you're taking too much of a medicine you're carrying with you,' the medium announced. 'He's going to...'

There was a crash, as a bottle of Atophan was thrown violently against the wall, shattering into small pieces. It was the bottle the woman had been carrying inside her handbag.

'Oswaldo Cruz says,' Mirabelli went on, unperturbed, 'that you got a prescription from a medium. You can go on taking the medicine that the spirit prescribed for you.' Whereupon another bottle, this time of Antimopolis and also from the startled lady's handbag, was thrown onto the floor without breaking.

There seems to have been no limit to what the man could produce, in or out of trance. His artistic output in the latter condition was fairly impressive; he could paint in a number of different styles, produce portraits of dead people which were identified by surviving relatives (fifty paintings of his were once exhibited in Amsterdam), and also conjure musical phenomena out of thin air. Witnesses recall having heard ethereal concerts in his presence, ranging from snatches of opera to military fanfares, while the musically untrained Mirabelli (who was untrained in practically everything else as well, come to that), would sing lengthy arias in a number of languages, often while doing something else at the same time, like writing or painting.

His inspiration could also take a practical turn; once he was lamenting the fact that his record player was out of action, whereupon the machine switched itself on and the needle placed itself on the disc - this before the invention of the automatic turntable.

What, it may be asked, was the point of all this sort of thing? The apparent purpose behind the Mirabelli manifestations was to prove the existence of spirits and the validity of the Spiritist doctrine as drawn up by Kardec. This is the purpose of all Spiritist meetings, though nowadays physical phenomena are regarded as rather old-fashioned stuff, no longer needed to support the faith of veteran Kardecists.

The only evidence for Mirabelli's doctrinaire intentions comes from the examples of his automatic writing, many of which have been published in Brazil, and of which I have seen several photocopies but unfortunately no originals. These are thought to exist, but after his death there was some confusion in the family as to who inherited what, and even the two of Mirabelli's sons I was able to locate had no idea where they were.

At one typical 1928 session, Mirabelli produced messages purporting to come from Saint-Simon, St Bernard of Clairvaux and Louis XII (all in French), Martin Luther (German) and a fellow who signs himself G. Knox The Quaker (English).

Saint-Simon comes across in elegant French, making an earnest plea for concentration on the principles of Spiritism and concluding 'Voilà, mourir ... et revivre encore, cette est la Loi établie par Allan Kardec.' The others say much the same thing in their own languages, while the final message, from Mr Knox, concludes: Therefore I can do no more than confirm all M. Bernard de Clairvaux's doctrines, for its author knows better than I what is truth, as he already reached the lightest places in sky among the angels and nearer of God than I'm [*sic*]. Good bye. Bible and sword.'

Messages would come through in all usual European languages, plus a few less usual ones such as Catalan, Albanian and Bulgarian; also in a number of oriental languages including Japanese and Chinese. Most of them are neatly written, though spelling mistakes are common, and their subject matter varies enormously. De Goes lists discourses on Great Britain and the Irish Question, Slav psychology, the Russo-Japanese war, inhabitable planets and Buddha among several others. They contain nothing revelationary, but show evidence of more knowledge than a busy man with no special educational qualifications would be expected to have amassed in his spare time.

Some of the messages have an intriguing ring of authenticity. Cromwell, for instance, gives a long and rambling account of a nightmare he had in which King Charles had cut *his* head off, which is quite an entertaining little essay in its own right.

Joan of Arc comes over with a stirring denunciation of the Church. 'Je nie et renie mille fois,' she writes, 'la basse et noire croyance qui est l'église catholique, qui malgré avoir été causatrice de ma mort, joue le colin-maillard avec mes cendres et ossements! ... La victime d'hier est santifiée par ses propres bourreaux et mise sur l'auteuil.' Messages such as these made little impression on the Society of Psychical Research, which noticed a collection of them in its Journal for October 1927, dismissing them along with accounts of other Mirabelli miracles as 'preposterous'; hardly a scientific attitude, and especially curious coming from Mrs Helen Salter, herself a prolific automatic writer and member of the team that produced the celebrated 'Myers cross-correspondences', some of the best evidence for human survival of bodily death ever gathered.

Another collection of Mirabelliana was reviewed by Theodore Besterman in the SPR Journal for November 1930. He pointed out reasonably that there was no evidence of supernormal knowledge in the messages, but overstated his case by claiming that there was nothing in them beyond the reach of Mirabelli's 'linguistic associations and comparatively good education'. All witnesses I have interviewed agree without hesitation that Mirabelli could not even speak either of his own languages (Italian and Portuguese) correctly.

A more open-minded attitude was expressed by Dr E. J. Dingwall, in a review of a German translation of an early Mirabelli book that came out in 1960. He laments the fact that the Mirabelli case 'remains another of those unsolved mysteries with which the history of parapsychology abounds', and takes his former SPR colleagues to task for not having collected evidence from eye-witnesses of the phenomena.[3]

Fortunately, I was able to collect some evidence that might help at least partially solve the Great Mirabelli Mystery. I set out in 1973 to track down survivors of Mirabelli sessions who had witnessed paranormal phenomena at first hand, and were prepared to talk about them. It was no easy task. Though many of my friends in the Spiritist movement were able to produce a wealth of secondhand evidence (one eminent São Paulo surgeon assured me that his father had seen Mirabelli leave the floor while sitting in a chair), I could find only a handful of men who had known him over a long period of time, and most of these were too old to remember anything clearly except that the medium had been a source of inspiration to their spiritual development. This was comforting, but of little evidential value. It did suggest that Mirabelli was an effective saver of souls after his unusual fashion, a point not to be overlooked.

The general picture that soon began to emerge was that Mirabelli definitely had abilities as a medium, though he did not develop them fully and very probably resorted to trickery on his off days. He also attracted a definitely second-rate variety of spirit, I was assured.

An oculist, who should be able to believe his own eyes, described a partial materialization he had witnessed, of a human figure that began to form inside a circle of people holding hands, including Mirabelli, but suddenly vanished before it took identifiable shape.

This was an encouraging start, and after much further inquiry I was able to gather far more detailed evidence from two of Mirabelli's sons, insisting to each that they only describe what they saw with their own eyes, and making allowances for the fact that no son is likely to denounce his own father as a fraud.

First, I sought out Regene Mirabelli, a businessman and accomplished amateur hypnotist with a keen interest in the scientific rather than the spiritual side of psychical research. Regene had no doubts whatsoever as to his father's abilities, and flatly denied my suggestion that hypnotism had played any part in them.

Since his parents had separated amicably shortly after his birth, Regene saw little of his father until he was ten years old. Almost on their first meeting, things began to happen.

'I was sitting on the arm of a heavy renaissance-style sofa,' Regene told me. 'Father liked me to stroke his hair, and I was doing this when the sofa simply began to move, with both of us sitting on it. Then I clearly saw the shadow of a figure on the floor in front of us; there was sunlight coming through a heavy glass window beside the sofa. Then the door of the cupboard across the room opened and a quill pen came out and was shot into the wooden floor like an arrow.' All of which sent young Regene rushing out of the room in terror, screaming for his mother. But there was more to come.

'Out in the hallway there was a heavy brass cuspidor that had fallen over, blocking the passage. We heard loud bangs and crashes coming from a room beyond, and when I rushed in, there was Mother lying on the floor with every piece of the furniture in the room on top of her. She wasn't hurt because "they" had the consideration to place a thick mattress over her first!' One night, when Mirabelli's old friend Miguel Karl was staying in the house, Regene happened to peep through a crack in the door to have a look at the visitor, who was sitting on the bed with the light on, his arms folded in front of him in a position of meditation.

'As I watched him,' he told me, 'his body began to rise up in the air, without changing position. Then he just stayed there, in mid-air, about a metre off the bed, his arms and legs still crossed ... That was enough for me, and I ran off to tell Mother as fast as I could.' Mother, however, was quite used to this sort of thing, and one can appreciate why she had opted out of the family.

'You can imagine what it was like for her,' Regene said, 'spending half an hour laying the table, for instance, and then when her back was turned finding everything flung all over the room. How could you run a kitchen in a house like that?' Another evening, Regene joined a session consisting of the family and a dozen friends, which was being held to help a bedridden invalid in another room. This was an occasion he will never forget.

'Father told us all to form a current, and he said not to worry about any phenomena that might happen. I was sitting about two metres from a table where there were three bottles of water, corked. This was to be "fluidized" and used to treat the sick man. We all sat there, and suddenly the bottles rose into the air, about thirty centimetres, and we heard three clinks as each struck the other. Then the bottles slowly began to turn over in mid-air, and stayed like that, upside down for a moment or two. I could see them very clearly, and the water inside them seemed to have gone solid, for it stayed in position, with a gap just under the cork. Then all the bottles fell hard onto the table and rolled about, although they did not break.' Regene Mirabelli assured me that none of his family have inherited any of his father's talents, though of those talents there could be no doubt at all.

'He was the greatest medium since Jesus Christ,' he summed up.

Cesar Augusto Mirabelli, the medium's youngest son, provided me with the kind of clear and straightforward evidence that would make research of this kind easy if there were more of it to be had from key witnesses. Providing clear evidence was indeed part of his job as an investigator in the São Paulo police force flying squad.

As we discussed his father's mediumship, Cesar would think hard before answering, choosing his words as if giving evidence in court, as he often had to do. He made it clear at the start of our interview that he was far from sympathetic towards Spiritism in general.

'I have always accepted Spiritist facts,' he told me. 'But I never accepted the Spiritist religion. Ninety-nine per cent of what is known as Spiritism is deceit, mystification or bad faith. If my father were a fraud, I would certainly say so.' As an investigator himself, I asked, was he fully satisfied that his father had really caused psychic phenomena without any possible collusion or trickery of any kind?

'Well,' Cesar replied with a smile, 'I'm a suspect when it comes to testifying to the authenticity and honesty of these phenomena, being his son. But, you may not believe it, I would never take part in a conspiracy aimed at deceiving so many people.

'The facts really were true. Fraud was impossible, bearing in mind the locations - even out in the street in broad daylight where there was no chance of previous preparation. The phenomena were often produced just for us, the family. Now, if there had been any intention to mystify people, this should have been done to others, but why us?'

One night, for instance, Cesar was coming home with his mother and father after a visit to friends. As they entered the house, a shower of rose petals fell on their heads just inside the door. This struck me as something that could easily have been prepared beforehand, but I could not say the same of the next phenomenon Cesar recalled for me:

'We had an ornamental porcelain vase, about 60 centimetres high, weighing I suppose three to four kilos, standing on a kind of tripod. There were only us in the house. Suddenly, Father started to look at the corner where the vase was, and I started to look as well. Then the vase just rose into the air, about 40 centimetres up. Then all at once it turned, picked up speed and smashed itself to pieces against the wall, two metres away.' Wasn't he curious about this sort of thing at the time? I wondered.

'Yes I was,' he replied, 'but I thought it quite natural because of the frequency and the naturalness of the phenomena. They just happened almost every day, any time and any place.'

'Were these phenomena connected with what your father was doing at the time?' I asked.

'Some things that happened were unforeseen, even by him,' Cesar answered.

'Could he provoke a phenomenon deliberately?'

'Yes, he could if he concentrated. But sometimes they occurred independently of his will.'

Finally, I mentioned the question of levitation, one of the most difficult of all phenomena to accept for anybody like myself who has never seen one. Cesar told me he had not been present on the celebrated occasion his father was supposed to have been levitated almost to the ceiling during a session at Rua Natal 9, the building constructed to house the Spiritist centre next door to the family home at No 11. (On a visit to this house, I checked the background of a photograph showing Mirabelli in mid-air and found it exactly matched, the same light fitting being still there today. Eurico de Goes accepted the photo as genuine, though the shadow on the wall seems to have been retouched, as I will describe later.)

'But,' Cesar went on, 'since levitation means the displacement of the mass of any body with relation to its gravity ...' Here again was the professional investigator speaking, rather than the son of a Spiritist medium. '... I did have the opportunity to witness other examples of objects that moved from one place to another.'

There was, he said, one particular occasion he would never forget. Some building work was being done in the house, and a pile of bricks stood in the corridor.

'I started to imitate Father's gestures, just for fun, because at times I really used to think his attitudes were rather comic. Then a brick suddenly fell on the floor beside me. I looked around - there was nobody there and then another brick fell, and another. I started to run, and bricks began to fly all over the place. I ran and ran, all round the house, and at the end of the passage there was a big iron door. As I was trying to get it open, another brick was flung against it ...'

'Didn't that scare the life out of you,' I interrupted to ask.

'Well, although I was only a child, I distinctly felt that the bricks were not exactly being aimed at me. Whoever was throwing them didn't want to hit me. Anyway, I finally got outside and ran across the road to a small football pitch we had there. Then I started to yell; I was afraid to go home. Father appeared at the window and I told him to stay there and keep a lookout while I went back into the house. At first, I thought he must have been playing tricks with me because he was all covered with brick dust as well - he had been sitting on his rocking chair and bricks had been dropped all over him, though he wasn't hurt. He couldn't have been throwing them himself, though, as I had really been running all over the place.'

Cesar's most vivid memory of his father was a tragic one; that of the day he was killed.

It was April 30th, 1951, and the two of them were on their way to the cinema when Mirabelli decided to cross the road to buy something. Cesar stayed chatting with a shoe-shine boy, and as his father was walking across the road, a car came round a bend and hit him, causing a cranial lesion that put him into a coma from which he never recovered.

'It was a black 1938 Ford,' said Cesar, ever the conscientious observer.

One man who had not forgotten Mirabelli more than twenty years after his death was Fenelon Alves Feitosa, a courteous and kindly Brazilian of the old school now rapidly vanishing in ultra-materialistic São Paulo, who ran his real estate business from an office in the heart of the city's commercial district.

When I called to see him, he opened the top drawer of his desk and produced a small pile of literature on Mirabelli, as if it were the most urgent business of the day even now.

For my benefit, Fenelon recalled an outing he had spent with 'the Professor' as Mirabelli was known to all thirty years previously, remembering it as clearly as if it had taken place the day before and giving a vivid impression of what life with Mirabelli had really been like.

One day in 1943, for example, Mirabelli invited Fenelon to join him on a trip to Ibirá, some 250 miles from São Paulo, to visit a certain

Joaquim Seixas who lived there. The two of them took the night train, arriving early in the morning and being warmly welcomed by Mr Seixas and his family. Fenelon had slept little during the journey, and immediately went to take a bath and clean himself up. He was still in the bath and covered with soap when he heard Mirabelli calling: 'Fenelon! Fenelon! Come here quickly!'

'I dried myself and dressed hurriedly,' Fenelon recalled, 'and ran into the living room, where I found the Professor linked by a chain of hands to Mr and Mrs Seixas and two or three other members of their family. As I came in, the Professor cried: "Fenelon! Fix your thoughts on Jesus, please!" 'Then he cried "Come!" in a loud voice, and we heard the sharp sound of something hitting a china bowl there in the room and falling onto the floor. Soon we saw what it was; a revolver bullet. Five more times, the Professor called out "Come!", and on each occasion other bullets fell one by one until there were six of them on the floor.

'The Professor asked whose bullets they were, and Mr Seixas picked them up and examined them. "They look like the ones from my revolver," he said, "but they can't be, because it's locked up in a drawer." 'No sooner had he spoken when a revolver fell loudly onto the floor in front of our eyes. Mr Seixas recognized it at once as his own, inexplicably transported from its locked drawer. He bent down, picked it up, and was amazed to find that there were no bullets in the chamber, whereas there should have been six.'

At this point, amid general expressions of astonishment, Fenelon tried to persuade Mirabelli, who was sweating profusely and had turned pale, to have a rest or take a bath. But the 'Professor' did not seem to hear him, and with a jerk he suddenly slumped into a chair, staring vaguely at the ceiling. Fenelon realized he had gone into a trance.

'Then,' Fenelon continued, 'he got to his feet as if drawn by an outside force, and drew our attention to an object that was passing over our heads towards the master bedroom. This was connected by a door to the room we were in. We all ran into the next room and the first thing we saw was Mrs Seixas, who was weeping and pointing to the bedside table, crying "Look! My St Anthony has come back! Here he is!" 'There was indeed a statue of St Anthony on the bedside table, and according to Mrs Seixas it had disappeared more than eight years previously. This was the object that had passed over our heads, on its way back to its original position.'

They went back into the living room, and a few moments later Mirabelli called out the words 'Schmidt! Long barrel, black handle!' They all joined hands again, and Mirabelli led them back into the bedroom, opening a drawer with one hand (while Mr Seixas held the other) and producing a brand new Schmidt revolver, with a long barrel and black bakelite handle. This he handed to Mr Seixas and told him to keep it.

Mirabelli then sat down again and asked who was in the habit of making up his bed.

'The maids see to that,' Seixas replied. 'Why do you ask?'

'I wanted to know,' Mirabelli explained, 'so as to be able to tell you that what we are about to see is not the work of your maids.' Nobody understood what he was talking about, but Mirabelli called for a knife, and going back into the bedroom he pulled the sheets and blankets aside and thrust the knife into the centre of the mattress, prodding around with its point until it was heard to strike something metallic-sounding.

'Ah!' he said, 'here it is.' Whereupon he put his hands inside the mattress and pulled out an old pair of scissors with both blades broken. 'I just wanted you to know that this was not put here by your maid,' he observed. 'You can throw it away, it's no longer any use, especially for sleeping on!' It was still early in the morning, and the party had not even had breakfast. As they went into the dining room, Mirabelli asked for a bottle of water. Explaining that he was receiving instructions to fluidify it, he began to make passes over it with his hands.

'Look!' somebody exclaimed, 'the water is turning pink!' 'We were surprised to see,' said Fenelon, 'that the water really was becoming discoloured.' After that episode, the party set off to visit the farm belonging to Mr Seixas's son-in-law, José Maria. Fenelon takes up the story.

'When we got there, we didn't even have time to sit down. José Maria introduced us to members of his family, including his own son-in-law, a boy of about twenty, telling us in confidence that he had been showing suicidal tendencies. The Professor at once went into one of the bedrooms, reached behind a wardrobe and pulled out a dusty picture, all covered with cobwebs.

' "Whose picture is that?" the Professor asked.

' "That's my late brother-in-law," Jose Maria replied. "He committed suicide."

' "Exactly, and that's why the boy wants to do the same. You must pray hard for him and for your brother-in-law, so that he doesn't stay attached to him, influencing him without meaning to with ideas of suicide."

'Then Mirabelli turned to me and said, "Fenelon, put your hand on the boy's head, set your thoughts and don't move." He left us and went into another room some distance away. I could hear him talking loudly at the other end of the house, and thinking something interesting might be happening that I didn't want to miss, I took my hand off the boy's head, telling him to stay where he was and think of Jesus. But I hadn't taken more than two or three steps when I heard the Professor call out "Fenelon! Get back!", although we were in rooms far apart and there was no way he could be watching me.' At that moment, Fenelon later learned, a plaster saint from the nearby chapel had been flung against Mirabelli's legs, giving him a cut that took ten days to heal properly.

Fenelon felt himself to blame for this, by disobeying orders and taking his hand off the boy's head. But Mirabelli was in high spirits as the group sat down to lunch, in spite of the damage to his leg. He seemed to regard this as all part of the occupational hazards of his job.

'While we were eating,' Fenelon continued, 'something passed over our heads at tremendous speed and went into the next room. Then came a deafening crash. The Professor immediately got up and we all followed him into the next room, where there was nobody else at the time. We saw the lid of a water cooler wobbling around on top of the table, amid the shattered remains of the cooler itself, which was in pieces after spilling its water all over the table. We were still admiring this phenomenon when something heavy fell at the Professor's feet.

'José Maria stared at it and exclaimed, "But that's my revolver! But how on earth? It was safely put away inside its cover!" He picked it up, examined it and confirmed that it was indeed his. Just then, something hit the Professor on the back and fell to the floor. It was the cover of José Maria's revolver, no more no less.'

After lunch, the group went back to the centre of Ibirá and sat down on benches in the little town's main square. But Mirabelli, for all the entertainment he had already provided in two different houses, neither of which he had visited previously, was still not through for the day.

'Suddenly,' Fenelon went on, 'rifle bullets began to fall to the ground, one after the other. José Maria stared at them and said they must come from his farm, because he had a store of bullets of the same calibre. Next, another object came floating out of nowhere and landed at our feet. It was a pen, which Jose Maria also recognized as his.

' "That's right," said the Professor, "this pen was brought here so that we can sign the minutes this evening!"' Fenelon himself wrote out this account of his memorable outing with Mirabelli, which he signed and presented to the IBPP.

Mirabelli's reported feats make an interesting comparison with those of the nineteenth-century medium D. D. Home, as painstakingly recorded by Sir William Crookes.[4]

Crookes divided the phenomena he had personally witnessed into 13 classes. These were the production of sounds, alteration of weight of bodies, movements of heavy substances at a distance, levitation of objects and human beings, movement of objects without contact with any person, luminous appearances, materialization of hands, forms and faces and miscellaneous phenomena such as accordions playing themselves and bells ringing. The other class was of instances that, as Crookes put it, seemed to point to the agency of an exterior intelligence.

No scientist of Crookes's stature has ever made such thorough studies of so many different phenomena, and his findings deserve attention by anybody seriously interested in such things. Desperate efforts have been made in recent times to discredit Crookes, claiming that he was having an affair with his favourite medium, Florence Cook, and wrote a lot of rubbish in an attempt to cover up his behaviour.

This I find unlikely, since Crookes was devoted to his wife Nellie, who was usually present at his sessions (held in his own house) and remained on good terms with Florence after her marriage. Since much of Crookes's research was carried out with other mediums, notably Kate Fox and Daniel Home, should we assume he was having affairs with them as well?

Or was the poor fellow simply soft in the head? More than one scientist has suggested to me that this may have been the case. Let us look at some facts; Crookes's research into what he called 'the phenomena of spiritualism' was restricted to the years 1870-1874, at which time he was at the height of his career. (He turned forty in 1872.) True, his greatest discovery, that of thallium, was behind him; but over the 45 years after his psychical research period his record does not read like that of a madman.

He became president of the Chemical Society (1887), the Institution of Electrical Engineers (1890), the British Association (1898), the Society of Chemical Industry (1913), and finally the Royal Society itself (1913). He was knighted in 1897 and awarded Britain's highest civil honour, the Order of Merit, in 1910. At the age of 86 he produced a paper for the Royal Society on the 'Arc Spectra of Scandium'. If he did go soft in the head, he left it extremely late.

I mention all this to make the point that Mirabelli did very little that has not been witnessed elsewhere by a man with far more professional qualifications than any other psychical researcher in history. A historical precedent is as useful in psychical research as in a court of law.

All the same, if anybody of Crookes's stature had investigated Mirabelli, I doubt if anybody would have believed him, just as few believed Crookes. As a contemporary of his observed, 'either the facts must be admitted to be such as are reported, or the possibility of certifying facts by human testimony must be given up.'

Resisting the temptation to give up, I will end by summarizing what I consider the best evidence available for and against Mirabelli. There is plenty of both.

The largest quantity of evidence against, if not the best, comes from the newspaper *Correio Paulistano*, which ran a series of diatribes against Mirabelli and everything he stood for in almost every issue from May to July 1916. They are notable for the almost total absence of any evidence in his favour, and can hardly be considered balanced or convincing. Their main theme is that Mirabelli refused to take part in experiments of the anonymous author's devising, and to judge from the tone of the articles, one can hardly blame him.

Theodore Besterman's long report on his August 1934 visit to Brazil contains allegations of outright fraud, and does at least give examples of incidents he witnessed himself that he reckoned were faked.

He states that he saw Mirabelli throw various small objects around the room after distracting everybody's attention by making them look at the ceiling. He also accuses Mirabelli's wife of being an accomplice in an act that involved the discovery of flowers draped around a chandelier in another room. Since she had left the room while her husband was making a speech, this does seem circumstantially possible. Some rather feeble bottle-clinking went on in the dark, spectacles moved on a table, a ruler was pulled from Besterman's hand and some paper torn while he was holding it. All this, he concluded, must be done by the use of threads, although 'notwithstanding every effort' he never found any.

Next, a coin was made to appear in a pocket of Besterman's choice. Dropping coins in people's pockets is no harder than picking them, but as Dr Dingwall pointed out, what would have happened if Besterman had asked for the coin to appear in the heel of his shoe? [5,6]

Then we come to what Besterman describes as 'the only really impressive part' of the sittings he attended.

Mirabelli took a blackboard measuring about 70 by 80 cm., one centimetre thick and weighing 3.65 kilos, and placed it on top of a bottle. A group of sitters, including the medium himself, then held their hands over the board, which after a minute or two began to revolve, turning about one and a half full circles before it fell off the bottle. On a second attempt, at another session, the board made three whole revolutions before falling, and the phenomenon was repeated with a cane 60 cm. long. All of this took place in a 'brilliant' light, though not brilliant enough to enable Besterman to get good results with his ciné camera, which Mirabelli allowed him to use without objection.

Besterman tried later to repeat the board-revolving effect by blowing, and found he could not. He was satisfied at least on this occasion that no threads were used, and admits that 'any other fraudulent method is difficult to conceive'.

Finally, Besterman was treated to a display of Mirabelli's skill at automatic writing. He records that the medium produced just under 1800 words in French in 53 minutes, giving an average of 34 words per minute. This is not bad going; I can write 50 words in a minute in my own language, but I could not keep it up for 53 minutes, and I could certainly not do so in French although unlike Mirabelli I have a university degree in that language. Yet Besterman finds nothing difficult, let alone paranormal about this feat.

He sums up his findings as follows: 'He is either a fraud pure and simple, or else he possesses a certain narrowly-defined paranormal faculty, round which he has erected, for commercial purposes, an elaborate structure of fraud.' There did appear to be, he admitted, 'a prima facie case for the second possibility', subject to numerous reservations. (Later, as we shall see, he changed his mind).

Besterman's evidence is inconclusive, but since it is just about all we have of its kind it deserves some study. He does at least suggest that Mirabelli cheated on occasions, though this is no proof at all that he always did. It may be that Mirabelli was anxious to put on a good show for his foreign visitor, and that he appeared to help out the genuine phenomena with a few wholly normal ones.

Yet the question of fraudulent mediumship is a lot more complicated than it may seem to some, including Besterman. You simply cannot catch mediums cheating just once and then denounce them as total phonies.

Take the case of Eusapia Palladino. This astonishing Neapolitan convinced experienced researchers over and over again that inexplicable phenomena could and did take place in her presence. She also convinced practically everybody who attended her sessions that she would appear to cheat shamelessly whenever she could. Yet when Everard Feilding investigated her (in 1908) under almost ideal conditions, he found that the tighter the controls, the less she cheated and the more genuine phenomena she caused to take place, as his two co-investigators Hereward Carrington and Wortley Baggaly, both experts in magic and trickery, agreed.[7]

William James has pointed out that for fraud in any form to exist, there must have been a genuine original. He confesses that he once cheated himself, by projecting the shadow of a turtle onto a screen during a physiology lecture, showing its heart apparently beating. The turtle was in fact dead, and the movement of its heart was caused by James's finger. Should everything he wrote since be discredited because of this?[8]

Mirabelli may well have performed a few simple conjuring tricks now and then, perhaps not knowing what he was doing. There is plenty of evidence to suggest that mediums 'cheat' without consciously knowing they are doing so. But to claim Mirabelli was totally fraudulent, as Besterman did (see below), seems unreasonable. To prove such a claim, it is necessary to show or at least suggest how he did everything he was thought to do, and Besterman admits he cannot explain even the few phenomena he witnessed himself.

One is reminded of Crookes's reply to his critics: 'Prove it to be an error by showing where the error lies, or, if a trick, by showing how the trick is performed. Try the experiment fully and fairly. If fraud be found, expose it; if it be a truth, proclaim it. This is the only true scientific procedure, and this it is that I purpose steadily to pursue.' Besterman duly exposed some fraud, but he was never able to show how the blackboard trick was done.

However, nearly forty years later he was able to tell me in a letter that 'what I do remember very clearly was that Mirabelli left me in no doubt that he was purely and simply fraudulent.'

'Once I had expressed this opinion,' he added, 'none of his followers would talk to me, so that I was unable to get any firsthand impression of their role in his performance.'[9]

In fairness to Besterman, it must be said that little useful research can be done in two or three weeks in Brazil even today, and even when one speaks Portuguese, as I do and he did not. In 1934 there was a strong tide of nationalism in Brazil in the wake of the 1930 revolution, and even if Besterman had interviewed witnesses before denouncing Mirabelli, (which might have been worth trying), I doubt if they would have immediately described their personal experiences to an unknown foreigner. Enormous patience and very careful handling of sensibilities are called for if one is to get anything out of Brazilian Spiritists.

There is a very curious discrepancy between Besterman's published account of the five special meetings Mirabelli held for his benefit and the official minutes of the same meetings, which Eurico de Goes prints in full in his book.

At the very first meeting, according to the minutes, Mirabelli announced that he could see an entity named Zabelle, whom he described in detail. Besterman said he had known a lady of that name in London who was now dead, and when he asked for a sign of her presence, bottles began to jump around on a table, one of them even falling on to the floor at his request. Besterman mentions the bottles, but not the mysterious Zabelle.

At the second meeting, Zabelle again dropped in and became visible enough for Dr Thadeu de Medeiros to take a photograph of her. This is reproduced in de Goes's book, and is one of the more credible materialization photographs I have seen. (The lady is not even wearing an Arab headdress, for once!) According to the minutes, which de Goes reports Besterman as having signed, Zabelle performed a number of feats to prove her presence.

In the minutes of the third meeting, we are told that Besterman examined the photograph of Zabelle and declared that there was a strong resemblance to the lady he had known. The face on the photograph is extremely clear, more so than in most pictures of this kind.

It is surprising that Besterman makes no mention of this episode. It is clear from his lengthy published report that he was anxious to miss no opportunity to discredit Mirabelli's powers, and if the Zabelle story were untrue, here was an excellent opportunity to do so.

If, on the other hand, it was true, then Besterman is guilty of suppressing strong evidence in favour of the medium. As so often happens, an attempt to investigate paranormal phenomena led to raising more doubts instead of solving any problems.

Next, we turn to the brief but meticulously presented evidence of Professor Hans Driesch, who as I have already mentioned was the most distinguished foreigner ever to see Mirabelli in action.

Driesch met him on a brief visit to São Paulo in August, 1928. His impressions were contained in a five-page letter he wrote to an SPR colleague some three months later. This letter has never been published, and I am most grateful to the Council of the SPR for allowing me to quote from it here, for the first time.

Mirabelli, says Driesch, was 'quite a nice and jolly fellow, of an Italian or Spanish type', although he surprised the multilingual German embryologist by claiming not to understand Italian, which was certainly not true. There followed, however, a long discourse in Italian, which Driesch found 'very indifferent', purporting to come from the spirit of Mirabelli's deceased father.

After this unimpressive start, Mirabelli's performance improved somewhat when a mirror fell from a table with nobody less than six feet from it, a bottle moved and fell over in another room, and a metal pot did the same thing in the kitchen.

'There was also a vase with flowers,' Driesch writes. 'All the flowers fell to the ground; one of them moved towards Mrs Driesch.' An enormous knife also fell to the ground, but 'most impressive of all' was a double door that closed itself in response to Mirabelli's appeal to one of his favourite saints for 'a sign'.

Driesch made it clear that conditions were not scientific, but he was undoubtedly impressed by what he saw. The phenomena had taken place in the private house of a German banker ('who is personally beyond all doubts') in a good light, and though they were trivial stuff compared to almost any of the sessions described by Eurico de Goes, they were enough for Driesch to invite Mirabelli to visit Europe to be investigated properly.

Mirabelli agreed at once, provided he could take his wife and his friend de Goes with him. He did not demand a fee.

However, the project fell through, and the only further contact Mirabelli was to have with the SPR was through the inconclusive investigations of Theodore Besterman already described. A great opportunity was lost, but at least we have evidence that Mirabelli could be found 'impressive' by a former president of the Society.[10]

Now we consider the best published evidence available for the defence of Mirabelli, which comes from a wholly unexpected quarter; the late Carlos Imbassahy, one of the most widely respected pillars of orthodox Brazilian Spiritism and author of a monumental history of psychical phenomena that appeared in 1935.[11]

The 377 footnotes scattered through the pages of this well-written book show that its author was thoroughly familiar with psychical research in Britain, France and the US, though he has nothing to say about research in Brazil for the simple reason that there had never been any. He does however devote four pages to Mirabelli, making it quite clear at the start that he strongly disapproved of the man and had no desire at all even to meet him.

As a highly orthodox Spiritist, Imbassahy regarded Mirabelli as either a vulgar fraud, a skilful conjuror, or at most a medium who had got mixed up in the wrong company, both incarnate and discarnate. Worst of all, everything seemed to get smashed up when he was around, and Imbassahy had no wish to get involved in 'this perilous mediumship'.

One day, Imbassahy (who had made his opinion of Mirabelli well known to his friends) was at home with a businessman friend called Daniel de Brito, when who should turn up out of the blue but Mirabelli himself! He had been brought along by another friend of Imbassahy's who was convinced of the medium's genuineness.

'I must have looked like a farmer who has just seen a swarm of locusts on the horizon,' he writes. A member of the household was ill at the time, and 'there was nobody I less wanted to see.' Mirabelli nevertheless made himself at home at once, seating himself in a rocking chair and promptly launching into a speech in 'detestable Italian mixed with Portuguese and Spanish words'. This purported to come from Cesare Lombroso, and Imbassahy sat through it, deciding that the medium was a 'grotesque charlatan', but consoling himself with the thought that at least his crockery was still intact on the shelves.

Upon finishing his speech, Mirabelli immediately turned to Brito and proceeded to give the startled businessman an account of his life from the cradle onwards. Brito had never met him before, and was not a well-known figure himself, but the medium seemed to know all there was to know about him. Imbassahy was reluctantly impressed.

'Once more, I began to worry about the fate of my plates,' he adds.

Next, upon hearing that there was a sick person in the house, Mirabelli called for some bottles of water, which a housemaid brought in and placed on a table four or five metres from where he was sitting. He never touched them, and the four men joined hands to form a current, so as to help the spirits 'fluidify' the water.

'Immediately, in full view of us all,' Imbassahy writes, 'one of the bottles rose half way up the height of the others, and hit them with full force for five or ten seconds, before returning to its place. We thought they must have been cracked. This was clearly seen and heard, with no shadow of hesitation. People in the next room also heard it, and the patient became extremely alarmed!' So did everybody else, as Mirabelli then announced that a phalange of obsessing spirits had arrived. Oh Lord, Imbassahy thought, there goes the glassware! But at that point, the patient leaped out of bed and begged them to end the session, which they did accordingly. Mirabelli left soon afterwards.

Imbassahy slumped exhausted and sweating into an armchair, though relieved that his precious crockery had survived intact. The patient, incidentally, got worse at once.

'As consolation,' he concludes, 'we were left with the unshakable certainty of Mirabelli's mediumistic gifts.' Trickery was out of the question; nobody had touched the bottles except the maid, the room was lit by two 100watt bulbs, and there had been no time for Mirabelli to prepare any tricks. His hands had been held while the bottles moved and he had been far back from the table.

Against his previous judgment, Imbassahy concluded that Mirabelli was a medium after all, though not one that he ever wanted to have in the house again.

There are three possible verdicts on Mirabelli. One is that he was a total fraud. The second is that he was one of the greatest mediums of all time, capable of producing almost every mental or physical paranormal effect known to psi-research.

The third verdict is that he had the 'unknown power' as few have ever had it. but he did not fully understand it or make proper use of it. On his off days, which mediums have like anybody else, he was capable of producing some innocuous conjuring tricks, perhaps unconsciously, in order not to disappoint his audience. This is the verdict I prefer. There is insufficient evidence for the first two, though there is far more in favour of the second than the first.

However, evidence came to light in 1990 that Mirabelli was party to deliberate deception on at least one occasion. Earlier, I mentioned the photograph that purports to show him in mid-air. This was reproduced for the first time outside Brazil, as far as I know, in the first edition of this book, and I noted in my original caption that 'the author is unable to authenticate the photo' and that 'it could have been faked'.

An original print discovered in the archives of the Society for Psychical Research shows clear signs of fakery in the form of retouching to remove the ladder on which Mirabelli was standing. The print is signed by Mirabelli and inscribed 'To Mr Theodore Besterman' (who surprisingly does not mention it in his report). I can hardly disagree with Gordon Stein, the American researcher who found it, that Mirabelli 'knowingly passed off a fraudulent photo of himself as authentic.'[12]

Once a cheat, always a cheat? Besterman, who met the man, certainly considered him 'purely and simply fraudulent', and if a man is known to have cheated once, it is reasonable to suppose that he might have cheated more than once, but it is not reasonable to allege that he cheated all the time.

In the case of Mirabelli, this has not been proven, and it is just as reasonable to suppose that a medium whose powers are not always available when needed will try to perpetuate his reputation by any means available. Stars of sport and entertainment have been known to have their off-days, or carry on well past their sell-by dates. Also, as a lawyer friend of mine pointed out, if you want to debunk somebody like Mirabelli, you have to find normal explanations for *everything* he is alleged to have done.

I find it unlikely that Mirabelli was a total fraud. The testimony of his family and close friends is too abundant and too consistent, especially that of the two of his sons I was able to interview, as is that of at least one of his enemies, the orthodox Spiritist Carlos Imbassahy.

Brazilian Spiritists feel that Mirabelli broke some of their basic rules by charging for his services, which he definitely did at times, and by allowing a personality cult to grow around him yet he was not a bad man. He never did anybody any harm, to my knowledge, and he unquestionably brought much comfort and inspiration into the lives of a large number of people. He made a great many converts to Spiritism, and he would not be the first evangelist to use dubious means to further a praiseworthy end.

Allan Kardec, who had a great deal of experience of mediumistic phenomena, was one of the first to point out that the quality of such phenomena depends on the personal qualities of the medium. It is a case of like attracting like. Exalted spirits, therefore, will be attracted to such developed and self-effacing mediums as Peixotinho or Chico Xavier; mischievous ones will fasten onto less developed extroverts like Mirabelli; while the lowest form of spirit life will gravitate towards those unfortunate neurotics who keep turning up on poltergeist cases.

There is nothing inferior spirits enjoy more than a good joke, says Kardec. I often wonder which they find most hilarious: the faithful Spiritists who swallow everything offered them as the literal truth, the parapsychologist who ransacks libraries in search of rational and materialist explanations for innocent spirit-pranks, or the researcher

who never could figure out how a blackboard went round and round
on top of a bottle ...

# 3

## OTILIA DIOGO

N ow we come to one of the most lamentable chapters in the brief history of psychical research in Brazil. It concerns the widely publicized full-form materializations of a certain Sister Josefa, plus assorted Indians and discarnate doctors, through the mediumship of a woman named Otília Diogo.

I include this episode to show that fraudulent mediums do stand a reasonable chance of being found out and exposed in Brazil, where some might have reason to suppose at this stage that anything goes, and that Lincoln was wrong in claiming that all the people cannot be fooled all the time.

The story began hitting headlines all over the country towards the end of 1963, after a picture magazine had announced that a team of ten doctors had just 'scientifically proved' some 15 types of psychic phenomena, the most dramatic (and photogenic) being the materialization of Sister Josefa. She was said to be an Italian-born nun who died in 1946, after a lifetime of charitable work which had made her widely loved.[1]

The ten doctors (all named) occupied prominent positions in their respective fields. Most of them came from Uberaba, where the sessions took place, though one or two were from São Paulo; one being a hospital director from the interior of the state. Their credentials seemed impeccable, especially those of the group's spokesman, Dr Waldo Vieira, a long time friend and associate of the one and only Chico Xavier, about whom no suggestion of personal dishonesty had ever been made even by the severest critics of Spiritism.

Dr Vieira, among his other good works, ran a private clinic in Uberaba that was a kind of one-man welfare service. The sign outside the door simply read 'Dr Waldo Vieira. Free Consultations'. In addition to being a fully qualified doctor, Vieira was an articulate and intelligent man who gave every impression of being devoted to the task of establishing Spiritist phenomena by careful scientific methods. He was also one of the country's best-known automatic writers next to Chico Xavier, with whom he had collaborated on several books.

All the right precautions seemed to have been taken. The medium, a fifty-year-old mother of two children who claimed to be, of all things, the daughter of the beloved Sister Josefa, had been given the full treatment. She had been searched, chained to her chair, even enclosed in a cage, while everybody present had also been searched and forbidden to bring anything in except essential clothing and spectacles.

A total of about 400 photographs had been taken of paranormal phenomena, to be included in a large book that Vieira hoped would become a classic of correct and methodical research by qualified experts into the phenomenon of physical-effects mediumship. He made it clear that his interest in studying such a subject was in finding ways to cure the sick on a large scale with help from the spirit world. There was no suggestion that he sought to gain personally by exploiting Otília Diogo or anyone else. He accepted no money either for his medical or writing work, and was widely known as a model of militant Spiritist charity.

So far, so good. Brazil seemed to be entering the dawn of a new era of revelations, with Vieira as the Brazilian Crookes. The whole materialisation thing was being brought out in public, and about time too. A television programme shown in November 1963 increased public interest, and soon afterwards the weekly magazine *O Cruzeiro* joined in the fun, sending a reporter to Uberaba to see what was going on.

This magazine, at that time the widest read in Brazil, devoted fourteen pages of an early 1964 edition to the story. This was entirely based, as the magazine took pains to point out, on material supplied by the doctors themselves.[2]

Dr Vieira and his colleagues can scarcely have hoped to deceive a magazine like *O Cruzeiro*, pioneer of Brazilian photo-journalism which specialized in general muckraking and would certainly not hesitate to expose any fraud that came its way. The magazine was invited to send a reporter and a photographer, to attend a special session, the sixth in the Sister Josefa series. When, accordingly, six writers and photographers instead of the two invited turned up on Dr Vieira's doorstep, they were well received and somehow fitted into the small session room.

Everything went wrong from the start. The way the reporters described it, the doctors' examination of the medium was a complete farce. Her clothes were given a summary patting, a suspicious bulge around her middle was left unexplained, she refused to remove her underwear alleging that she was menstruating at the time, and she was allowed to go to the bathroom unaccompanied. An experienced investigator at this stage would probably have taken the next bus out of Uberaba. But worse was to come.

The journalists claimed they were refused permission to spread talcum powder on the floor of the medium's cabin, to check for footprints. They were told that the cage, through which Sister Josefa had been apparently passing in some of the photographs taken at previous sessions, would not be used again 'because it put the medium off'. They were told they could only take pictures themselves when given permission.

Anyway, the session began and Otília duly did her stuff. Compared to the phenomena witnessed around the mediumship of Peixotinho and Fabio Machado, second-rate stuff it was. Whereas Sheila and her friends had managed to materialize luminously, make uplifting speeches, treat the sick and generally radiate goodwill as well as make themselves useful, the supposed Sister Josefa evidently assumed that the medium was the whole message.

She restricted her performance to stumbling round the room, occasionally striking a pose for the photographers, and muttering a few words of greeting. The good sister, who had died in 1946, even pretended not to know what a 'reporter' was! The reporters, however, thought they knew what a phony medium was when they saw one, and at the end of the session they unanimously announced that they considered the whole show a fraud. Dr Vieira took this quite calmly, and offered to arrange 'as many more sessions as you like until you are convinced'. But O Cruzeiro had had enough.

Otília Diogo's face duly made the cover of the magazine. In fact it appeared twice on the same cover, once as herself and once, in colour, as Sister Josefa. The colour film clearly brought out the familiar features of the medium behind her veil, with her long pointed nose and tightly set lips.

Not satisfied with this revelation, the magazine called upon a top criminologist to examine the photos from earlier sessions, and also a piece of thread they claimed to have found in the medium's cabin after the session. The expert had no difficulty in reaching a verdict of total fraud. Among many other incriminating details, he pointed out that the medium's large bunion on her left foot was all too plainly visible on the alleged 'Dr Veloso', who also seemed to have unusually large breasts for a man.

The final blow was struck six years later, after (unbelievable as it may seem) Diogo had managed to continue her career on the less respectable branches of the Spiritist circuit, even making something of a comeback in the eyes of the diehard faithful. The IBPP has a picture taken at one of these post-Uberaba sessions, in which the medium is wearing a thick sweater, although the audience is in its shirtsleeves, and has the most obvious-looking roll of bandage stuffed up her nostril. Many photos of ectoplasm look like fakes, but this one especially so. I have never seen anything of its kind less convincing.

The man who finally claimed to have unmasked the old trouper was a well-known São Paulo plastic surgeon, who had gone along to see the show at the centre in Campinas where Otília was then working. He must have been quite impressed by what he saw, for when the medium later asked him to give her a face-lift, he agreed to do so free of charge, and invited her to stay at his home.

The medium got her face job, and naturally offered a performance in exchange. The surgeon noticed that all the time she was in his house, she never let her little black suitcase out of her sight. Very suspicious. After the performance, the medium had a few Scotches (something orthodox mediums never do) and finally staggered off to bed after acting in a generally strange manner.

The doctor decided to have a look inside that black bag at all costs. With his wife, he searched Otília's bedroom for the key to no avail. Then his wife poked under the *soutien* of the snoring medium and found it tucked away there. The case was opened, and there it all was: the complete do-it-yourself materialization kit; veils, robes, harmonica, crucifix, ether and perfume sprays ... the whole works.

The following morning, Otília Diogo awoke to find the doctor and his family surrounding her bed. Spread out on the floor, like the exhibits in a criminal case, were the contents of her precious black bag.

She sprang out of bed, crying 'Sister Josefa, why have you forsaken me?' and bursting into a flood of insults and abuse, only calming down when the disgusted doctor threatened to hand her over to the police without more ado.

Finally, when she saw the game was up, out came the confession: 'I lost my mediumship in 1965, but I thought I should go on doing materializations. I didn't want anybody to notice. I did exercises, training my arms and legs for some time, until I felt I could go back to work. I know none of it was true, but I went on ...' Then, pointing to the remains of her stage props lying on the floor, she made one final plea: 'Do me a favour - burn the lot!'[3]

It only remained for *O Cruzeiro* to make the 500-mile trek from Rio de Janeiro to Uberaba once more, to see what Chico Xavier had to say about the affair, now that it seemed to be over once and for all.

Chico had been closely involved in the original sessions, and had been photographed holding the shrouded hand of the apparition. He was a close friend of Dr Vieira, with whom he had collaborated on seventeen books, and he was Brazil's best known and most highly respected medium.

The reporters expected a hostile reception, but were warmly greeted by Chico, whose kindness of heart seemed inexhaustible. He had no objections at all to giving his views on the affair at great length, answering all their questions without hesitation.

He was prepared to admit that there had been fraud, but was adamant in insisting that Otília Diogo had been genuine to start with. This is perfectly possible; she would not be the first medium thought to have had a record of fraud preceded by honesty.

'Mediumship,' Chico explained, 'is like a strong flow of water that is suitable for the production of energy. If a hydroelectric power plant is not constructed, this force is lost in nature, when it might be serving mankind.' Otília's spiritual power plant had to be reconstructed, he said, so that she could carry on with her work. Chico not only made it clear that she was welcome in Uberaba at any time 'to start all over again', but even invited the reporters to come back and attend any future sessions with her.[4]

Nearly ten years after the original Uberaba sessions, I managed to locate one of the original team of doctors involved, who now holds a lecturing post at a leading São Paulo state hospital. I was in for a surprise:

'Otília Diogo was the greatest Brazilian medium of all time,' he told me at once. 'The only fraud involved was on the part of the press, which set out to destroy her from the start, just as they tried to destroy Arigó, or any other medium who becomes too well-known.'

'But,' I objected, 'the photographs clearly showed ...'

'That she was genuine,' the doctor interrupted sternly.

'Look at the photo where she is supposed to be kneeling, as the caption says. She wasn't kneeling at all, but materialized in miniature.'

I duly checked my files, and the picture he mentioned did indeed look more like a miniature figure than a full-sized kneeling one. But then there was the unmistakable resemblance between the faces of the medium and the supposed Sister Josefa.

'Mediums' features can be materialized in their spirit doubles on occasions,' the doctor replied. 'You'll find historical precedents for that!' He was right again. I looked where he told me to look, and found an account of the extraordinary experiences of a young schoolteacher named Emilia Sagée, who lost her job at a girls' school in Latvia in 1846, because she had the disconcerting habit of appearing in front of her classes beside herself, her second body being identical with the first. The bewildered pupils could not tell which was which. Upon being fired, Miss Sagée had exclaimed: 'Oh, I can't bear it! This is the nineteenth time!' This is a well documented case, which was observed over an 18-month period by an entire school, staff and pupils.[5]

The doctor also drew my attention to a statement that had been issued by his colleagues shortly after the original *O Cruzeiro* denunciation, which the magazine had not published and which had attracted little attention. The statement contained items that must be taken into account before any attempt to solve the great Uberaba mystery.[6]

Among them: Otília Diogo had been found securely bound after the session, with the marked seals still in place. No reporter had found any of the clothing allegedly used during the materializations, although they searched the whole house for it. While doing so, they did find a small crucifix which they had not found previously. Searching of persons attending the session had been thorough; no flasks or bottles allowed, yet there had been a strong smell of roses and ether during the phenomena. The fact that the medium's features resembled those of the supposed spirit proved nothing. Not only Aksakof but also Crookes, Richet and Lombroso had witnessed similar duplication effects.

The doctors pointed out nine incorrect statements in the reporters' copy, noting that they had not even been able to measure the room correctly, and accusing them of providing the piece of thread they had sent for analysis themselves. Ectoplasm does not leave threads behind, they claimed. Furthermore, they pointed to several discrepancies in the six reporters' original statements. Finally, they stated that they had publicly invited the reporters to take part in a TV debate, but their invitation had been declined.

Otília Diogo, like Mirabelli, undoubtedly did cheat on occasions. But again, this is no proof whatsoever that she always did. I find it hard to believe that a total of nineteen qualified doctors who attended one or other of the original five sessions can all have been deceived. At no stage was their behaviour suspicious; they never sought publicity in the first place but made no objections when it sought them.

As far as I have been able to gather, phenomena witnessed at the first five sessions were far more impressive than those produced for the reporters from *O Cruzeiro.*

Can this be a case of what Barrett meant, as I have already suggested of investigators unconsciously producing the fraud they are looking for? The moral of this sad little story seems to be that, as every serious investigator is well aware, fraud must always be borne in mind as a possibility when researching any form of paranormal phenomenon.

Not only on the part of the medium, I might add, but also on the part of the investigators.

# PART II

# 1

## PSYCHIC SURGERY

EARLY in the 1960s, reports began to come from both Brazil and the Philippines of a phenomenon that most sane people still have no difficulty in finding totally unbelievable; psychic surgery, or actual operations on human bodies by untrained 'surgeons'. The two most widely publicized practitioners of this bizarre profession have been the Brazilian known as Arigó, who died in 1971, and a Filipino named Tony Agpaoa.

Conditions for research into psychic surgery seem to be much better in the Philippines than they are in Brazil, and in 1966 the veteran researcher Harold Sherman produced the first major study of the subject, based on his own amazing experiences with Agpaoa and other healers who worked within, or in association with, the large Filipino Spiritist movement. Meanwhile, another enterprising American researcher, Dr Andrija Puharich, was making several visits to Brazil to observe Arigó, though he was to withhold publication of his findings for several years.[1,2]

Psychic surgeons differ from other types of unorthodox healer in that they actually seem to perform surgical interventions on the human body while in a state of trance and under the control of a guiding spirit; in the case of Arigó this was a certain Dr Adolf Fritz. They may use conventional surgical equipment, ordinary kitchen knives and nail scissors, or in some cases nothing but their own bare hands.

Investigating this particular field is no easy task. As in the case of flying saucers, seeing is not necessarily believing, and getting anybody else to believe is no easy task either. Psychic surgery is something you have to see for yourself, as I have on many occasions as both observer and patient, and have no doubt whatsoever that the phenomenon exists.

It is often objected by sceptics that Spiritist phenomena tend to be trivial. Many indeed are, but surely there is no human activity that is less trivial than our attempts to heal each other of disease? If there is any evidence at all - never mind about proof for the time being - that people can be cured of organic disease by methods not explicable in terms of our present knowledge, then these methods should be examined, however strange they may appear, and as we shall see some of them appear to be very strange indeed.

This is not easy. In unconventional healing, as for that matter in conventional healing, the problem is that without very full records of what was wrong with the patient to begin with, including X-rays and pathological sections, it can be practically impossible to judge whether the treatment has actually caused the improvement, or even if there has been any improvement at all other than in the mind of the patient. (Which may be all that was needed in the first place.)

In addition to faith and spirit healing, many other techniques have provided evidence for cure by seemingly inexplicable methods. Some of these, such as acupuncture, are now becoming widely accepted as normal by many conventional doctors in the West. Hypnosis is another, and in my opinion a very poorly understood and under-utilised one.[3]

Psychic surgery, however, is certainly not accepted as normal or even genuine except by those who have witnessed it. There are three separate questions to be asked here; can people like Arigó and Agpaoa really operate on the physical body, can they make accurate diagnoses, and can their patients get better as a direct result of their actions? The answer to all three questions is yes, though it cannot yet be said that repeatable proof of the latter assertion has yet been obtained under controlled conditions.

What would constitute such proof? Surely there are enough case reports by now to convince anybody that Arigó, for one, really did cure people? Everybody in Brazil seems to know somebody's mother-in-law whose life was saved by him. 'Oh yes,' they assure you, 'she was given up by all the doctors, but after Dr Fritz had a go at her she fully recovered. She can tell you all about it.'

She can indeed, but in my experience she cannot prove anything. She may sincerely believe that she was cured of cancer or whatever, which in itself is something, but proof positive is something else. We will only have it when so many cases of psychic surgery have been witnessed by qualified doctors, before and after (and preferably also during), that it will be evident that there is some pattern behind its workings, and that it can be effective. When that day comes, there are plenty of open-minded doctors around, at least in Brazil, who will gladly put their official seal of approval on the findings of the researchers.

I see no chance of such proof being forthcoming for many years. Let me give an idea of some of the problems involved. Many are similar to those of investigating any phenomena connected with Spiritist mediums. When mediums become well known, they invariably become surrounded by a team of assistants whose duties include keeping people at arm's length, for like any other celebrity the medium is constantly being pestered by seekers of favours. Everybody has a problem of some kind most of the time, and if there is a medium on hand who has the reputation of being able to help people, it is natural that demand will soon exceed availability.

Having penetrated the protective ring around the medium, the researcher may find that the medium does not particularly want to be investigated. They have every right to feel this way, especially if they are doing something technically illegal like psychic surgery. Even if they show an interest in serious research, they may simply not have time to lend themselves to it. Moreover, the average Spiritist in Brazil is none too concerned whether outsiders are convinced of the truths of their faith or not. They are the least aggressive of evangelists, and the most tolerant towards other beliefs, but however helpful they may wish to be, they cannot be expected to hand over their private centres for the purpose of full-scale research, especially if conducted by foreigners. It takes a great deal of time and patience even to get near a really outstanding medium, and stay near for any length of time.

A special problem regarding psychic surgeons is that however obliging they may be as their normal selves, they seldom have the faintest idea what goes on when they are entranced and on the job, so are no more able to tell researchers what they do and how they do it than sleepwalkers are able to say where they have been when they wake up. Worse still, psychic surgeons tend to talk a lot of nonsense while in trance, as I have proved in one case by asking specially prepared questions to which the answers are not known, at least in this world. One of these questions concerned the production of antibodies, and the doctor who set the question for me commented on the lengthy and apparently complete reply: 'His remarks show that he, or whoever he gets it from, has absolutely no idea what antibodies are.'

Whatever else they may do, psychic surgeons are not likely to push back many frontiers of medical knowledge with their trance utterances. The fact that they are often astonishingly accurate when it comes to diagnosing does not make them omniscient, as they certainly can appear at times.

I cannot estimate how many psychic surgeons there are or have been in Brazil. I have seen three at work, seen films of two more, and heard first-hand testimony of a sixth in addition to second-hand accounts of four or five more.

None of the latter will be included here for lack of corroborative evidence. In the following chapters I will describe only those of whom I have either personal experience or for whom there is what I regard as trustworthy evidence.

Now for a word about fraud, which applies to many phenomena described elsewhere in this book. The first thing that must be understood is that psychic gifts have been observed to come and go in cycles. Dr J. B. Rhine has shown that there is a curve of decline and emergence in telepathy, and this also applies to psychic surgery and Spiritist mediumship in general. In Zener card guessing, the telepathy involved may come and go at short intervals, whereas with physical-effects mediumship there may be a long period of supremacy followed by an equally long decline. Let us examine some of the factors that affect this curve of ups and downs, and see where the question of fraud comes in.

Whatever the source of the extraordinary power that some psychic surgeons have been observed to possess may turn out to be, it seems clear that the moral character of the medium concerned has a great deal to do with its continuing supply. A basic tenet of Brazilian Spiritism is that once you make use of your paranormal powers for your own benefit, you lose them. Its believers insist that one should freely give what one has freely received, and that under no circumstances at all should mediums charge money for their services.

It is difficult to stop people giving presents to mediums, however, and only a man with the moral qualities of a Chico Xavier (who once gave away an expensive imported piano an admirer had sent him, although he loved music) can resist this form of temptation to acquire material riches. Mediums are only human, and the better they are at their job the more people will want to give them presents; the more lavish these are the greater their corrupting influence will be. A fondness for material wealth, even unasked, can have an effect on the curve of a medium's abilities. It is a tough vocation, making often unbearable demands on its practitioners, and once a medium's powers have declined they tend to stay that way, possibly with occasional reminders of the old power.

Perhaps the most important factor bearing on the curve of mediumistic ability is that of environment. Very few mediums, and no psychic surgeons that I know of in Brazil, work entirely on their own. They tend to be surrounded by a group of helpers, on whom the mediums depend to a great extent to tell them what they do while they are in trance. If they are genuine, or if at least if they were to start with, trance mediums' only sources of reliable information about their own work are those present during the trance state. To be able to assemble such a group in the first place, it seems probable that a medium must at some time have shown genuine gifts, for it cannot be easy to begin as a deliberate fraud from scratch.

Thus mediums will gradually come to know what is expected of them, and feel obliged, even if subconsciously, to provide the phenomena their customers or patients have come to see. Then comes the day when they find they have not got the necessary power. Now if this happened to a concert pianist, for instance, there would be nothing for it but to cancel the concert. You cannot very well pretend to play a piano concerto if you have forgotten it.

Yet the medium can pretend to be a medium, knowing that there is a good chance nobody will notice the difference, since so much of a medium's work deals with the invisible. When they have one of their bad days, they can either cheat on purpose or unconsciously; or if they are honest they can call off the session altogether. If there are two or three hundred people waiting to see them, perhaps people who have made a contribution to the centre where they work, they may feel obliged to perform just to satisfy their audience, even if they know they cannot produce the genuine effects they have come to see.

You too can be a psychic surgeon, if not for long. Here is how.

There are many ways in which psychic surgeons can, and do, cheat. The most common, which has been observed in the Philippines but not as yet in Brazil, is to tape two small cellophane bags in the palms of your hands, one containing chicken blood and the other pure ether. You slap the hand with the blood in it on the patient's stomach, having punctured it with a tiny pin attached to your thumbnail, making a terrible mess. Then you start prodding away with your fingers, perhaps even making a 'cut' beforehand with a blunt knife so as to leave a nice red line on the skin. Then, when you have finished 'operating', you burst the ether bag in your other hand and mop up the blood, most of which will appear to evaporate, helped perhaps by your assistant's casual dabs with damp cotton wool.

A far easier way of cheating for beginners is to claim that you are only going to operate on the perispirit body, or in the astral plane. Here, all you have to do is wave your hands in the air above the body, manipulate invisible scissors, knives and other implements, muttering instructions to your unseen helpers. These, of course, will not reply, but everybody present will understand that they are on the astral plane and only you can hear them.

As for diagnosis, you use the time-honoured methods of muscle reading and fishing. Chances are your patients have something wrong in the stomach area, so you simply prod around here and write out a prescription for anything you like, preferably something totally harmless. Assure your patients that your spirit guides will slip something into the medicine to make it work better, slap them on the back and order God to be with them. You may find that some will actually get better. If you come up against a really tough case, you always have karma to fall back on. Supposing an attractive young lady comes up and says: 'Oh, Dr Wu' (that's your spirit guide), I'm desperate. I've got cancer of the uterus, colon, stomach, lungs, neck, nose and big toe. I've been given three weeks to live. Help!' In cases like this you prod her around a little, look at the ceiling, cock your ear to the voice of your invisible mentor and reply:

'Yes, my dear sister. Your problem is one of karma. In your past incarnation you were a prison guard in Siberia, and before that you were one of the assistants who threw Christians to the lions in Rome. Before that you were a mass murderer in Atlantis, and in the Mesolithic Age you were a child rapist. In this lifetime, you have been given a great chance to pay off all your past debts at once. God is good. Next patient, please!'

This will never fail. Karma is karma, and with luck your patient will obediently go away and die, convinced she is doing herself a favour. Your spiritual wisdom and understanding will be widely praised, especially if you murmur a prayer for the girl's soul and wish it better luck next time round.

In general, would-be psychic surgeons must remember the cardinal rules of conjuring: don't tell your audience what you are going to do, and never try the same trick twice on the same evening. But there is something else amateur surgeons must do: namely, bring off some genuine cures now and then, otherwise they will be out of business, for the only way they can advertise is by word of mouth. They are also warned that sooner or later somebody will try to film them at work, or bring along a real doctor to watch. When that happens, they had better say their guides are taking the evening off, and do likewise themselves.

A very serious warning must be given here to would-be patients. Although Brazil welcomes tourists, there are two very good reasons why foreigners suffering from serious diseases should not go there in search of help. One is that Brazil, like many countries, has strict immigration laws, and will not issue a visa to anybody who is dangerously ill. The other is that alternative healing is widely practised in many other countries, especially Britain and the US, so readers from those areas are advised to seek out their own local healers instead of adding themselves to the long waiting lists of Brazil's already overburdened psychics. There is no indication whatever that Brazilian healers can do anything that reputable healers in other countries cannot also do; they just use different methods.

Another point to consider is that since the persecution and imprisonment of Arigó there has been a tendency for psychic surgeons to try to remain anonymous, avoid publicity and work in near secrecy. They have in fact mostly gone underground, and it might take a newcomer months even to find one.

Here then, is a short account of a few of the best-known Brazilian psychic surgeons, and a longer account of my own experiences with one of them.

# 2

# ARIGÓ

THE small town of Congonhas do Campo, 250 miles north of Rio de Janeiro in the state of Minas Gerais, is famous throughout Brazil for two very different reasons. It contains some of the finest work of the crippled sculptor known as Aleijadinho, whose real name was Antonio Francisco Lisboa (1738-1814). Tourists and pilgrims still flock to see his dramatic group of prophets, carved from the local soapstone, that stands on the terrace of the church of Bom Jesus de Matosinhos, a masterpiece of Brazilian baroque architecture that was built in 1773.

The other tourist attraction is, or was, the Centro Espírita Jesus Nazareno a few blocks downhill from the church; a modest Spiritist centre like thousands of others all over the country that attracted up to a thousand visitors a day who used to come in hopes of seeing the resident healing medium, a simple and friendly fellow called José Pedro de Freitas, better known by the nickname Zé Arigó, a sort of Brazilian equivalent of 'Johnny Appleseed'.

Arigó was only 49 years old when he died in a head-on collision in January 1971. In his relatively short career as a psychic consultant and surgeon, he had attended to an estimated two million people from all walks of life, including a member of a President of the Republic's own family, several distinguished personalities from the entertainment and political worlds, and countless and mostly anonymous ordinary men and women who helped give him the reputation of being the world's leading practitioner of his peculiar art.

With the exception of Chico Xavier, no Brazilian medium has ever been more of a public figure than Arigó. At least six books have been written about him, in addition to countless newspaper and magazine articles. His unbelievable feats with a terrifying assortment of kitchen knives and rusty pairs of scissors were witnessed at point-blank range by some of the country's leading doctors, and fortunately for posterity he became the first and only Brazilian medium to undergo anything like a serious scrutiny by a qualified scientist. This was not a Brazilian, but a visiting American, Dr Andrija Puharich, one of the few psi researchers of recent times who was prepared to go hunting in the field for interesting cases.

Arigó always worked in public, under normal lighting conditions and in full view of whoever happened to have filed into the centre to await their turn for consultation or treatment. When doctors were present, he would see they had a good view and often let them stand next to him and even hold the patient's head in their hands. Chatting away in the German accent of his supposed spirit guide Dr Fritz, he would often come out with medical language scarcely to be expected from a barely literate son of Congonhas do Campo. He was never accused of fraud by anybody who had actually seen him at work, and it is unlikely that any other Brazilian medium will ever offer such opportunities for research again, opportunities only an American was enterprising enough to grasp.

José Pedro de Freitas was born on October 18th, 1921 on the modest farm of his parents near Congonhas do Campo, the first of a family of ten. He worked in the fields as a child, managing to get through only three years of primary school by way of formal education, after which he could barely read or write. Later, he spent some six years working as a miner of iron ore, after an unsuccessful attempt to run a bar and restaurant, which failed due to Arigó's willingness to sell food and drink on credit.

During his time as a miner, he won a reputation as a labour organizer and was accused of having Communist sympathies, as was then standard practice in Brazil when anybody showed concern for the conditions of the poor. He made some political enemies at this time, some of whom later tried without success to discredit him as a healer, even threatening to kill him.

In 1942, Arigó married his cousin Arlete Soares, who gave him six children, and for about 14 years he held down a regular job in the local pensions office, working from midday to six in the evening.

Accounts of the first manifestations of his mediumship differ widely. Brazilian writers tend to have a horror of such things as dates, place names, witnesses or indeed any form of concrete fact, but what seems known for certain is that in 1956 a well-known senator named Lucio Bittencourt announced in public that he had been operated on by Arigó in a room at the Hotel Itatiaia in Belo Horizonte, the capital of Minas Gerais. Since both the senator and Arigó appeared to have been asleep at the time, it is not clear just what happened, though Bittencourt said he had been suffering from a tumour of the lung, which was certainly not there when he went back to his doctor for X-rays.

Arigó later told the writer J. Herculano Pires (one of the few Brazilian parapsychologists ever to have attempted original research of any kind) that he recalled nothing whatsoever of this incident, and that at the time he had been a devout Catholic with a horror of any form of Spiritism, from which he had fled 'like the Devil from the cross'.[1]

He did, however, claim that since childhood he had experienced strange visions, usually of a kind of luminous cloud floating in space, and had heard voices talking to him, sometimes in what he took to be German. He had also seen his subsequent mentor, Dr Fritz, whose first manifestation had scared him stiff. 'He was a monster with a huge belly and a German-looking face!'

Arigó's first public performance, according to himself (as told to Pires), was an operation on the stomach of an old woman in Congonhas from which he extracted a tumour, using only a kitchen knife and his bare hands, in full view of several witnesses. This was probably also in 1956.

Not surprisingly, his fame as a healer spread rapidly, and before long the whole of Brazil seemed to be beating a path to the door of the Spiritist centre that had been formed by a group of Arigó's friends, once the medium himself had accepted his fate and gradually moved away from Catholicism to Spiritism.

He managed to remain on good terms with his former church. Father Virgilio, parish priest of Congonhas who had known him since childhood, told one of Arigó's biographers that he had always regarded him as a model of Christian charity and humane sentiments, whose main aim in life was to help his fellow men. 'How can we condemn him for wishing his neighbour well?' the priest asked, showing tolerance seldom expressed by Catholics towards Spiritist mediums.[2]

The good priest's sentiments were not shared by all, and in 1958 Arigó had his first clash with the law of the land, under which the illegal practice of medicine was punishable, as in many countries, by a jail sentence. The Minas Gerais Medical Association managed to get him into court and sentenced to thirty months, although he was saved at the last minute by no less than the President of the Republic, Juscelino Kubitschek.

Though a practising Catholic and qualified medical doctor, Kubitschek knew his people well and was always sympathetic towards Spiritism. It was during his term of office that Brazil became the only country in the world to issue a special postage stamp to mark the 100th anniversary of the publication of Kardec's *The Spirits' Book*, and when one of his daughters became seriously ill, he had no hesitation in summoning Arigó to the presidential home in Copacabana to examine her.

'He came in and looked at her,' the former president recalled in a 1972 interview, 'and without knowing anything about her disease said she was suffering from a serious kidney complaint and needed an immediate operation.' Arigó advised the president to let his daughter go ahead with the operation that had already been arranged in the US, assuring him that she would be all right and that he would hold himself responsible for the result. Marcia Kubitschek duly went to the United States, had her kidney operation, and returned fully cured. 'All I can say is that I believed in Zé Arigó,' her father recalled. 'I never heard of anyone suffering under his hands. He did nothing but good. I collected evidence from thousands of people, and they all considered him charitable and kind. So I pardoned him.'[3]

This episode reveals the degree to which Spiritist phenomena can be accepted in Brazil even when they appear to go against the law. But Arigó was less fortunate the next time the law went after him, which was in 1964, the year of the military-backed revolution that among other things deprived Kubitschek of his political rights. (To their credit, successive military governments after 1964 never interfered with Spiritism; another Kardec stamp was issued in 1969 during the extremely tough Costa e Silva administration, but they were far too busy in their first year of office to worry about the fate of Arigó).

This time he did go to prison, rejecting his friends' offer of a campaign to secure another pardon from high places. Once behind bars, Arigó showed no hard feelings, only complaining of the conditions his fellow prisoners had to live in; he himself was given a number of privileges in view of his status as a national celebrity. 'The judge who sentenced me was only doing his duty,' he told reporters who flocked to see him behind bars. 'We all have a mission here on earth, and mine is to heal.' Indeed, at his formal sentencing, Arigó had kissed the magistrate's hand, apologized for all the trouble he had caused and reminded him that 'I have a job to do as well, you know!'

Despite his own refusal to plead for a reduction in his sentence, Arigó immediately became a *cause célèbre*, attracting so many visitors to the town of Conselheiro Lafaiete, where he was held, that he jokingly suggested they should build a special prison for him in Congonhas, 'where at least I can be near my wife and children'.

He referred to his prison as 'paradise', where he was free from all the pressures of his work at the Spiritist centre. 'Here, I'm a free man,' he said. Some of his admirers even felt he must have done something wrong in a previous incarnation and was now being allowed to adjust his karma. Anyway, he was freed after serving seven months and four days of his 16-month sentence, and his return home to Congonhas provoked wild scenes of celebration.

As he quickly became re-established as the most famous surgeon in the country, he began to attract the attention of members of the profession considerably better qualified than himself. Fortunately for posterity, many of these came not to denounce him, but to study his methods with open minds. There is probably more eyewitness testimony on public record to Arigó's work than to that of any similar healer in history, and much of it comes from qualified doctors.

One distinguished Brazilian surgeon who is fully satisfied with the evidence of his own eyes is Dr Ary Lex, author of one of the standard textbooks used by Brazilian medical students, and an active member of several professional associations. When I approached him in September 1973, Dr Lex unhesitatingly confirmed the lengthy and detailed account of his experiences with Arigó that had already been widely quoted. His evidence is of special interest in that he admitted he originally went to see Arigó in an extremely sceptical frame of mind.

'I was fully prepared to debunk him if necessary,' he told me. 'But there was no trickery at all. It was the small details that really stuck in my mind; the way Arigó would simply turn his back on the patient in the middle of an operation, the way he would just touch some blood flowing from an eye and it would stop at once, or the way he would pull an eye right out of its socket without causing a trace of pain.'

Dr Lex witnessed a total of four operations in the space of about half an hour, during one of which he was actually holding the patient's head in his hands. The first was for the draining of a cyst on the patient's wrist, which was done without any preparation whatsoever (as in every reported operation of Arigó's), no anaesthesia, no kind of sterilization, and no hint of hypnosis or suggestion. Next came the removal of a lipoma (a benign tumour made up largely of fatty cells) from a woman's arm. While Dr Lex held the arm, Arigó simply rubbed the back of his knife over the skin without attempting to cut it, until the skin appeared to open of its own accord, upon which Arigó squeezed the lipoma and brought it out intact. Dr Lex had the presence of mind to time the operation, which took place about a foot in front of his eyes in a good light, and found the whole process took thirty seconds. He reckoned that fifteen minutes would be an average time for a similar operation under conventional conditions.

The third operation was the same as the second, and Dr Lex again pointed out that he had a perfectly clear and unobstructed view. Out popped another lipoma in half a minute. I have seen the colour film of a similar operation made by the São Paulo journalist Jorge Rizzini, and can fully support Dr Lex's testimony. So could Dr Puharich, who was himself the patient on this occasion.

Next came one of Arigó's traditional specialities; the ablation or removal of a pterygium from a woman's eye. This was done with an ordinary pair of nail scissors, and when blood began to trickle from the eye, Arigó simply dabbed at it with cotton wool and told it to stop, which it did. I have also seen this on film, and Dr Lex assures me that he knows of no way in which the amount of blood he saw can normally be made to coagulate so quickly.

What really shook Dr Lex (and me, while watching Rizzini's film), was the incredible roughness, at times amounting to violence, of Arigó's surgical techniques. He would pick up his knife, which looked like an ordinary table knife, and simply shove it under the eyeball, sometimes taking his hand away and letting it hang there. The patient would appear apprehensive, though showing no sign at all of pain. Worst of all was Arigó's disconcerting habit of appearing to take little interest in what he was doing, frequently looking over his shoulder while poking around with somebody's eyeball half out of its socket.

An important point regarding Dr Lex's testimony is that he was himself an active Spiritist and a frequent speaker at the São Paulo Spiritist Federation, where a favourite theme of his was the need to expose fraudulent mediums who only served to discredit the movement. He did not strike me as a man one can describe as credulous, for he had examined several other alleged medium healers and remained unimpressed by any of them.

He was also sharply critical of Arigó's prescriptions, some of which he was able to examine on the spot.

They were absolutely ridiculous,' he told me. 'Some of them were for obsolete medicines which were only still being made because he prescribed them.' He mentioned one, known in Brazil as Kanamicina, which he considered not only obsolete but actually dangerous. He also told me that Arigó would prescribe alarmingly large quantities of medicines, which quite apart from their possible side effects were extremely expensive. He estimated the cost of one prescription he saw as equal to about one hundred US dollars.

Dr Lex made an attempt to set up some sort of scientific test with Arigó, 'but I was given the impression he was not interested'. Future investigators are advised that they are likely to get better results with psychic surgeons when they are out of trance, when some of them are perfectly normal people. When they are entranced they can be very different, and although in my own experience a medium in trance will stand by a promise made out of trance, the reverse is not always true. It is all very confusing, and it is only too easy for researchers of psychic surgery to give up in despair.

Dr Lex made it unmistakably clear to me that he had witnessed the reality of paranormal surgery. Zé Arigó was genuine. He offered me no evidence for lasting cures, and reminded me that the real significance of the work of people like Arigó was often misunderstood. 'He was sent for a mission far greater than the healing of a few bad eyes,' he told me. Just what that mission was must be a matter of personal opinion, but I can only point out that after witnessing phenomena such as those described above, especially for the first time, few people are able to resist the impulse to revise their opinions of some of the greater mysteries of life. Having experienced psychic surgery myself, I am forced to take the Spiritist explanation seriously, at least as a working hypothesis, if only because any other hypothesis seems even more unlikely.

Many people, I suspect, would take psychic surgeons more seriously if there were strong evidence that anybody had been cured of a fatal disease by one. Such evidence is hard to find. Harry Edwards has pointed out that it is in fact almost impossible, because any patient who is considered incurable must have had some medical treatment, and if there is a recovery after paranormal healing it will always be claimed that this was due to the medical treatment. Or, of course, the original diagnosis may have been wrong.[4]

What we need is a case where full medical records were compiled, the patient was declared incurable by more than one specialist, and then made a full recovery after unorthodox healing.

Here it is.

This case history was given me by Dr José Hortencio de Medeiros, a specialist in radiology of the heart who held several important posts in São Paulo hospitals, including that of lecturer at the state cardiology institute. The patient, a woman of 28, was carried into a São Paulo emergency ward one day in 1961, suffering from severe intestinal obstruction. Examinations revealed that she had two tumours in her transverse colon, one of which was blocking it completely. They were removed, sent for analysis, and found to be cancerous. Two further examinations by independent pathologists confirmed that the woman was incurable. She was given two months to live at the most, and for temporary relief a colostomy operation was performed to allow excretion to pass from her colon.

As Dr Medeiros was telling me the story, he suddenly grabbed my notebook and pen, and drew a diagram of a colon, indicating the site of the tumours.

'There were metastases all over the place,' he said, drawing fifteen circles around the colon. 'One was the size of a hen's egg. She simply hadn't a chance. Three specialists were agreed on that.'

'Was there any possibility of spontaneous regression?' I asked timidly.

Dr Medeiros snorted, as if a student had asked a particularly silly question. 'I wouldn't say so,' he replied, before going on with his story.

'The woman's husband decided not to give up. He took his wife to Congonhas by air; she was too weak to travel by road, since her normal weight of 58 kilos was down to less than 30. Arigó took one look at her and wrote out a prescription for four medicines: Kanamicina, Olobintin, Neurorubin and Dexteoxina; heavy doses of each.' Two of these, I noticed, were among the medicines Dr Lex had condemned as either obsolete or dangerous.

'The patient took the medicines as ordered by Arigó, and began to improve at once. After only a week she had put on ten kilos and was getting out of bed and walking around. Six weeks later she was weighing 60 kilos; two kilos above her former normal weight.' The woman seemed to have been cured, but she went back to Congonhas just to make sure. Arigó told her she had been saved, but gave her two more prescriptions, including Gamaclorex, Cloromycetin Metio-Scil and Albamicina-GU, an antibiotic for the urinary passages. The latter struck Dr Medeiros as interesting, for the blockage in the woman's colon had caused trouble in her urinary system as well.[5]

Back she went for a third check-up, whereupon Arigó announced that she was cured. That was in August 1961. The woman who had been given two months to live eventually died in January 1968. She had been back to see Arigó shortly before her death, but the prescription he had given her was no use.

'The phenomenon had fallen off by then,' Dr Medeiros told me, confirming other reports I had heard to the effect that towards the end of his career Arigó had lost some of his earlier powers. 'But there is no doubt that she lived over six years because of him; no doubt at all.' Every detail of every stage of this case is on file at the hospitals where the woman was originally examined. It is not a perfect case, since she was never actually operated on by Arigó, at least not visibly, and she did eventually die while still only in her thirties. It reminded me of other cases with which I was familiar of patients who had apparently been cured by psychic surgeons but had suffered relapses later. Psychic surgeons unquestionably have powers, but these seem limited by factors beyond even their control.

Dr Medeiros was able to watch Arigó at work on several occasions, witnessing two of the eye operations for which he was best known.

'He was really violent,' he told me. 'I cannot think how he avoided cutting the muscles, the way he moved the knife around, sometimes even without looking at what he was doing. Anybody else would have hurt the patient seriously, but patients showed no sign of pain at all.'

There was an interesting sequel to Arigó's cure of the woman's cancer of the colon. In 1961, Dr Medeiros went on television to describe the case, after it was apparent that the woman's life had been saved by unconventional methods. As might be expected, he was immediately bombarded with requests for the magic prescriptions that Arigó had given her.

'There were at least fifty of them, mostly people who had been given up by their doctors. I gave them all the prescriptions, as I felt obliged to do for humanitarian reasons, but I made it very clear that I could not be held responsible for results.

'The results were very interesting. In some cases there was no improvement at all; in others the patients lived for a further six months or so, but in three cases the patients were cured for at least three or four years, after which I lost touch with them. Now the interesting feature is that these three, who were all women, were precisely the most understanding and highly spiritualized of them all. One of them, who had terminal cancer of the uterus, with no chance of living more than a couple of months, was a real saint, a radiant personality. It shows that there must be a relation between the patient's attitude and the disease, even when it is cancer. Without faith and good vibrations, you get nowhere.'

It makes you wonder. Can all disease be cured by the faith of the patient? And are visible psychic operations really necessary? Dr Medeiros mentioned a case where a woman with a previously X-rayed cancerous tumour in her stomach had recovered after a visit to Arigó in which he had not only not operated, but had not even given her a prescription. He had simply sent her away with the assurance that she would recover and the mysterious comment 'I'll have you surrounded!'

Is it all done by suggestion? There can be no doubt that many of those who flocked to Congonhas do Campo were fully convinced that Arigó (or Dr Fritz, or whoever) was going to save their lives. There is probably a psychosomatic element in all disease, and confidence on the part of the patient is obviously a help rather than a hindrance during treatment. Animal lovers will know what remarkable 'miracle cures' their pets are able to achieve without any help from us humans. A friend of mine had a dog that was bitten by a jararaca, the most dangerous snake in Brazil that can kill a man in fifteen minutes. The dog stumbled off into the forest as if to die, but came bounding home four days later with no trace of the hideous wound the snake had inflicted. The look on its face seemed to be saying 'There! We dogs know a thing or two about healing that you don't!' Yet, bearing the question of suggestion in mind, the fact remains that Arigó was seen to do things that are supposed to be impossible.

First, there was the way he would work on patients without any form of anaesthesia, hypnosis, sterilization precautions or spoken suggestion. Yet nobody ever complained of pain or died of blood poisoning. If there had been one single case of a patient dying under Arigó's rusty knife or blunt scissors, the story would have been all over the country overnight, and Arigó would have faced jail for life.

Next, and most impressive of all, was his uncanny way of closing up incisions. Dr Medeiros and Dr Lex were just two of several doctors who were able to watch this happening under good lighting conditions, and made their opinions known publicly. Once, after removing a synovial cyst from a woman's arm, cutting tissue with his usual pair of nail scissors, Arigó simply pressed the edges of the flesh together with his fingers and joined them 'as if by magic', in the words of Dr Medeiros who, as a radiologist, is accustomed to careful observation. This is one of the great mysteries of psychic surgery, yet I have seen it happen both on film and in the flesh (mine included). The flesh simply comes together leaving a faint red line, which subsequently disappears altogether, where the incision was made.

Finally, there was the rapidity with which Arigó could make accurate diagnoses. He would work with the speed of an assembly line worker on piece rates, often treating patients with considerable roughness or making unkind jokes at their expense. 'There's nothing wrong with you at all,' he told one elderly spinster. 'What you need is to get married. Well then, go away and get married!' To Arigó, it was a matter of doing the job in hand as quickly as possible and getting on with the next one, working standing up for hours on end without showing signs of fatigue. He never seemed to pause to think. He would casually prod the patient with one hand while scribbling off a complicated prescription with the other. He could deal with consultations at the rate of one a minute; diagnosis, prescription and all. As to the accuracy of the diagnoses, Dr Puharich and his team were able to follow up more than five hundred cases and confirm Arigó's findings as 95% correct. [6]

What first strikes everybody who is able to witness psychic surgery is the amazing speed at which some, but not all, surgeons work, and the complete self-confidence they all show in the process. The impression really is of another force guiding their hands, especially when, as so often happens, they are not even looking at what their hands are doing.

How do they do it? Strangely enough, few Brazilians have ever asked, and those that have were usually told a lot of incoherent nonsense. I have been assured by Spiritist friends that what often happens is what they call partial incorporation, whereby the mediums' hands are controlled by spirits while their minds, conscious or otherwise, remain largely responsible for the stream of mystifying chatter they may keep up.

Arigó was always apparently incorporated by the spirit of the late Dr Adolf Fritz, who is supposed to have been born in Munich, brought up in Poland and later arrested after an unsuccessful operation on a General's daughter. Eventually, he is said to have fled to Estonia and died there in 1918. No supporting evidence for the existence of Dr Fritz has ever been found, and I suspect it never will be.

In general, psychic surgeons seem to have telepathic access to information regarding the patient in front of them, but little else. It is no use asking them to reveal the secrets of the universe, though very occasionally there are glimmerings of a breakthrough in this direction. After one of Arigó's routine operations, an enterprising onlooker once asked how it was done, and the reply in Dr Fritz's gruff German accent was to the following effect: 'We disconnect the biomagnetic organizing fields that link the perispirit body to matter (i.e. the physical body), so that the tissues become an amorphous mass. Then we remove the foreign matter, which is not connected to the structure of the organism, and reconnect the fields.' My source for this information was a reliable witness who was none too sure what Arigó was talking about at the time, but simply did his best to remember his exact words.

The quotation brings to mind Chico Xavier's insistence, in *Evolution in Two Worlds*, upon the reality of an organizing force behind all living matter. It will make more sense in the context of Hernani Guimarães Andrade's corpuscular spirit, or psi matter, theory which we will examine at the end of this book.

Briefly, this theory is a concept worked out to explain the organization of molecules into organic matter along predetermined lines as established by a biological organizing model (BOM). Since these lines do not include disease, damaged tissues are not governed by the model, and if there is some way of making contact with the BOM, living tissue can be recreated, much in the way that a cook can bake a new cake after the first has collapsed in the oven, using the same mould. This may sound fairly far out, but it will have to do until a better hypothesis comes along. It can only be said at this stage that much of what psychic surgeons have been observed to do appears to support it, and if there were a normal explanation for what they do we should have had it by now.

We might have had it if Puharich's pioneering research of the 1960s had been followed up. He and his colleagues established the fact that psychic surgery is a genuine phenomenon, at least as practiced by Arigó and others to be mentioned later. There is more than enough evidence, much of it on film and video, in addition to testimony from qualified doctors, to dismiss the allegation we still hear from the diehard sceptics that it is all deception and illusion. A huge field, which may contain countless hitherto buried treasures awaits further exploration.

# 3

## ANTONIO SALES

Antonio Sales was the quiet man of psychic surgery. Little is known about him except that he was born near Caratinga, Minas Gerais, in 1928 and lived there for most of his life; that he was barely literate, and that his only profession other than psychic surgeon was that of bricklayer. According to one source he never even got that far, having worked only as a bricklayer's assistant. He began to develop his talents as a medium around 1949, after working on the construction of a Spiritist centre where he was told he had mediumistic qualities that should be trained. He began his career in psychic surgery in the early nineteen fifties, moving to the Dias da Cruz Spiritist centre in 1966, where he remained as full-time medium and healer. He was married with three daughters and a son named Joseph Gleber after one of the spirit doctors who were said to guide him.

Despite his lack of formal education, Sales was a distinguished-looking man who might almost pass for a normal surgeon. He worked in a white coat, used conventional surgical equipment, and the walls of his surgery were lined with shelves of ordinary medicines, neatly stacked and labelled. Former patients have described him to me as a calm and friendly man who treated them much more kindly than Arigó used to.

'Arigo was very crude indeed,' one woman told me. 'Sales is just like any other doctor. He puts you at your ease, talking about your problem, and behaving like a real professional.'

'There is a wonderful atmosphere of doing good at his centre,' another former patient said. 'Nobody ever asked me for money there. I

didn't like Arigó at all, but Sales was really charming.' This is interesting, because Sales and Arigó had one thing in common: Dr Fritz. There
were so many Dr Fritzes popping up all over Brazil since Arigó's death
that reports of a new manifestation of him tended to be regarded with
scepticism even by the most credulous. Sales, nevertheless, invariably
spoke with the Fritz accent while at work (except when one of his other
doctor spirits was in charge), and appeared to have done so since some
time after Arigó began performing fewer operations after his second
prison sentence and restricted his work to diagnosis and prescription.
This, I understand, was a condition of his early release.

A Rio de Janeiro woman who visited Arigó had been given pills for
inflammation of her ovaries. Later, after Arigó's death, she went to see
Sales for another problem and was surprised to hear a Germanic voice
addressing her and saying 'Ah, I'm glad you took those pills,' mentioning the same pills by name. It sounded like the same old Fritz.

Sales was also noted for his eye operations, which was always Arigó's
speciality. His techniques were considerably more normal, however, and
the only apparent difference between him and a normal surgeon is the
speed with which he worked, apart from the fact that like all psychic
surgeons he used no visible methods of sterilization or anaesthesia.

I have no reliable evidence that Sales actually opened bodies, though
there is no doubt he could perform highly skilful feats during trance.
A woman has told me how she went to him suffering from a permanently painful slipped disc, and was told to lie on the bed, whereupon
Sales seized her and gave her spine a terrific wrench.

'Help!' she cried. 'You're killing me!'

'Don't worry,' came the gruff reply. 'Fritz knows what he is doing.'
This was just as well, for an unskilled bone manipulator can easily
paralyse a person for life. The woman assured me that her pain went
at once.

Another witness has described to me how Sales operated on the
throat of a girl apparently suffering from tonsillitis. 'He thrust a pair
of scissors into her mouth and started cutting away, telling the girl not
to worry because everything was sterilized. I noticed a smell of ether
around the place, but saw no sign of anybody sterilizing anything at
all. Some blood came out of the girl's mouth, but very little, and two
hours later she was eating a huge steak.' The same girl had been told to
take massive doses of antibiotics, but had found no chemist willing to
make up the prescription. She soon became ill with a high fever, and
only after her desperate family had persuaded a nervous family doctor

to rewrite the prescription was she able to get hold of the antibiotics. These, I was assured, cured her.

Another woman was also apparently cured of a serious skin disease. 'Look at my hands,' she invited me. 'Aren't they beautiful?' I stroked her skin with a finger. It was soft and silky, and the woman herself was youthful-looking and attractive, although she had a grown-up daughter.

'Before I went to see Sales, I had to wear gloves,' she told me. 'My arms and hands were simply hideous with a sort of rash that nobody could cure.' From her description, she seemed to have had a form of psoriasis, which was then generally thought to be incurable, at least in Brazil. Members of her family agreed that she had always worn long-sleeved dresses and gloves.

Sales seemed to have suffered the same fate as Arigó, though to a lesser extent. In 1971 a series of articles in a Brazilian weekly magazine earned him nation-wide publicity, and visitors to Caratinga after that date have told me that he was still giving consultations but doing no more operations. The magazine printed a picture of Sales examining an eye with a normal-looking surgical knife, while other pictures showed faint lines on a stomach that could easily have been produced by scratching the surface, although the patient concerned was quoted as saying he had felt something being removed from his stomach. However, since the whole operation took place in total darkness we have little reliable evidence to go on in this case.[1]

Another visitor to Caratinga, a devout Spiritist medium, told me that Sales lost his healing powers, and the whole set-up there was what she called 'a case for the police'. We must remember, though, that mediumistic powers come and go, and my friend may have simply caught Sales on one of his off days, or even in an off year.

It is not fair to judge any medium's performance from one visit, or even from a dozen. There was a time when the Society for Psychical Research were in favour of rejecting out of hand any medium they caught cheating, which in my opinion was a mistaken attitude. If I had not been able to observe psychic surgery for myself over a period of more than two years, I would have been unable to write anything about it at all that sounded convincing even to myself.

On the evidence I have been able to gather, it seems that Antonio Sales once had considerable gifts as a healing medium, for which he never charged, and which included skills that qualify him for inclusion in this section on psychic surgery. However, it seems that after 1971 he entered a period of decline, and I heard no more about him.

# 4

# LOURIVAL DE FREITAS

THE most unconventional and spectacular of all psychic surgeons, Lourival de Freitas deserves a whole book to himself, and thanks to British journalist Anne Dooley, who knew him for many years and was herself operated on by him, he has at least several chapters in one.[1]

The most gregarious and sociable of mediums, he seems to have had no objections to publicity or observation while at work. There were few possibilities of investigating him in Brazil, however, since most of his operating was done on his frequent trips to England and other European countries, where he was better known than he was in Brazil. There he is said to have lived in fear of arrest, and carried out his healing work in considerable secrecy. As it happens, he used to do some of it in a house a short walk from mine in the Santa Teresa district of Rio de Janeiro, though I only heard about it later from a neighbour. So, having missed a chance to witness psychic surgery almost on my doorstep, I did my best to collect first-hand evidence for his activities.

Lourival was unlike any other psychic surgeon I know of in practically every respect. He had no connection with any Spiritist movement; he worked in conditions that have been well described as a 'surgeon's nightmare', and the evidence for his ability to perform the most dramatic feats of surgical intervention on the body is overwhelming. There is also solid evidence, including some from qualified doctors, that he could cure serious diseases, of which the case of Anne Dooley is among the most convincing yet published. Above all, he was a wildly eccentric individual who had been seen to down an entire bottle of Scotch before operating, and whose only other apparent preparation for work was playing his guitar and singing songs.

My neighbour described for me how Lourival operated on a young girl who was suffering from saturation of the lungs and was gradually being choked to death, being considered an inoperable case. Lourival had insisted on the operation being performed in a yacht, of all places, moored in the Bay of Guanabara some distance from the beaches of Rio de Janeiro. As the small boat swayed to and fro, Lourival plunged a pair of scissors down the girl's throat with considerable violence and began to make cutting movements and sounds. At this point, one onlooker rushed out on deck in terror, and later refused even to discuss the affair with me, saying that even thinking about it made her feel sick.

The patient showed signs of considerable pain for a few minutes, but Lourival then picked her up by her legs and held her upside down, upon which quantities of liquid flowed out of her mouth on to the floor of the cabin. After this experience, the girl made an apparently complete recovery and was able to go out to parties and to dance, which she had been too weak to do previously. After about a year, however, she felt signs that her old problem was returning, after which I lost touch with her. This is not the only case where cures by psychic surgery appear to have been only temporary.

Larry Carr, the Hollywood actor whom I mentioned in my Introduction, has told me he watched Lourival extract an apparent tumour from a woman by simply pressing a glass against her skin. A lump of dark tissue appeared to come through the skin into the glass without leaving any mark on the skin itself. A similar performance is described by Anne Dooley. Brazilian journalist Jorge Rizzini has shown me a film made under strong light in which Lourival performs several operations on various stomachs, giving a nerve-shatteringly realistic impression of cutting skin with his knife, putting his hands inside the body, and pulling out pieces of tissue. Blood-coloured liquid is plainly visible; at one stage Lourival playfully smears a red stain on the patient's forehead that remains after the operation is over, as do the marks along the line of incision. The film also shows him placing a bandage over the scar, pulling it off moments later to reveal nothing except a faint reddish stain around the wound. If this is conjuring, its performer could make a fortune on any stage.

Lourival came from a little fishing village near Rio de Janeiro called Coroa Grande. He was born in 1929, an orphan who believed he was of Russian descent, and was given the family name of the couple who adopted him. He had almost no formal education, and worked as a bus ticket collector, salvage salesman and apparently also as a police detective, a job for which educational requirements in Brazil cannot be very high. His mediumship dated from about 1934, when he is supposed to have performed an operation on a plantation owner with an ordinary pocket knife. If true, this would make him the youngest psychic surgeon on record. Since childhood, he was under the impression that his spirit guide was the former Roman emperor Nero.

One person who was thoroughly convinced of his powers was his English wife Charm, who married him after he had cured her six-year-old daughter (by a previous marriage) of a bronchial complaint that had beset her since the age of eighteen months. This was in 1966, while Lourival was on one of his European trips. In July of that year he gave a demonstration of his powers at the Spiritualist Association premises in London, to which several prominent British healers were invited. Harry Edwards, the most reputable of these, later accused him outright of fraud, while Gordon Turner was quoted as hoping that 'we have seen the last' of this form of alleged healing. He could not believe, he said, that the Great Spirit required table knives in order to heal.

Mr Turner may be right, if his own impressive record of healing is anything to go by. It is unfortunate, though, that nobody in London seems to have tried to investigate Lourival seriously, for there was quite enough evidence of his powers to warrant such a step. As for the Great Spirit, it is known to move in mysterious ways.

I now pass on to three psychic surgeons of whom I had first-hand knowledge. Collecting accounts from witnesses of psychic surgery is one thing, even from your next-door neighbours, but seeing it for yourself and undergoing it is another.

Luckily, I was able to do both.

# 5

## ZECA

I FIRST saw Zeca (the nickname by which he was known) at work in a crowded Spiritist centre in the Lapa district of São Paulo one evening in November 1973. With a fellow researcher, I arrived at 8 p.m. to find him already at work in front of at least 200 people who filled the rows of wooden benches in the room, which was about eight yards by ten and brightly lit by five bulbs of at least 60 watts each. At the far end of the room, a portrait of Jesus was topped by a weaker blue bulb, and beneath this were two iron beds, beside which Zeca was standing with his back to the wall. The beds were placed end to end and parallel with the back wall.

Two helpers were smoothing sheets over the patients awaiting their turn for operation. Near the beds, on the side closest to the audience, there was a large table at which seven or eight mediums were seated, their eyes closed or covered by their hands. From time to time one of these would get up and be replaced by another, and occasionally somebody would make a short speech to the audience, asking us to concentrate our thoughts on Jesus, keep quiet and leave the area around the door clear.

I was immediately disappointed to find that while Zeca was actually touching his patients, the helpers would hold up the sheet so that patients could not be seen from the main part of the hall, where I was standing, although we could see under and around the beds. Plenty could be heard, however, and when I later compared notes with my colleague, who had edged her way round to the other side of the room from where I was, we were satisfied that considerable anomalous activity had taken place.

87

Zeca, whose only known profession was that of dealer in second-hand oil drums, was wearing a short-sleeved sweater, and frequently went to wash his hands in a bucket of dirty-looking water. This was the first evidence I had that psychic surgeons take any sort of notice of the rules of elementary hygiene.

He was a tall and handsome-looking fellow, aged about forty, with dark hair and a calm expression on his suntanned face. He spoke hardly a word throughout the three hours I watched him at work, nor did he rest for a single moment, moving from one bed back to the other as patients came forward when their names were called. I saw a total of eighteen people receive treatment, and learned that more had been attended to before my arrival.

Several features of his performance struck me as interesting. His operations took a very long time by psi-surgical standards, some lasting up to ten minutes, and occasionally patients would make realistic noises suggesting either nervousness, acute discomfort, or real pain. Zeca appeared to be using normal surgical equipment, snapping his fingers at an assistant to pass the tray of scissors, knives and cotton swabs much as an ordinary surgeon does.

He would take surgical scissors and make realistic cutting sounds behind the raised sheet. Several times I saw him take pincers and drop what looked like small pieces of meat into a plastic shopping bag an assistant held out for him. One such piece was far larger, about the size of a fair-sized piece of raw steak, the sight of which brought a gasp from the audience and a stern instruction from one of the mediums to fix our thoughts on Jesus. Zeca simply glanced at this hunk of matter and dropped it casually into the bag. I learned later that this bag was always thrown into a river after sessions. No free samples for researchers.

Zeca had little chance to conceal these pieces of what may well have been human tissue. The sheets were changed for every patient; he wore tightly fitting sleeves that only reached a few inches below his elbow, and he never put a hand in a pocket throughout the evening. I frequently caught sight of the palms of his hands, and could see no sign of anything concealed in them. He was almost always holding some implement in them, and he worked without a break, even for a glass of water, although the room was uncomfortably hot and stuffy.

Patients were of all ages and both sexes, and included a little boy of about four, who was carried to the bed in his father's arms, and who cried out loudly several times during his long operation. Each time he did so, we were urged to repeat the Lord's Prayer out loud, and I reminded myself it was time I learned this in Portuguese if I was to make a convincing impression as a member of the faithful on future occasions.

The most alarming moment came when Zeca took a small hammer and a kind of steel chisel and proceeded to make loud taps behind the raised sheet, as if cutting through a fair-sized bone. This patient, a middle-aged man, looked uncomfortable and nervous but showed no sign of serious pain. Zeca tapped away at least fifty times, very rapidly, and later dropped what looked very much like a piece of bone (from about four yards) into the plastic bag.

When he had performed the last operation of the evening, Zeca at once began to attend to patients who had been waiting for a consultation, although he had been either on his feet or resting briefly against a high stool for over three hours. To some of his patients, he gave what looked like acupuncture jabs with a very large needle, like a knitting needle, prodding at great speed into various parts of the neck and back, with impressive self-assurance and quite alarming violence.

To another patient, a smartly dressed man with a neat black moustache, he gave a frightening display of bone manipulation; locking his arms round the man's neck, he gave it a violent upward wrench, almost lifting the man from the floor. (An unarmed combat specialist has told me that this is similar to one of the easier ways to kill a man in a few seconds). Next, Zeca stood back to back with the man, grabbed his arms over his head and jerked himself forward, so that the startled man was lifted into a horizontal position in the air. Instead of subsequently crumpling into a heap on the floor as I feared he might, the man merely straightened his tie, smiled and walked out of the room.

This performance alone satisfied me that Zeca had unusual abilities, and had given a display of healing methods that no layman would dare attempt in public. But I could naturally not feel fully satisfied until I had good evidence of what went on behind those raised sheets.

After many enquiries, I got what I wanted; an eye witness account of a genuine surgical intervention by a fully qualified doctor, who agreed to describe her experience with Zeca on condition that I did not reveal her name.

Dr S. was a young graduate from one of Brazil's leading medical faculties, who subsequently completed a postgraduate course in psychiatry and opened her own clinic. She had a whole wall of framed diplomas, including that of membership of the São Paulo Association of Spiritist Medicine. She was also a medium, and therefore interested in psychic surgery from both sides, so to speak. She was one of the very few people outside Zeca's own circle of helpers (who won't talk to strangers) who have seen him at work from the other side of the raised sheet.

The operation she watched took place in a private house in São Paulo on a Saturday afternoon in May 1973. Dr S., a friend of the patient's family, was present along with five or six other people of good social standing. As a medium, she was asked to sit at the table and help provide the necessary 'current' by prayer and concentration.

'I sat at the table with my back to the couch where the patient was lying,' she told me as we sat in her clinic one hot November afternoon. 'I couldn't see anything, of course, because I had my eyes closed like all the others at the table. But now and then I would sort of squint round to see what was going on. I could see a normal tray of surgical equipment, including a pair of trochanter scissors - that's a type of surgical scissors for cutting through cartilage and small bones, and at one stage I could clearly hear the sound of this instrument being used.

'I became quite alarmed, and finally I turned my head right round and looked. The assistants were holding the sheet up, so that I couldn't see anything, but Zeca saw me and asked what was the matter. I told him that as a doctor I felt I had an obligation to know what was happening, and asked if I could come round and watch, because I simply could not concentrate properly at the table.

'He said I could, and at once I got up and went to stand right beside him. I looked down at the patient, a man of 38 who had been diagnosed as suffering from a heart condition, and I saw that an incision about fifteen centimetres long had been made right down his costal edge.

'Then Zeca just separated the flesh and plunged both his hands inside, or rather just his fingers, and began to manipulate quite violently. Then he took a pair of pincers and pulled out a piece of tissue, which he dropped into a metal container. Next, he simply pressed the two sides of the opening together - that's the only way I can describe it, and the skin just closed up. Zeca took a roll of plaster and was about to bandage the man's chest when I asked if I could have a closer look at the scar. He let me do this, and I clearly saw a reddish line exactly corresponding to where I had seen the chest open.

'At one stage I remember the patient seemed to be in pain, and Zeca immediately told the mediums at the table that they must concentrate harder, and say the Lord's Prayer out loud to help him.'

'Were you completely satisfied that Zeca really opened the man's body?' I asked Dr S. 'Satisfied as a doctor, not only as a medium and a Spiritist?'

'Completely,' she replied without hesitation. 'The room was well lit by natural light, and I was only a few feet away like this!' She opened her arms to indicate a space of about a yard.

'And that was not all he did. Right at the end of the session, for instance, when the atmosphere was quite normal, with nobody at the table praying or anything like that, a man went up to Zeca and showed him a nevus - that's a sort of birthmark about one centimetre long and at least half a centimetre wide at the base, just over the nipple of his left breast. Zeca laughed and said it wasn't anything very serious, but he would take it off if the man wanted him to.

'Then he picked up a scalpel and just slashed it off in one stroke, and put his thumb over the stump for a few seconds. When he took it away there was no sign of bleeding at all, although a cut like that should need several stitches.

'Under normal conditions, what he did would have been absolutely impossible.'

# 6

## MARIA

**E**VERY psychic surgeon I came across seemed to bring a personal touch to the profession. Some used ordinary equipment, some used kitchen knives, others used their bare hands. The woman known simply as Maria introduced a refinement that even I, with two years' experience in the field when I first met her, had never imagined possible. She did what I am sure no other surgeon in the history of medicine has ever done - she did her operations with her eyes tightly closed.

I had heard various accounts of Maria's work before I was able to see it for myself. Some witnesses were impressed, others not. All agreed that she was a very pleasant woman, and that she neither sought publicity nor had any particular objections to being watched on the job by serious researchers. As far as her technique was concerned, it seemed she went through all the right motions when operating, using ordinary surgical equipment, but she had the disconcerting habit of preferring to work in dim light, with an assistant holding a sheet between patient and spectator, as I had observed in the case of Zeca.

A former patient of hers described his feelings to me at the time of operation, but these amounted to no more than a tickling sensation on the skin (he was supposed to be having a mitral valve transplant) and we agreed that this sensation should not be too difficult to produce, with nothing either psychic or even surgical involved.

Another witness told me that Maria had put her hand in the pocket of her white coat and produced a pill, telling him it had just been materialized for him. I do not like psychic surgeons who put their hands in pockets, and on the whole I heard very little about Maria that sounded very encouraging.

Moreover, a few days before I was due to visit the Spiritist centre where she was working, I had received a letter from Dr Eric J. Dingwall, the most experienced psychical researcher of his day, the very mention of whose name must have struck terror into the hearts of false mediums throughout the world for over fifty years. 'Surely you must realize by now that many of the stories about these surgeons are sheer nonsense,' he had written to me, leading me to suppose that stories I had been sending him about my own experiences were likely to prove equally nonsensical. (I should add here that 'Ding', as he liked to be known, later became a good friend as well as my severest critic).

Accordingly, it was in my best debunking frame of mind that I went along to see Maria, in the company of the same sharp-eyed and refreshingly sceptical colleague who had been with me on my visit to Zeca.

The boards creaked as we climbed the old staircase leading to the first-floor Spiritist centre, one of the oldest-established in São Paulo, only a few blocks from the main banking district. This centre had a reputation for sticking closely to traditional Kardecism and for its charitable work among the poor.

The meeting had already begun when we arrived. There were about a hundred people in the main room, seated in rows of wooden chairs facing the long white-covered table where the mediums were sitting. A man was reading from the Gospel of St Matthew, after which another medium made a little impromptu speech interpreting it and commenting on the theme for the evening, which was 'turn the other cheek'. Next, the spirits were invited to say a few words, as is usual at such meetings, and two or three of the mediums duly obliged. One exhorted us to love each other in such stentorian tones that I feared she was about to pelt us all with rotten bananas. She calmed down, however, wishing us all the peace of God, which was quite welcome by then, whereupon a lady announced that Dona Maria would now attend to patients in the other room.

Maria got up from the head of the table and left the room. She was a kindly-looking woman of about fifty, with a dark complexion. She reminded me of the old-fashioned type of village postmistress in England, who always had time for a friendly chat while she weighed out your four ounces of chocolate drops.

I had made arrangements beforehand to be allowed to watch an operation as a 'student of parapsychology', a phrase that tends to impress

Spiritists but also to make them slightly suspicious, since in Brazil the word parapsychology unfortunately became identified in Spiritist circles with the antics of the Jesuit priest Fr. Oscar Quevedo and his organization, the 'Latin American Parapsychology Council' known by its Portuguese acronym CLAP, a chief aim of which appeared to be to discredit Spiritism.

Maria greeted us on her way into the surgery (we had met very briefly a day or two earlier to make the appointment) and asked us to wait until we were called. We did so, sitting on a long bench in the corridor, in the company of the first patient of the evening. This was a mentally retarded boy who was wailing incessantly in his father's arms, the most pathetic little creature imaginable to whom it seemed the pleasures of normal life would be denied as long as he lived. I was impressed by the willingness with which Brazilian Spiritists will try and help even the most desperate cases.

After a few minutes, the father was called inside. The little boy gave me a blank stare that chilled me to the bones and wailed even louder as he passed us. Almost immediately, it seemed, he came out again, and whatever Maria had done to him had certainly quietened him down, for he left without a further sound as his father carried him gently down the old staircase and out into the street. That was an encouraging start to the evening's healing work.

A man stuck his head round the door and nodded at us. He seemed very unwilling to let us in, only doing so at Maria's own request. (We had only been given the appointment in the first place because of my friend's position as volunteer medium at the São Paulo Spiritist Federation.) Putting on my best devout and spiritual expression, I tiptoed through the waiting room and into the surgery at the back. It was a clean, orderly room about ten by fifteen feet, furnished only with a large wall shelf stocked with ordinary-looking medicines; a small table containing a few packets of cotton wool, some small bottles and a tray of surgical instruments; and a single bed.

The new patient was already lying on the bed, a sheet pulled up to her chin. She was an attractive woman of about thirty-five, her dark hair neatly set, who was staring at the ceiling in that state of pre-operative tension I knew so well from my experiences, to be described in the next chapter.

Two assistants stood by the bed, one at the head and the other with her back to me. Maria was on the other side of the bed, with her back to the plain wall, out of reach of either the shelf or the table. She was bending over the patient, massaging her neck gently with both hands. She showed no sign of recognizing me, although we had exchanged greetings less than ten minutes previously.

'Come on, woman,' I thought to myself somewhat impatiently. 'Do your stuff, whatever it is.'

'Fix the thoughts on Jesus, please!' one of the assistants said sternly, without looking at me. I did so, though keeping my eyes determinedly fixed on the patient's throat. The room was lit by the bright light coming through the open door that led from the waiting room. It would have been light enough to read twelve-point type by, and there was no difficulty in seeing everything in the room. Had I stretched out my left arm, I could easily have touched the woman's throat with my finger tips.

I had a perfect view of nothing worth seeing, at any rate not yet. Maria simply went on rubbing the woman's neck, saying nothing, occasionally throwing handfuls of invisible matter into an equally invisible receptacle. Oh dear, I thought, it's one of these invisible jobs.

I had been so intent upon watching the patient's neck and Maria's hands that I had not even glanced at the latter's face. When I did so I had the first surprise of the evening. Maria had removed her spectacles, her face was screwed up and her eyes were tightly closed.

Next, Maria asked for a piece of cotton wool, which one of the assistants handed her, pulling it from a box beside me. Then she took a pair of scissors in her right hand, holding the sheet up with her left hand a few inches above the patient's left side (the side farthest from where I was standing). She made some brief cutting motions, then put down the scissors, took the cotton wool and pressed it on the neck, handing it back at once to the assistant. There was a bright red blob in the middle of it.

I gave a start. There must be something hidden under the sheet. As if reading my thoughts, Maria immediately drew back the sheet, folding it back on itself at about the level of the patient's bust to reveal what I was afraid I was going to see, a completely unmistakable hole in the patient's neck, on the lower part of it just to the left of the windpipe.

The hole was about the size of a silver dollar in circumference, and it was partly full of dark liquid. I edged a little closer, nobody making any attempt to stop me. I stared at the hole for a good twenty seconds; it was a hole, and it contained liquid. I was close enough, and the light was good enough for there to be no doubt whatsoever. It was a hole, period.

'Pincers!' Maria ordered in a gruff voice. An assistant passed them over, and with my eyes glued to her right hand, Maria proceeded to plunge the pincers slowly and carefully into the hole, the tips of the pincers going at least an inch and a half below skin level. Immediately, the pincers came out again, holding a black object that reminded me of a small burnt sardine just over an inch long, which an assistant took in her fingers and dropped into a bucket on the floor.

'Hurting?' Maria asked quietly. The patient mumbled something that sounded rather negative. She was lying stiffly, obviously nervous, but making no sound suggestive of serious pain. Her eyes, unlike Maria's, were open and blinking throughout the operation.

Maria wiped the pincers casually on the sheet over the woman's stomach, leaving two clear red marks. She asked for more swabs, and to my total amazement proceeded to press one of them right inside the hole, tamping it down with the pincers until I could only just see the white of the cotton on the bottom of the hole, which looked almost an inch deep.

'There!' Maria exclaimed, relaxing the tension a little.

'Now how are we going to close the hole, eh?' This, the longest sentence I heard her speak on this occasion, must have been for my benefit, for neither of the two assistants made any suggestions. I also kept quiet, and for a few moments Maria just stood there as if waiting for something to happen by itself.

Then, very gently, she began to ease the cotton-wool swab out of the hole in the woman's neck. The patient made a few grunts as she did so, and Maria again asked if she felt pain. The reply was a contented 'uh-huh' sound.

'Say the Lord's Prayer out loud and fix the thoughts on Jesus,' one of the assistants ordered unexpectedly. From experience I knew this meant we were at the trickiest stage of the operation. With my thoughts about evenly divided between Jesus and Dr Dingwall (I hope both will understand), I managed to tag along about half a beat late as the *Pai Nosso* was recited by the assistants and my colleague. As we repeated the words, Maria slowly eased the swab up and out of the hole, handing it to an assistant, who took it and casually threw it towards the bucket on the floor. She missed, and the stained swab landed a few inches from my left shoe.

'Grab it and take it to the lab for tests!' I could hear Dr Dingwall's voice in my ear, but any ideas I had in this direction were dismissed when I caught sight of one of the centre's staff members standing right behind me. Lab tests would have to wait. I had seen the swab come out of the neck, enough proof for the time being that paranormal opening of a human body had taken place. Like the first one, this swab had a large red blob on it, and as the assistant had taken it from Maria's pincers right under my nose, I could see it was exactly the same colour as blood.

Maria bent over the hole. 'Look closely!' one of the assistants ordered. Now the first rule of psychical research is that when somebody tells you to look at something, you immediately look everywhere else. I did so, first at Maria's face, seeing her eyes still tightly closed, and then at her hands, which had not moved since she had put down the pincers.

Then the hole simply closed itself up. That is the only way I can describe it. One moment it was there and then it wasn't. Maria had done nothing at all after removing the swab. I had not taken my eyes off it for more than perhaps one second. The assistants had not moved except to hold the palms of their hands towards the hole, at least two feet away. The patient had remained motionless as a corpse. But the hole had gone.

An assistant reached for a bandage and Maria began to wind it round the woman's neck, muttering in her gruff trance voice that it was all over. Later I learned that this voice was supposed to be that of a well-known Austrian doctor who had practised for many years in São Paulo before his death there in about 1950. A former patient of this doctor, whose name I was given, had visited Maria and been recognized spontaneously. I can only testify that Maria's trance voice and manner were totally unlike her normal ones.

That's all,' said an assistant, pushing me gently towards the door.

'What was the operation for?' I managed to ask.

'Thyroiditis,' the woman replied, the tone of her voice not encouraging further questions.

We left, after it had been made clear that there would be no more operations for spectators that evening.

Out in the street, I immediately asked my colleague to describe everything she had seen. I then did the same for her, and our impressions matched exactly, except that from her position my friend had not been able to see the cotton wool actually leaving the hole, as I had. Neither of us could think of any way deception could have been practised.

Maria's hands had been visible throughout the operation once she had folded back the sheet. She had put neither hand in her pocket. We had both clearly seen the black object emerging from the hole. We agreed on the red spots on the cotton wool and the marks on the sheet. Even if anything had been hidden under the sheet beforehand, we should have been able to spot it. What could have been hidden, anyway? The essential point was that we had both seen a hole in a woman's neck, and we had seen something coming out of it. We had also seen it close itself. Neither of us had any doubt that we had seen a genuine psychic operation at point-blank range.

I hurried home in a taxi to write up my notes. One sometimes has difficulty in believing this kind of thing the morning after ...

Two days later, I paid a surprise visit to Maria in her home, the address of which I had been given by a friend I met at the centre. One of the advantages of São Paulo's (then) woefully deficient telephone and mail systems is that people did not usually mind being dropped in on unexpectedly.

Maria was enjoying a quiet Sunday afternoon in her very modest house, which contained nothing but the bare essentials and an ancient TV set, in front of which two of her six children were sprawled on the floor playing toy football.

She received me amiably, though she looked tired and had a slight cold. Like many healers, she seemed unable to cure her own ailments; it appears to be a rule that spirit doctors pay little attention to their mediums' needs.

We sat on the plastic-covered sofa, and after thanking Maria for letting me watch her at work, I asked how long she had been a healing medium.

'Oh, it must be about forty years now,' she replied. 'It began when I was a girl, about nine or ten. I used to see visions, of a lady in white with a blue sash, and I found that when I put my hands on sick people they would get better.'

'When did you do your first operation?' I asked.

'When I was about ten. It was a man who had trouble with his kidneys. He came to our house and I put my hands on him, and apparently I just opened him up, so Mother told me later. She was terrified.' She had been healing ever since, she told me, and had never accepted money for doing what she regarded as 'helping God's work'. I could see no sign in the house of any of the sort of presents psychic healers are often given, and which some have been known to ask for.

Maria worked every day in a government office from eight until two-thirty, she told me, then came home to attend to anybody who came to see her for help. At least twice a week she went out to work either at the centre or at a private house, and sometimes she would go to people's own homes to operate, if they were unable to leave their beds. She always worked with her eyes closed, she said, and had no memory at all of what she did during trance, except a vague awareness of the spirit doctors guiding her.

She listened with interest as I described the operation I had seen her perform two days previously...

# 7

## EDIVALDO

I WAITED to see Edivaldo sitting on a wooden bench in a ground-floor room in Rio de Janeiro that had been converted into a Spiritist centre. The building stood, or leaned, in a narrow side street of an area full of warehouses, gasworks and run-down bars; the kind of street you end up in when you get lost on the way to an airport. The narrow façade of the building fronted a precarious two-floor construction the demolition squads seemed to have overlooked. Its lower level had been opened up into one long room, with creaking floorboards, a few pictures of saints and inspirational quotations on the walls, and an altar at the far end hiding behind a blue curtain. Nothing could have been less like a surgeon's waiting room.

Yet there we all sat, about a hundred of us, clutching our numbered plastic *fichas*, or counters. They were in three colours - green was for a consultation, yellow for a check-up, and pink, of which only eight were handed out at each session, for an operation.

We had been handed our *fichas* at the door by a woman who had checked our names on her list and asked if we could make a 'contribution' of thirty cruzeiros, then worth about two pounds sterling. The money went into a plastic shopping bag to be used, she assured us, to buy clothing and equipment for a school in Edivaldo's home town. (On later visits, I was not asked for money, but to bring some children's sport shoes which Edivaldo would give to poor families in his home town. He was clearly not into psychic surgery for the money).

The waiting room was full of the sort of ordinary-looking people you might find waiting to catch a bus. There were men and women, young and old, and quite a few children. Some were obviously in a bad way, leaning on the shoulders of relatives or moaning quietly to themselves in corners. Others looked perfectly well and happy. Nobody complained because Edivaldo was late. We knew he had to drive more than 500 miles from his home town in the state of Bahia, as he had been doing every other weekend for at least a couple of years. (On alternate weekends he would go to Salvador or Recife, always leaving in time to get back to his regular job as a teacher.)

Finally he arrived, greeted the lady at the door and a few old friends, and immediately went straight to the small hut at the end of the back yard where his assistants were waiting for him. I caught a glimpse of a well-dressed man of medium height with dark hair, spectacles and a neat moustache who seemed unwilling to draw attention to himself. A few minutes later, an assistant peered through the door and called out 'Green fichas one to ten!' The first ten for consultation got up and went out into the back yard.

The atmosphere was quiet and businesslike, with no mass hypnosis, hysteria or speeches. The lady at the door quietly reminded us that Edivaldo's work would be helped if we kept quiet and prayed for him, mentalizing our problems as we did so.

I went out into the yard with the next group of ten, and as I waited outside the hut I could hear Edivaldo's voice coming through the open window covered by a thin curtain. He was speaking a mixture of Spanish and Portuguese with a lilting Bahia accent. That would be Dr Calazans the Spaniard, somebody told me, one of the spirits who regularly worked through his mediumship.

Then my group was called into the hut and I was able to get a better look at Edivaldo. He was slightly built, about forty years old, and had an intelligent and kind expression on his face. He was no crude country peasant, like Arigó. The first thing that struck me about him was his apparent normalness; he might have been a friendly bank manager, for he had a considerable air of authority and self-confidence about him.

He was sitting on a chair with his back to a small bed. The only other piece of furniture in the hut was a small table, where a helper was unpacking a paper parcel of bandages and cotton wool. Another assistant held a small tape recorder. Consultations of those in front of me were very rapid. Edivaldo would simply put his fingers on their stomachs and prod around rather vaguely for a few seconds. He would ask patients if they wanted to say anything, though giving the impression he knew what was wrong anyway. Sometimes he would say nothing and just start writing on his prescription pad. He both wrote and spoke at a terrific speed, hence the tape recorder, for patients to check their diagnoses later if necessary, and also for his colleague Firmino outside, whose job was to decipher the prescriptions. He gave me the impression of working frantically against time, as if aware that however many people he treated there would always be more waiting outside.

Finally it was my turn. The assistant motioned me forward and I stood face to face with the healer I had heard so much about. My first meeting with him was something of an anti-climax. His left hand went straight to the spot on my abdomen that had been bothering me on and off for three years. I began to mutter the Portuguese equivalent of 'It's my digestion, Doctor...'

'I know. That's where I'm looking,' he interrupted brusquely but not unkindly. Then he scribbled off a prescription, rattled off a list of things I should not eat or drink (the same list, incidentally, he had recited for every previous patient) and told me to come back for *una pequeña operación*. A small operation! That was all. At once he called for *otra consulta* - next patient, please.

Out in the yard, Firmino translated my prescription into legible Portuguese. I noticed that some of the pills were the same as those my conventional doctor had prescribed for my digestion problem. They had worked for a time, but the pains had kept coming back, preventing me from sleeping properly and consequently affecting my work. Firmino told me exactly how many of which pill to take, and when, and so ended my first personal encounter with a psychic surgeon.

It made little impression on me at the time. I had many doubts. This was in 1971, before my move to São Paulo and before I had any experience with the healers described in the previous chapters, and I felt somewhat disappointed by the total lack of showmanship on the lines of what I would have expected from Arigó or Lourival, the only other psychic healers known to me at that time. The whole atmosphere seemed far too normal, and my consultation had been so rapid that I had simply had no time to be impressed, although in retrospect it seemed no mean feat to have produced a diagnosis and a prescription in about thirty seconds although I had given no indication as to what my problem was. Unreasonably, I felt let down because Edivaldo had neither cured me on the spot nor worked any other kind of miracle. Nor had he given me a brief account of my past and future, as he had done to a friend of mine.

Anyway, I went off and bought the pills, which were easy to find and quite inexpensive. I was luckier in this respect than another friend who had been told her pills could only be found in Italy, which proved to be true, though extremely difficult even in Rome.

I did not worry too much at first about that *pequeña operación* Edivaldo had said I needed. This may seem a casual attitude, but it is difficult to live long in Brazil without coming to accept psychic surgery as something that quite possibly happened, if preferably to other people. I went along with the general attitude, similar to that expressed in the Spanish saying *'no creo en las brujas, pero que las hay, las hay!'* I didn't believe in witches either, but I knew they existed all right. As for psychic surgery, here was my chance to see if it too existed; whether it did or not I was unlikely to come to any physical harm.

'I simply can't believe it' is the usual reaction to the kind of experience I will be describing shortly. I understand this point of view, since I shared it even after my own operations. What people believe is their own affair, and knowing something to be true is somehow not the same thing. Also, whether any psychical phenomena are true or not is of little importance to most of us, for it is possible to live a long and happy life without worrying about such things at all. Unless, of course, one happens to you. In this case, you can either forget about it or try to work it out, and I have chosen the latter course. The great majority of Brazilians either take the former, or put all such phenomena, including psychic surgery, down to divine power, ask no further questions and, as the witch told Macbeth, 'seek to know no more.'

I would like to be able to claim that I was desperately ill when I went to Edivaldo for treatment, and that he worked a miracle cure on me. Neither claim would be true, however. I was simply being bothered by recurrent stomach problems, and felt that it would be interesting, if nothing else, to see what he could do to help. I half suspected the 'operation' would consist of no more than the laying on of hands, a heavy dose of auto-suggestion or even hypnosis, a few words of spiritual comfort and some placebo pills thrown in for good measure.

I could not have been more completely wrong.

Five months passed, and at last the day set for my *pequeña operación* came round.

This was it. I lay on the narrow bed in the same little hut in the back yard. The atmosphere was the same as before; it was just another working weekend for Edivaldo.

I had approached my operation day much as one approaches a vital examination or a visit to the dentist; it might not be too pleasant at the time, and it would be good to get it over and done with.

I was lucky, or perhaps unlucky, in being able to watch another one taking place before it was my own turn. What had happened was this; clutching my precious pink *ficha* outside the hut, I was trying to keep as calm as everybody else seemed to be. My fellow patients looked about as nervous as they would waiting for a bank to open.

Several people were in front of me in the line for operations, and so far only the first had been called inside. He was a very thin man of at least sixty, with an expression of serenity on his face that gave me much-needed confidence.

Suddenly the door of the hut opened and one of the helpers, a young Japanese-Brazilian with long hair and a permanent friendly smile, asked the crowd in general for a *testemunha*, or witness, for the first operation of the day.

I had never heard of this happening before. Though operations were performed in the same room as consultations and checkups, often almost at the same time, I had the impression that it was considered bad form to stare while one was in progress.

Nobody in the crowd moved forward, and the Nissei hippie seemed to be looking straight at me. So in I went.

The elderly man was lying on his back on the bed, his shirt unbuttoned to leave his whole abdomen bare. By the time I had made my way round to the bed, the operation had already begun. In fact it was nearly over.

The hut was dimly lit by such light as filtered through the thin curtain that covered the window opening, but it was quite light enough to see what was going on. Edivaldo and two of his helpers were leaning over the bed, one holding the microphone and another with a large bandage ready. I rested my hands on the rail at the foot of the bed and stared in complete bewilderment at about two square feet of what looked like exposed innards. It was only a fleeting glance, as several hands intermittently blocked my view. But it was the kind of sight one does not forget in a hurry; the old man's abdomen seemed to have been ripped wide open. There were a few spots of what looked like blood on the skin to either side of the opening, and the rest was a sickening bloody mess.

'It tickles a bit when I cut here, doesn't it?' Edivaldo observed amiably, much as a dentist tells you your tooth may be 'a little sensitive'.

The man seemed in no mood for conversation, but he grunted an affirmative-sounding reply. He was fully conscious and in evident discomfort, but not pain.

My first sight of a paranormally opened body was an overwhelming shock. Instinctively, I looked away, and when I looked again the man's stomach was all neat and tidy and being covered by the bandage the helper had slapped on. Then the man's wife came forward, helped him to his feet and led him out.

This really happened, I told myself, although I was none too sure. I am not accustomed to hallucinations. Nobody was trying to hypnotize me. Nobody was projecting colour slides from the ceiling (as a British researcher later seriously suggested!). I had seen a psychic operation. They really happened.

(I should add here that I later saw several videos of allegedly bogus psychic surgeons at work, and noted their technique of apparently fixing small plastic bags of animal blood and ether to their palms, which they would puncture with a well sharpened thumbnail. Yet I never saw Edivaldo doing anything remotely resembling this trick). As to why I had been asked to watch: I was told later that I was there to give a blood transfusion to the old man. You can't believe everything they tell you in the psychic healing business.

I made my way round to the door, half wanting to escape from the whole scene. All right, it was all true. It happened. But I was beginning to wonder if it should happen to me. Then one of the helpers stopped me. 'You're waiting for an operation, aren't you?'

I admitted I was, but said there were several other people in front of me in the line outside.

'Never mind,' said the assistant casually. 'Now you're here you may as well have yours next. Lie down on the bed.'

There seemed to be no escape, so I took off my coat and looked for somewhere to hang it. I was wearing my best suit, for that morning I had been to visit ex-president Juscelino Kubitschek in his Copacabana apartment, to discuss an English translation of his memoirs, which he was then writing. As we talked, I sipped a very excellent Scotch, wondering if one should drink before being opened up. Then some other people had arrived and I was invited to stay for lunch.

One does not lightly refuse a presidential invitation, especially from such a courteous host as 'JK', as all Brazil knew him, but I had to get across town to the centre in about an hour. It was impossible to stay, so I sought refuge in the only possible excuse; the truth.

'Thank you very much, *Senhor Presidente*,' I remember saying, 'but I have to go and have an operation.' Kubitschek seemed to accept this, and took me to the elevator. As a former doctor himself, he must have known that Saturday afternoon was a funny time for a walking patient to be off to an operation, unless it was at a Spiritist centre. I think he knew what I was up to.

So I had eaten a quick lunch at a Chinese place on Avenida Atlantica across from Copacabana beach, grabbed a taxi and just made it in time to collect my pink counter, deposit my contribution in the bag, and wait to be called.

There was indeed nowhere to hang my jacket, but the Nissei hippie put it somewhere, with my best tie stuffed in the pocket. I lay down on the bed and tried to relax. It had been quite a day already. My meeting with Kubitschek had not been a success, since I had been unable to give the matter in hand my full attention. I remember telling him I thought he should confine his memoirs to the building of Brasilia, for which he was mainly responsible, and to events since the 1964 revolution, which was hardly what he wanted to hear.

Edivaldo was giving consultations at great speed, scribbling away on his prescription pad and talking his usual mixture of Spanish and Portuguese. He seemed to say much the same thing to each patient, though he spoke so fast that he easily outpaced my knowledge of Spanish.

An assistant tapped Edivaldo on the shoulder and pointed to the bed I was lying on. 'There's another operation waiting, Doctor,' she said.

Edivaldo showed not the slightest interest in me. 'Later,' he rapped. 'Send in more consultations.' So all I could do was lie and wait. I started to undo my shirt buttons, beginning at the top. It was my best shirt, bought on my last trip to London, and I didn't want blood all over it. I had managed to get two rather stiff new buttons undone when suddenly I began to feel really frightened.

I had just witnessed an operation, but now that it was my turn another set of reactions began to take effect. I only wanted to escape, to go home and forget all about psychic healing. I could always go back to the kind old Hungarian doctor who had done his best to solve my digestion problem. If he tried everything he would cure it eventually. At least you could talk to him; he gave you as much of his time as you wanted for his modest fee.

Yet Edivaldo's set-up was so impersonal, cold and businesslike. Nobody cared about me in the least. I had never been operated on before; and had only visited a doctor about six times in my life. If I was going to be carved open, I wanted a pretty nurse to hold my hand and assure me there was nothing to worry about.

But nobody held my hand, and there was plenty to worry about. I seriously considered the thought that I was going to die, overlooking the fact that this would make me the first person ever to do so under psychic surgery, unless previous cases had been well hushed up. Well, perhaps they had been hushed up.

Luckily, I got over this nervous crisis and began to undo my third shirt button. What a fool I would feel if I missed an opportunity like this, I told myself. Wasn't I supposed to be a writer? So, start counting the crowd! Before I could finish doing this - I estimated the crowd at about eight - Edivaldo suddenly swung round in his chair, got up and hurried over to the bed, holding out his hands as if he had just made up his mind to strangle me. I began to tear at the shirt buttons in a sudden effort to be cooperative and not keep Doctor waiting. The most vivid detail of the whole affair I recalled later was that I never got to the seventh and last button. The hands just came at me and began to feel around the belly area.

Then came the unmistakable moment of truth. Edivaldo's hands seemed to find what they were looking for, the thumbs pressed down hard, and I felt a very distinct plop as they penetrated the skin and went inside. My stomach immediately felt wet all over, as if I were bleeding to death.

I could feel a sort of tickling inside, but no pain at all. The most unusual sensation was a sudden strong smell of ether, which seemed to come from my stomach area and drift upwards past my nose.

Then it was all over, as suddenly as it had begun. Edivaldo muttered something I could not understand, a bandage was slapped casually and quite hard on my belly, and a helper said I could get up and go home.

Easier said than done. I was completely rigid all over my middle area. I had difficulty in breathing properly, and still had the sensation of having a hole in my stomach.

Somebody gave me a hand and I managed to get my legs on the floor, and finally the rest of my body on the legs. Walking seemed easier than getting up had been. The hippie helped me on with my coat and tie, and repeated in intelligible Portuguese what Edivaldo had muttered before turning his back on me and getting on with the next consultation. Total rest and no food for 24 hours, I was told, and no heavy food for the next few days. I walked stiffly out of the hut and was just wondering how I was going to get home unaided when the assistant came

Part of the crowd of up to 15,000 awaiting special distributions of food and clothing held four times a year at Chico Xavier's Spiritist Centre in Uberaba.

Chico's fans fill a large gymnasium as they wait their turn for a handshake, a red rose and an autograph at a 1973 launching of yet another of his books.

Alan Kardec's stern but kindly features have appeared on three separate stamp issues, an honour seldom awarded to anyone in any country. The centenary of his Gospel, that of his first book in 1957.

Stamp issued in 2010 to commemorate the centenary of Chico Xavier's birth. The text reads: *"Always love. And when you are on the point of disbelieving in the power of love, remember Christ."*

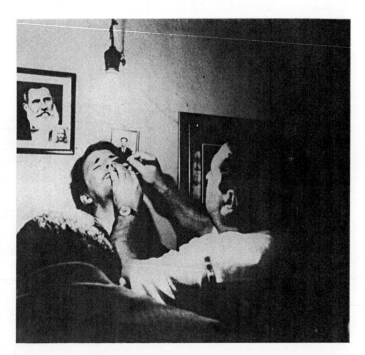

Noted Brazilian photographer Claudia Andujar took this dramatic shot of the late Zé Arigó jabbing his penknife into a patient's eye.

Carapicuiba, Brazil, September 1974. The author examines damage done to heavy roof tiles on two houses. In the lower picture, several tiles have clearly been recently replaced, after three weeks of steady bombardment by an invisible assailant.

It was this roof that was the target of the shower of stones thrown while the author was standing a few feet away on his first visit to the site. Local police agreed with all residents involved that no normal explanation for the attacks could be found.

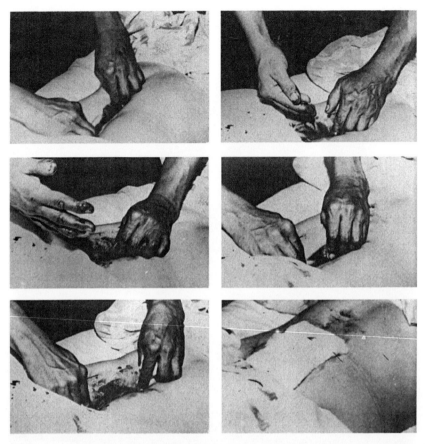

This sequence of photographs, hitherto unpublished, shows psychic surgeon Edivaldo Oliveira Silva's hands as they rip open the abdomen of a woman patient (1), the depression in her skin remaining clearly visible even when one hand is removed (2,3). The patient's hand appears in (4), suggesting that she is fully conscious. As the operation nears its end (5) a bandage held by an assistant is slapped roughly on the skin (6). The author did not witness the operation shown here, but has observed several similar operations at close range, and regards this one as, if anything, less messy than the average. *Photos courtesy of Edivaldo Oliveira Silva.*

The stool photographed by the sleepy author seconds after it had crashed downstairs and woken him up.

The poltergeist in action: Suzuko Hashizume's raincoat as she found it after she had spent the night on a sofa less than four yards away.

Heavy wooden shelf photographed minutes after it had been thrown from normal position against the wall of an empty room.

Suzuko Hashizume examines a shirt damaged by paranormal spontaneous combustion.

The Mogi das Cruzes polter-geist caused the near-total destruction of the family home.

A typical scorch mark found inside a closed drawer.

IBPP director Hernani Guimaraes Antrade collects first-hand testimony on the Suzano poltergeist case from the local police chief.

The teenage girl who is thought to be at the epicenter.

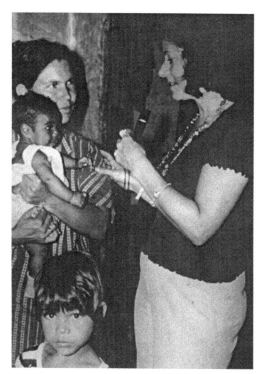

The little baby whose mother is being interviewed by IBPP researcher Carmen Marinho is lucky to be alive. She was snatched from a para-normally burning laundry basket just in time...

Reporter Kazunaro Akaki took this photo shortly after the Toyota jeep he had parked apparently jumped uphill for 40 metres without leaving tyre marks.

Mirabelli levitating? The caption in the first edition of this book stated that this photo 'could have been faked', and following the discovery of an original print (see p.48) it is now clear that it was, the ladder on which Mirabelli was standing having been removed by retouching.

An example of automatic writing by Mirabelli. This message in Japanese purports to be from a man named Iwagoro Matsumoto. His date of death is given as October 10th, 1916, and includes the full address of his former home in the southern city of Kagoshima.

Allan Kardec (1804-1896), the 'calm, cautious and unimaginative' French schoolmaster whose writings inspired Brazil's most active religious movement. His main works are among the most comprehensive treaties on the psi world yet published.

Francisco Candido ('Chico') Xavier, Brazil's leading medium who has produced over 130 books in forty years of automatic writing, though he left school at thirteen.

Hernani Guimaraes Antrade, Brazil's foremost psi researcher and founder of the IBPP. Scientist, teacher, author and investigator of paranormal phenomena of all types, he has formulated a detailed theory of 'psi matter' which is presented in the appendix specially written for this book.

Photos taken by the author while Luiz Antonio Gasparetto was being filmed in June 1974 by the IBPP. Normally he draws and paints in near darkness.

Gasparetto rarely watches his hand as it flies over the paper, often producing a completed drawing in less than a minute.

A vivid portrait of a child drawn in front of the author in about 30 seconds.

Gasparetto draws two heads at once, using both hands. He worked at the same speed the special film lighting is on or off.

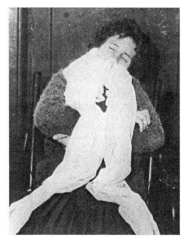

Otilia Diogo, wearing a thick sweater despite the heat and expelling 'ectoplasm' similar to a surgical bandage, made international headlines before being unmasked as a fraud.

Celia, the lady from Pompeii, as a Spanish dancer and (inset) at the age of six when she first began to recall other lives. Note gypsy-like position of hands on hips.

Celia took this photo of "her' street in Pompeii when she went there in 1970. It was the street along which she had rushed to her death when the city was destroyed.

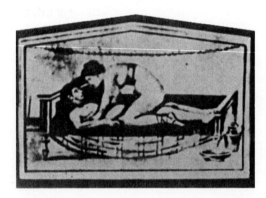

Even as a young girl, Celia would have visions of erotic scenes.

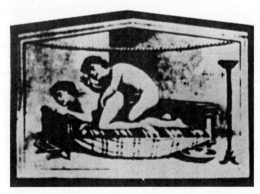

Two of the wall paintings from Celia's house in Pompeii — the city's brothel. Celia 'rediscovered' them in 1971.

up and asked if I had brought anybody with me. Operation cases were supposed to do this, but nobody had remembered to tell me. The woman promptly disappeared and produced a cheerful young Englishman, who introduced himself as an executive with a local British company (a very well-known one), and offered to drive me home. Since he was waiting for his wife, who was in line for a check-up after her previous operation, I suggested he go and find a taxi for me instead, so that I could get home quicker, which he kindly did.

Miraculously, the taxi driver was one of the few in Rio who could both drive safely and find their way about town, and after a calm ride I walked unsteadily down my garden path, immensely relieved that it was all over.

I felt very stiff. Bending to unlace my shoes proved impossible, so I had to force them off with my feet. I felt that any sudden movement might make me fall to pieces altogether. But once safely in bed, settling down to listen to the BBC World Service play, I peeled off the bandage on my stomach, using nail scissors to cut it free from the hairs.

There was a bright red mark on the place where Edivaldo had pressed with his thumbs, and nearby there were two bright red dots. The red line was not a scar, just a jagged line only about three inches long, above and to the left of the navel. By the following morning the line had faded (unfortunately I had not enough strength to make the effort to photograph it), and within two days it had disappeared. The red dots, however, took much longer to go away.

I rested for 24 hours as ordered, and the following day I felt just about normal. I had no wish to tell anybody about my experience, other than the friend who had introduced me to Edivaldo in the first place, whom I asked to keep it to himself. I did not want to discuss the affair until I knew more about it all. But a few days later we met at the house of a mutual friend, a Brazilian doctor, and the subject of my operation was mentioned. The doctor refused to believe a word of it. The red dots, which I showed him, could be anything, he said. The rest was pure imagination.

I almost believed him at the time. Fortunately, when I went back for my second operation, I took more precautions. I brought a friend with me, showing her my two red dots before the second operation and the four after it. She was also able to see the red line before it too faded in a couple of days.

The second operation took place about five months after the first. I had been back several times for check-ups after taking several lots of pills, which seemed to have done some good without totally removing the problem.

After Edivaldo had told me I needed a second operation, I went back twice without being treated at all; on both occasions he had suddenly stood up before the end of the session, saying he could do no more that day, for reasons never made clear to me. On one of these occasions a heavy thunderstorm was building up, and I assumed that even psychic surgeons prefer not to work with water pouring through the roof, as indeed it did. I wondered why Edivaldo could not find a better place to work in.

Eventually all went well, and once again I lay down on the bed, this time in a slightly larger hut beside the usual one. Edivaldo was in a very cheerful mood, and I was a lot less nervous. I was starting to take my shoes off, when he interrupted me.

'No need to take them off. I'm not going to operate on your feet, am I?' Some moments later, however, he seemed to have forgotten where he was going to operate. He stood up, came over to the bed and looked at me absent-mindedly, then turned to his assistant and asked her what he was supposed to be going to do. This, I thought, was too much. Anyway, the woman told him, and I pointed to the spot just to make sure, though once those hands were laid on my stomach there was no doubt that Edivaldo knew what he was doing. Or that somebody knew, at least.

He chatted away happily, asking why I wasn't married and advising me to find a nice *brasileña* and settle down. Then, after his hands had probed around for a few moments, again I felt that plop as they went inside.

At once, the tone of his voice changed from good-natured banter to strict professionalism.

This is going to hurt,' he stated flatly.

That really shook me. I had understood that psychic anaesthetics, however invisible, were always totally effective.

But I need not have been alarmed. It did hurt, very slightly, far less than the average tooth being drilled, and for much less time. I felt a firm wrench in my innards deep down, not just on the surface, and there was a slight pain, though not enough to make me yell. I had the curious sensation that there were two sets of hands at work on me; Edivaldo seemed to be doing no more than just keep his hands there while another invisible pair did the actual work.

His cheerful mood infected me, and the second operation was a thoroughly enjoyable affair. I had a friend waiting to help me home, and none of the fear of the unknown that had beset me on the previous occasion. I felt I was becoming an old hand at this sort of thing. I was an initiate, and no longer a nervous novice.

After the second operation, I went back for two more check-ups. At the first, Edivaldo told me I was 90% cured, and after taking what I hoped would be my last lot of pills I went back again to be greeted with a hearty slap on the chest and the exclamation *manda brasa!* a common Brazilian expression I would translate in this context as 'away you go!', with the implication that I was fully cured, as indeed I was, remaining so for over a year. This was far longer than any of my pain-free periods over the previous three years.

My next task was to interview Edivaldo. This was not easy, for two reasons. The first was that he simply had no time. He would arrive in Rio on alternate Saturday mornings after a twelve-hour overnight drive from his home town in Bahia, he would start work at once and go on until almost midnight. Then he would drive out to the flat in a distant suburb a friend lent him for his Rio visits, sleep a few hours there and be back at work early Sunday morning for another full day of consulting and operating.

Sunday nights he would drive another five hundred miles home in time to teach his Monday classes at his local secondary school.

The second reason was that he did not give interviews to anyone. He was aware of what had happened to Arigó, and to some extent Antonio Sales, after the Brazilian press had made them national figures. He had no wish to advertise, since he was already handling as many people as he possibly could.

After several months, thanks largely to the kindness and cooperation of the woman who booked appointments for him in Rio, I was invited to go out to his flat after a Saturday-night healing session in town, and to bring my tape recorder. I was to be the first person ever to be allowed to interview him, and as it turned out I was probably also the last.

Edivaldo greeted me like an old friend, gave me a cup of coffee and tried out a few words of his precarious English, immediately offering to answer any questions I cared to ask, the only condition being that I should publish nothing about him in Brazil.

He was forty-two years old, he told me (in July 1972), and a native of Vitoria da Conquista in the state of Bahia. By profession he was a secondary school teacher, entomologist and taxidermist, and despite his age he was also studying both medicine and law. He had travelled abroad twice; to England in the 1950s to study taxidermy, and to Argentina to demonstrate his psychic powers at a La Plata university faculty. He had also been invited to visit the Soviet Union by an official of the embassy in Brazil, which confirmed my suspicion that the Soviets were taking a more serious interest at official level in psychical phenomena than one might have thought. (I learned later that Chico Xavier had also been invited to the USSR but had declined – or rather his spirit guide had declined on his behalf).

In ten years of healing he had attended to an estimated 65,000 'clients', as he called them. More than half of these were in Salvador, capital city of his home state, and the rest in Rio de Janeiro, Niteroi, Belo Horizonte, Recife and Aracaju (all capitals of other Brazilian states). His clients included one marshal of the army, eight generals and over fifty doctors. He had treated a number of foreigners, including about thirty Portuguese who had come to Brazil specially to see him.

The first of many surprises he had in store for me concerned his religion. I had assumed him to be a Spiritist, for he certainly behaved like one.

'No, I'm not a Spiritist,' he said firmly. 'Spiritism is too refined, and I'm too coarse! I'm a Christian; I believe in the existence of Christ, and I try to love my neighbour and do what I can within my limits.' It all sounded very simple, and I said so.

'Of course!' Edivaldo replied excitedly. 'Being a Christian is too easy! What does it mean? It means following the commandments of Christ for the benefit of others. Begin by loving your neighbour. Whoever loves also understands and helps, you see?' This brief and simple statement of faith seemed, as we sat in the quiet suburban sitting-room, capable of solving most of the world's problems overnight. It also sounded very much like the faith of a Kardecist Spiritist. I asked how Edivaldo's relations were with the Church.

'I was brought up a Roman Catholic,' he answered. 'I am a Catholic in the sense that society expects everyone to have a religion. But the Church doesn't want to know about me. It has always sought a monopoly and that's why it's coming to an end. The Church doesn't do anything; priests least of all!' This was stated without rancour, merely as a fact of life. I began to see why official statistics on the number of Catholics in Brazil could be misleading.

Once, he said, a priest had told him he was possessed by a devil. 'I replied that if the devil can relieve pain, open up a stomach and remove an ulcer, then I prefer the devil!' I asked him if he had studied

parapsychology, and if he was familiar with the work of other reputable healing mediums, such as Edgar Cayce. He had never heard of
Cayce, nor of any other healers except Arigó, to whom he insisted he
was not the successor.

He had little interest in parapsychology as such. 'It only studies the
soul,' he observed. 'Mediumship shows what the soul can do.' As for
reading matter in general, his favourite was *Tio Patinhas*, the Brazilian version of Donald Duck, and he surprised me still further by saying he did not even read the Bible.

'Don't give me one,' he exclaimed, 'because I won't read it. They say
the Bible was written to unite people with God. Well, all it does is just
the opposite. Look at Northern Ireland! Now if all that discord comes
out of the Bible, then I won't read it. I want to believe in Christ in my
own way.' So much for established religion, I thought.

Next, I wanted to know how he had become a medium. These, it would
seem, tend to be made rather than born, or to have their strange talents
thrust upon them in curious ways. Cayce saw visions and heard voices, Pe-
ter Hurkos fell off a ladder, and Edivaldo was seized by a fit of madness.

'It was in 1962. A neighbour of mine, Dona Zelita, had gone tem-
porarily insane, so I went to sit with her while they fetched a doctor.
When we were alone together I suddenly went mad myself for about
an hour. I was completely unconscious; a spirit took me over and I became violent. When I recovered, there were broken things all over the
place, but the woman had got better.'

I could not imagine Edivaldo being violent. He seemed the gentlest
of souls, though I noticed a definite difference in personality between
that of the man I was talking to and the doctor I had consulted. The
'Calazans' voice was authoritative and brusque, though not harsh, and
his general manner came across as strong and demanding; quite unlike Edivaldo's.

'Soon afterwards,' he went on, 'something similar happened again.
I had gone to visit a lady who was suffering from rigidity all over the
body shortly after childbirth. Suddenly I went all rigid myself, while she
became normal. After these two experiences I feared I was going mad,
so I asked a doctor friend, who was also a psychiatrist, what I should
do. He said I was a medium and suggested I go to a Spiritist centre. I
didn't want to at first, but word got around town that I was possessed,
so finally I agreed to go along with a friend.'

That was the evening he performed his first operation. He recalled
none of the details, just as he had no conscious memory of any of the

healing work (not always involving operations) he reckoned he had performed subsequently some 65,000 times.

'On the way to the centre I felt my right leg go all stiff. Then afterwards there was this Portuguese fellow who was driving me home in a jeep, who said I had operated on him, to cure his alcoholism, on one of his internal secretion glands. He never drank again, anyway.'

That was all he remembered. 'I just have this condition, and I try to use it to do good,' he said, adding as if the information was relevant, 'I never drank, gambled, smoked or danced.'

He had never had any conscious contact with any of his attendant spirits, he said. These were said to include Dr Calazans, a Frenchman called Pierre, a Londoner called Johnson, the famous Dr Fritz from Germany, plus a Japanese, an Italian and a Brazilian. He only learned what he had been up to in trance by listening to tape recordings and looking at photographs, of which he had quite a large album. He was completely at a loss to explain how he did what he did.

He told me he had no special psychic gifts during his normal state, apart from the ability to control his mind to a high degree and shut it off completely when it was time to receive a spirit and go to work. He insisted that he never invoked spirits, and that according to both the Koran and the Bible (which he knew well, even if he no longer read it) one should never do this.

'I don't invoke anything,' he exclaimed. The spirits just come. I sit down and withdraw my own spirit, and Dr Calazans takes over. There isn't room for two spirits in one body, you see!'

When this happens, all Edivaldo feels is a strong light in his eyes, which he told me was like that of a welder's blowlamp, and then he is out. The first time he was introduced to his own wife while in trance he had no idea who she was. Nor, I was amazed to hear, had he any idea that he had operated on me. He was as surprised to learn this as I was to find he did not know.

He seemed quite concerned about me, and peered intently at the tiny red dots on my stomach. 'You could have asked Dr Calazans to leave the scar, you know,' he observed. 'He will if you ask him!' He was also anxious to make sure I did not feel I had been deceived in any way. 'Nobody tried to hypnotize you, did they? Or use any sort of auto-suggestion, or anything like that? Well, then!' He seemed as curious as I was to find out how it all worked.

'You must investigate, Guy. A few more like you, and Spiritism will either develop or disappear!' Unlike many Brazilian medium-healers,

Edivaldo is a well-educated and intelligent man, although you could not call him an intellectual. Although he knows little more than anybody else about how the healing power actually works, he was able to give me some fascinating insights into the methods he believed were involved.

Operations, he told me, can be either what he called plasmic or ectoplasmic. In the former, separation takes place of the red globules from the plasma, only the latter remaining visible. Ectoplasmic operations were totally invisible to our eyes. He assured me that operations were not performed as quickly as I had imagined. Patients, he said, were already being operated on as they waited in line, and the part where they lay on the bed was only the end of the process. The actual manipulation was only to convince them that they really had been operated on.

'How would the clients feel if they got onto the bed and were told their operation was over?' he asked me.

The spirits, it seemed, sometimes left permanent proof of their existence. At one point in our interview, Edivaldo suddenly stretched out his arm towards me.

'Feel this,' he said. 'It's a pin that Dr Fritz put there.' I felt. There was indeed a hard, thick object like a nail about an inch long just below the skin of his left forearm, which was unmarked. He told me the pin or nail (the word is the same in Portuguese) had been put there as a sign of his mediumship. I had known of other mediums being given what are known in the trade as apports, as a sign of appreciation for their services.

Dr Calazans, he told me, was quite a specialist in apports, which had included a bar of radium and a live snake. Another favourite habit of his was squeezing essence from roses, while another spirit had once materialized a pipe that had been found to be over 200 years old.

I steered the conversation back to healing. Could any disease be cured, I wanted to know, and had he ever failed? His reply was immediate. 'If I failed, would they still come to me? One failure would ruin everything. Don't forget I've been doing this for ten years.' Concerning incurable diseases, he reminded me that there were such things as karmic disorders, often given us at birth because of our behaviour in a previous life. (An orthodox Kardecist interpretation would be that we voluntarily choose such conditions in order to learn patience and sympathy for other sufferers.) These included epilepsy, deafness, dumbness and stunted growth, and tended to be incurable, though Edivaldo went on to claim he had 'controlled', as he put it, a number of cases of epilepsy.

There is the *petit mal* and the *grand mal*, he explained. I can only cure the first.' I asked if he had had any luck with cancer.

'I can give you the names of several cancer patients who are cured today,' he replied, and promptly did so. One was that of a member of the foreign consular corps, cured of cancer of the larynx. He also mentioned the case of a European woman cured of leukaemia, and that of a lady who had come over from Norway to be treated for psoriasis.

That's incurable, you know,' he said cheerfully. 'Anyway, she went home cured. Damned attractive she was, too!' Edivaldo's only regret is that he has not been able to spend a weekend with his wife and children for ten years.

'I wish there were more like me,' he said wistfully. So much healing seemed to be necessary.

I mentioned a BBC World Service broadcast I had heard in which the British healer Edward Fricker had said he longed for the day when every hospital would have a psychic ward where experienced healers could try and help terminal patients. Edivaldo thought this was a splendid idea.

'When medicine and mediums get together,' he exclaimed, 'humanity will get 70% better!' He reminded me that he had treated more than fifty doctors, few of whom could doubt his abilities, though winning over the medical profession as a whole was another matter.

I agreed this was a difficult task. Evidence for the reality of psychic healing would always be rejected, simply because researchers like myself were not qualified to collect and assess it.

At about two o'clock in the morning, Edivaldo began to yawn and I stood up to leave.

Two final questions; was he happy with his work?

'*Felicissimo!* ' he exclaimed. 'Very happy. Just what we did today ...'

And could he stop if he wanted to?

'No. Only they can stop. It is they who work, not me. I can't stop something I'm not doing. It's an extra-terrestrial condition I have, supernormal ... How I get it, I don't know ...'

I said good night and wandered out into the empty street to wait for a taxi. Providentially, one appeared at once, and sped me through the deserted suburbs to my hillside home in the city centre.

For me, Spiritism had begun to develop rather than disappear.

Two weeks later, buses and cars roared past as I waited in a busy street outside the house where I had arranged to meet Edivaldo again.

It was a large old house, one of the few of its kind in central Rio not to have been demolished to make way for apartment blocks. It belonged to a successful businessman who also ran a small Spiritist centre in his basement, where on alternate Saturdays Edivaldo would come with his team of helpers to diagnose, prescribe and where necessary operate.

Twenty or thirty people had already been admitted through the huge iron gate by the time Edivaldo and his party arrived. As on our previous meeting, he greeted me casually like an old friend. The owner of the house accepted me at once as a guest of Edivaldo's, and we all went down to the spacious basement.

Here, there was a calm atmosphere quite unlike the crush and near-squalor of the other centre. The room was clean and simply furnished with wooden chairs, a large dining table, the usual quotations on the wall, and a blue light in the ceiling. The far end of the room was closed off by a curtain, while soft music came from a loudspeaker in a corner.

The main part of the room was already full to standing capacity as Edivaldo picked his way through the crowd and went to join the half dozen mediums at the table, leaving me near the door.

There was a hush, as before the rising of a theatre curtain, and almost at once we heard Edivaldo clearing his throat loudly.

'Bonsoir, mes amis!' It was the voice of Dr Pierre, the French member of the team of spirits who work through the mediumship of Edivaldo. Speaking correct but very elementary French, he wished everybody well and gave way to an Italian voice, which was followed in turn by another voice saying 'good evening' in English with a strong Bahian accent. Finally, after a few Germanic noises from the legendary Dr Fritz, we were greeted in the fluent Spanish of Dr Calazans. Later I was told that he in fact did all the talking for the others, hence the variety of accents.

Edivaldo finished his brief greeting in the Calazans voice, then got up and went behind the curtain, calling for the first two patients; 'una consulta y una operación'. I was just wondering how I was going to get through the crowd and behind the curtain after my story, when suddenly I heard 'Calazans' (I will call Edivaldo while in trance by the name of his supposed control) calling loudly for the ingles.

I parted the curtains and went into the clinic area. There were two beds, a small table littered with bottles and bandages, and two chairs, on one of which Edivaldo was sitting beside his first operation case, a typical-looking Brazilian man of about thirty.

'So you're the parapsychologist, are you?' Calazans called out. 'Take a chair and come and sit by me.' I had barely had time to greet him in reply when he launched into a stream of very rapid Spanish, apparently explaining for my benefit how he worked. And my tape recorder was outside in the hall. (One does not turn on tape recorders at Spiritist meetings without specific permission if one ever wants to be invited again.)

I caught only isolated words and short phrases. '... separate the etheric double ... fourth dimension ... remove the plasma from the red corpuscles ... ectoplasm ...' I was fairly used to interviewing people under difficult conditions, but this time I had been caught off my guard. As if to gloat over my discomfiture, Calazans asked: 'Where's your tape recorder? Go and fetch it. I suppose you would go fishing without a fishing rod!' He chuckled happily as I left, and by the time I had fought my way back and set up the recorder he was already at work on his first patient for examination.

Again, he invited me to sit beside him, and asked if I could see well enough. I assured him I could; the blue light was subdued, but light enough to read by with difficulty. Handel's *Largo* wafted from the speaker.

Calazans waved his hands over the bare stomach of the man lying on the bed.

'Here we are over the human laboratory,' he said, as if lecturing a class of ignorant parapsychologists. 'This, the stomach, liver and pancreas, is where the body is made or destroyed. This is where the acids are mixed, the airs and the vessels ...' He broke off to ask again if I could see properly. I assured him I could.

'With the eyes, or with the mind?' he asked.

'Er, with the eyes at least,' I replied. Calazans seemed highly amused. 'So this isn't for parapsychology,' he observed, as if enjoying some private joke, as his hands already began to probe around the man's belly area.

'Feeling all right?' he asked the patient, getting a faint grunt in reply.

Calazans turned to me. 'Now he's feeling it open ...Not in the mind, but in the body itself, above the stomach ...' I noted he said above and not in the stomach, reminding me of theories I had heard to the effect that psychic operations are carried out on the perispirit body, not the physical one.

'Now we are putting in a drain,' he went on, though I could see nothing happening at all, 'to serve as tubing. Know what that is?' He turned to the young Brazilian doctor who was watching from the other side of the bed.

'Give him a medicine lesson!' he said, good-humouredly.

The doctor took no notice of me, perhaps afraid I would report him to the local medical association. Doctors, I had found, had to be very well established before they would talk to strangers about psychic surgery.

'How long should he rest?' an assistant asked.

'Forty-eight hours,' Calazans replied at once. It then turned out that the man had been planning to drive himself home, and had nobody with him. Calazans seemed to think this was extremely amusing. 'Only if you go by rocket!' he chuckled. 'Next patient, please!' The man climbed stiffly off the bed and slumped on the other bed. He looked dazed and weak. The whole operation had been entirely invisible to my eyes, but he had certainly felt something. He began to moan incoherent phrases to himself.

Meanwhile, the next patient had come forward, an Argentinian lady with whom Calazans chatted happily about the difference between Spaniards like himself and *los argentinos*, especially the latter's eating habits. While he diagnosed her problem and scribbled off a prescription, another patient for operation had climbed onto the bed. The previous one was still looking very helpless and trying to lie down on the other bed.

Calazans looked across at him. 'And he wanted to drive himself home!' he exclaimed callously. 'Ay, these Brazilians are difficult!' It was a huge joke, at least for him.

'Oh, by the way,' he said to the Argentine lady as she was leaving. 'Don't forget that your husband is going to meet a violent death in one of these Brazilian cars ...' (he named the make) '... a red one.' He might have been reminding her to buy the fish on the way home, and turned his attention at once to the next patient, while the woman anxiously discussed with an assistant whether it was worth contacting her husband, from whom she was separated, and warning him.

The man on the other bed was getting worse. Calazans told the doctor to give him a massage and make him take deep breaths. He turned to me.

'See the effect of the anaesthetic?' he asked, again as if addressing a beginners' class. 'Know what that is called? No? Shock, that's what. Anaphylactic, or postoperative shock.' The poor fellow really looked terrible. He was yawning, moaning and begging to be allowed to lie down. 'No!' Calazans rapped sternly. 'Sit upright and drink some coffee.' Then he added, as if really wanting to rub it in: 'And you still want to drive yourself home, eh? What's that - taxi? Well, that's better!' He turned to me. 'Go over and help him. Use your mind.' I went to the other bed and made soothing noises.

Calazans could be devastating at times. When one frail old lady told him she was feeling better, he exclaimed 'Better! You call this better?' Another patient, a young man with long hair, was startled on being asked: 'When did you last use narcotics?' Yet for all his exuberance and apparent rough treatment, there was no mistaking Calazans' concern for his patients.

The man on the other bed calmed down at last, and Calazans called me back to watch the next operation, after casually mentioning that he would have to change a kidney for the last one.

'How would you do that by parapsychology, eh?' he asked me, as he turned at last to the woman waiting for her operation. She was fully dressed; onlookers were always asked to leave the room when women's private parts were treated or examined. She had pulled her sweater up to reveal a bare stomach.

This operation, he told me, was going to be one of the visible ones. I put the microphone of the recorder on the floor and leaned forward. What happened next was enough to dispel any lingering doubts I may have had about the reality of psychic surgery.

Put your hand here,' he ordered. His own were already on the woman's stomach, prodding around. I could see nothing unusual as yet, though the area he was prodding seemed to be wet, glistening in the soft blue light.

Suddenly he rubbed a finger on her skin and almost stuffed it up my nose.

'Water!' he observed. 'Know this type of water?' The pungent smell of pure ether was unmistakable. There was absolutely nowhere that I could see, at least on this plane, where it could have come from. There was no sign that I could see of plastic sachets taped to his palms and punctured by sharpened thumbnails, which I had seen operators in the Philippines quite clearly doing on several pieces of video recording.

I looked at the patient's face. She was an attractive young woman with long dark hair. She seemed to take no notice of me, although her eyes were open, so after some hesitation I put my right hand on the nearest bare patch of stomach, beside the spot Calazans had been feeling.

Then Calazans got down to business. This was indeed to be an example of the other kind of operation; the messy kind. A few twists and wrenches, and suddenly his fingers were immersed in a pool of dark liquid that had simply appeared from nowhere. It had certainly not come from a palmed sachet.

'Go on,' Calazans insisted. Put your hand in!' He took his own hands away. The pool of liquid remained in position. It is not possible even to simulate this effect by normal methods. The slightest movement will spill the liquid over the side of the body. Moreover, if you press down on an abdomen you tend to get side-to-side depressions, not the top-to-bottom ones like the one I was seeing.

I managed to get about an inch of one finger into the dark pool. It was yet another moment of truth, not that I should have needed proof. The liquid was warm, and checking later that evening with water heated to blood temperature I found it felt very similar. It looked lighter and thinner than blood, and I remembered that phrase about separating the red corpuscles from the plasma.

'Oxygenated water!' Calazans ordered, and an assistant poured some liquid from a small bottle into the hole. It frothed and bubbled, and I snatched my finger away. It remained wet and sticky for some minutes, but was not discoloured.

Then the liquid pool on the woman's stomach simply vanished, like spilt water in an animated cartoon. Calazans was explaining to the young doctor what he had been doing.

'We took the etheric ... separated it ... closed, to retain the pains ... all this here, 30%-40% red ...' It was technical talk from one doctor to another, and not for my benefit. I transcribe the exact words as I recorded them on tape.

Then it was back to the production-line routine of consultations, some of which lasted less than half a minute. Hand on the stomach, scribbled prescription, and next patient, please! Calazans seemed to be able to diagnose instantaneously.

One woman, whom I knew to be suffering from ear trouble (I had brought her along as a test case), was given her prescription before she had time to open her mouth. One of the three medicines prescribed was Auricovit, which is specifically for ear trouble. Calazans had not even looked at her ears.

Another elderly patient complained of nervous problems.

'Nerves!' Calazans exclaimed, back to his ebullient self. 'You're on the verge of the lunatic asylum. This isn't nerves, it's schizothymia!'

'What do you suggest, doctor?' the old lady asked timidly.

'I'm not going to suggest anything,' Calazans snapped back. 'I'm going to treat you. Otherwise you'll end up in a sanatorium!' A few lightning scrawls on his prescription pad, and he handed her a sheet of paper to be deciphered by Firmino upstairs. Next patient, please ...

'Put the ingles at the table,' Calazans ordered suddenly.

I left the recorder running under the bed, went through the curtains and sat down at the table with the silent mediums, where I did my best to think positively.

Soon the last patient had been treated, and the last operation, for cancer of the uterus, performed. No doubt this was why I had been told to leave the operating area. Then Calazans came over to the table and sat with us for a few moments, said a brief prayer, muttered a few words in the voice of what sounded like a slave from Brazil's colonial times, and finally woke up, like Superman turning back into Clark Kent.

Edivaldo got up at once, looking fresh and cheerful. He slapped me on the back and asked if I had enjoyed myself, then went upstairs for a snack and a coffee. For him, it had been just another long day's work, the same as any Saturday or Sunday.

For me, it had been another evening of what Einstein calls 'humble admiration of the illimitable superior spirit who reveals himself in the slight details we are able to perceive with our frail and feeble minds'.

I was in the position of an ancient Greek rubbing two pieces of amber together, and producing what would be known as electricity nearly two thousand years later, without having any idea what he was doing.

Back home, I drank a welcome cold beer and searched my bookshelf for some of the answers to the many questions filling my head. Einstein was the only help.

'To know that what is impenetrable to us really exists, manifesting itself as the highest wisdom and the most radiant beauty which our dull faculties can comprehend only in their most primitive forms this knowledge, this feeling is at the centre of true religiousness ...'

It was good to know that some things were impenetrable even to Einstein. They certainly were to me.

There was a sad ending to the story of my investigation of Edivaldo Oliveira Silva. On 9 March 1974 he was making another of his lengthy drives to Rio for another weekend of healing when he was involved in a head-on collision with another vehicle. He died in hospital a couple of hours later, aged 43.

When I read the news I suddenly remembered a remark he had made when I had asked him if he didn't get tired on those long drives.

'No," he replied. "Sometimes I go to sleep and let the spirits take over...'

# PART III

# 1

# THE IBPP

S PIRITISM, said Allan Kardec, would be scientific or it would not
survive. I am afraid he was wrong, at least with regard to Brazil;
for although the doctrine he codified and popularized has definitely survived, relatively few of its followers can be described as scientific in their approach by the wildest stretch of the imagination. This
helps account for the fact that psychical research was late in arriving
in Brazil, and is still in its infancy. There are further reasons: Brazilian Spiritists tend to assume that all necessary scientific proof of their
faith has already been obtained.

Did not Sir William Crookes, Charles Richet, Frederic Myers, Gabriel
Delanne, Ernesto Bozzano and others satisfy themselves of the reality of
almost all common phenomena associated with it? Were they not scientific enough, especially the first two? As to the question of investigating
phenomena in present times, they point out that Spiritism is a religion
and a philosophy as well as a science. It has now grown out of its scientific stage, somehow surviving intact despite its critics' efforts, and should
be accepted as a religion on its own merits. Who, they ask, sets out to
investigate Roman Catholicism nowadays? How about trying to prove
scientifically some of the Pope's wilder dogmas? Most of Brazil's more
interesting psi phenomena have taken place in the past within the Spiritist movement, or closely connected with it. To those within, they have
been proved enough already; while to those without, the whole movement is a lot of nonsense and not worth investigating anyway.

On the whole, Brazilian Spiritists are none too concerned whether
other people accept their beliefs or not. They are too busy practising their

faith and setting what they hope will be an example to others of militant (but never aggressive) Christianity to worry about their critics.

They are also trusting souls, erring sometimes on the side of suggestibility and credulousness, but quick to take offence if doubts are cast on their personal integrity, let alone their sanity. Mediums, in particular, soon tend to gather groups of admirers or helpers round them, and these often feel it their duty to keep their idol protected from the curious at all costs; in my experience such admirers are far more of a problem than the mediums themselves. To them, anyone described as an investigator is assumed at first to be either a secret policeman or a journalist bent upon destroying Spiritism, and is treated accordingly.

The situation is far from hopeless, however. Brazilian Spiritists are the kindest and most charitable people imaginable, and if researchers approach them with the claim that they are trying to understand their religion rather than expose its side effects as fraud, they will be given a warm welcome and all the help they need, or most of it. There is a growing tendency today for Brazilians to feel that Spiritism is well enough entrenched to allow for more serious research into it than has been permitted in the past.

It is not so long ago since Spiritists in Brazil had to stay underground or literally fight for survival if they came into the open. When Kardecism was a salon affair in its early days, and was largely restricted to the private homes of the upper classes in Rio de Janeiro, a city where just about any kind of behaviour is tolerated, it attracted no serious opposition. But when it spread into the interior, it often came up against open hostility from the Catholic Church, which until the end of the nineteenth century had enjoyed a total monopoly over Brazilian souls, and like all monopolists was unwilling to give up without a fight.

Dr Rafael A. Ranieri told me that there was a time when it was quite common for Spiritist centres in the interior to be stoned by mobs. Once, he added, a procession had been organized by a local priest to the centre where he was working. 'They were out to kill me,' he recalled. Times have changed; when I interviewed him, Ranieri was one of São Paulo's highest-ranking police commissioners. (When I turned up to interview him in his office, he was sitting on his desk oiling his gun which, he told me proudly, he had never had to use on duty).

'You must remember,' he told me, 'that Brazilians are religious people. For more than three hundred years this was a Catholic country, and today most of our Spiritists come from recent Catholic backgrounds. They retain their respect for religion, and when science looks like clashing with religion they will opt for the latter. Don't forget that the Brazilian Spiritist is a missionary, helping prepare his country for a very serious mission; the founding of a civilization of human fraternity and a world of real peace.'

Ranieri added that in his long experience mediums had rarely objected to being researched by outsiders, though often their surrounding groups had been less willing. He also made the point that the better class of Spiritist group, where the more dramatic effects were obtained, was usually restricted to a small number of advanced Spiritists who knew each other well, and were reluctant to admit outsiders to their sessions even if they were Spiritists, let alone non-Spiritist investigators.

An American team once turned up in São Paulo to investigate a very reputable medium, armed with the whole works from Faraday cage to handcuffs and all sorts of electrical gadgets. The poor medium was scared out of her wits, though anxious to help, and produced nothing at all under the conditions she was subjected to. The Americans concluded that she was a fraud. (I later concluded just the opposite; the medium in question was the psychic surgeon I have called Maria and described in a previous chapter.) Researchers in Brazil must make haste very slowly and tactfully. They are in the position of outsiders trying to join a club; that inner core of the Spiritist movement where the really interesting things happen. To join any club one must provide valid reasons for wanting to do so, and if members misbehave they get thrown out. This has happened quite often to foreigners who step off the plane at Rio or São Paulo airports and demand to see the psychic action right away. Those who take their time, like Dr Puharich, end up with what they want, as to some extent I also did.

The individual most responsible for the improvement in serious researchers' prospects in Brazil was Chico Xavier. He always welcomed publicity of any kind, though he never sought it; and he showed Spiritists that they had nothing to fear if they were genuine, as he most unquestionably was. Much of Chico's life was lived in public, and he is never known to have refused an interview; the more publicity he was given the more converts he won over. Dr Ranieri also played an important part in making Spiritism both respectable and researchable. He was one of the first Brazilian Spiritists to write about his own experiences in a straightforward and honest, if hardly scientific, manner. Pride of first place in serious scientific research into paranormal phenomena in Brazil must go, however, to a foreigner; Andrija Puharich. It was he who had the patience to seek out Arigó and persuade him, over a lengthy period, to submit himself to organized investigation.

The Uberaba affair, which I have already described, was a serious setback for researchers, since it left many Spiritists with the feeling that so-called scientific research was only a means by which the Catholic press sought to discredit their religion. Yet while this sordid controversy was at its height, a São Paulo civil servant and engineer quietly announced the foundation, in December 1963, of the *Instituto Brasileiro de Pesquisas Psicobiofísicas* (IBPP) or Brazilian Institute for Psycho-Biophysical Research. The somewhat unwieldy name was chosen in order to make it clear that the institute intended to explore biological and physical as well as purely psychical phenomena. The most significant thing about it was that it emerged from within the Spiritist movement itself.

Hernani Guimarães Andrade, its founder and the pioneer of serious psychical research in Brazil by Brazilians, was born in 1913 in the town of Araguari in the state of Minas Gerais. This is the state that has also produced many of Brazil's most outstanding mediums, including Chico Xavier and Arigó, and is generally regarded as the country's most psychic state. The rich mineral deposits that give the state its name (General Mines) are thought to have something to do with it. The *mineiros* (miners), as its natives are called, are known for their extreme caution, jokes about them being similar to those made by Englishmen about the Scots.

Andrade graduated from Brazil's leading university, that of São Paulo, in civil engineering in 1941. After a brief period working for state authorities there, and a year with the Standard Electric Company in Rio de Janeiro, he went to Volta Redonda to join the team that was helping set up Brazil's National Steel Company plant, the first of its kind in the country. He stayed more than seven years, rising to the position of chief in four different departments, and he also taught physics for three years at the special technical college set up at the works to train future employees of what was soon to become Brazil's most important industrial plant.

In 1952, he came to São Paulo to work for the state's Water and Electricity Department, later serving on a number of state and federal government commissions. In 1968, he became technical director of the department's electricity and telephone division. In short, he had a good scientific background.

He also had a good Spiritist one, becoming an active one at the age of seventeen. He told me how this came about. One evening in 1930 he was at a friend's house when the discussion turned to the subject of life after death. Hernani announced, when his opinion was asked for, that he regarded life as an essence independent of the physical body that animated it, and that after bodily death this essence went away to reappear in another living being awaiting birth. On hearing this, his friend's father had leapt from his chair and rushed out of the room, returning with a book in his hand.

'Go home and read this,' he ordered. 'You've got advanced ideas for your age!'

The book was Allan Kardec's What is Spiritism? and young Hernani was somewhat hesitant about reading it, for he came from a strictly Catholic family and was a student in a high school run by Catholic priests. He read it at a sitting, however, and immediately read everything else by Kardec.

'I found I had been a Spiritist all along without knowing it,' he told me.

Before long, he was regularly attending Spiritist sessions, welcoming his newly-revealed faith yet retaining a critical eye. At one session held in his own home, a prominent local Spiritist put on an impressive display of physical effects in a darkened room, making a record player perform, lights move and voices speak, provoking cries of ecstasy from the small audience. After the session was over, Hernani went back into the room and did a few experiments, calling to his friends a few moments later: 'Hey! I've discovered I'm a physical effects medium, too. Come back in here and see!'

They all duly trooped back into the room. Hernani turned the light out and proceeded to reproduce everything the group had just witnessed. After suitable verbal preparation in his best graveyard voice, he hoisted the record player onto his shoulder, making the first bars of the record play with the edge of his finger nail while holding a small torch in his mouth and ringing a bell with his other hand. At the same time, he managed to boom out some platitudes in a cavernous voice, until soon the room was resounding with cries of thanks to God for this magnificent display of His power. He kept up the performance until the end, and never revealed to his friends that he had tricked them.

Instead, he began to educate himself to become a proper researcher in the field of what used to be known as metaphysics. He taught himself enough French and English to be able to read the standard works on the subject, and before long became convinced that here in Brazil he had something that no would-be researcher before him had ever had; a ready abundance of genuine original material to study. Not all the sessions he attended were fakes, and though he never witnessed any really startling phenomena himself in his youth, he was convinced at an early age that Spiritism was a valid doctrine, and that some of its basic tenets, such as reincarnation and the possibility of communication with spirits, should be verifiable by scientific methods.

His first book, *The Corpuscular Spirit Theory*, appeared in 1958 and quickly sold out two editions. It was followed in 1960 by *New Ways Towards Spiritist Experimentation*. The two books were the result of thirty years of self education, observation and a great deal of thought. In them, he put forward the hypothesis that the spirit world could be described by a scientific terminology parallel to that used to describe physical matter. It was a real thing, with its own atomic and molecular structure and its own mechanism of interacting with the physical world.

The first book contained what was probably the first detailed hypothesis of the reincarnation process to be published anywhere, examined from the biological, physical and chemical points of view as well as the spiritual. The chapter on heredity was for some time the only material available in Portuguese that included an account of the work on the DNA molecular structure that won a Nobel prize for Messrs Crick, Wilkins and Watson in 1962. For a time, it was used as a textbook in a biology class at the University of São Paulo, where students and professors alike could find no fault in the presentation of the scientific data, however surprised they may have been by the title of the book, with its suggestion that the spirit world was as real as the physical one.

Although Andrade's corpuscular spirit theory is highly complex, the initial stated aims of the IBPP were extremely simple. 'Our fundamental objective is the study of paranormal facts and systematic research into the laws, properties and potential of the spirit by scientific methods.' Its five founder members were all Spiritists, but they made it clear that their work was not to be tied to any religious considerations. It was to be an impartial examination of the facts.

In his second book, Andrade described some of the methods by which the scientific department of the IBPP, his special responsibility, was to go after the facts.

The first piece of equipment to be built was called the Electromagnetic Space Condenser, designed to examine the effects of a biomagnetic field on the reproduction of bacteria.

The second was what has become known as a Kirlian camera, a device invented by Soviet electrician Semyon Kirlian and his wife Valentina to photograph effluvia from animate and inanimate objects through the use of a thing called a Tesla coil, which makes effects visible that cannot be seen by the naked eye. The IBPP built three Kirlian devices, probably the first outside the former USSR, the largest of which could photograph objects the size of a human hand.

While work was going ahead on these and number of other devices in the Andrade family garage, IBPP members were out in the field gathering all the information they could on anything that seemed relevant to psychical research. It was the first time this had been done in an organised manner in Brazil. Hernani and his small unfinanced team were doing what Frederic Myers and his more prosperous colleagues were doing when they founded the Society for Psychical Research in London.

The two most profitable lines of enquiry at first were those of poltergeists and reincarnation. Each had been well studied elsewhere, and there was plenty of published information to give the researchers an idea of what to look for. Brazil seemed to have an unusual amount of poltergeist activity causing havoc all over the place, and also a number of people who could remember what they thought might be a previous existence. It was time, Andrade and his colleagues felt, that such incidents and experiences were thouroughly examined, fully documented and where possible published.

While gathering evidence in these two fields, the IBPP also tried its hand at a full-scale investigation of a single incident, a supposed spirit communication involving a dead soldier named Ruytemberg Rocha, who 'dropped in' uninvited on a Spiritist meeting in São Paulo in 1961, providing a mass of verifiable information, though an amateur medium, about his life and death almost thirty years previously that Andrade and his colleagues were able to confirm from Brazilian army archives. (A full report on this remarkable case is now available in an English translation). 1

By its tenth birthday, in December 1973, the IBPP had three filing cabinets bulging with first-hand material, including tape recordings, photographs and personal accounts of unusual happenings. By that date its executive council consisted of eleven people, including three qualified engineers, three school-teachers, a doctor and an engineering student, Ricardo Andrade, who was to follow his father and two elder brothers into the engineering profession.

The IBPP managed to stay on good terms with other Spiritists, mainly because of its cautious attitude towards publicity; Andrade was often approached for interviews by the Brazilian press, and usually declined politely. He was reluctant to discuss anything in public that could not be supported by evidence in the institute's files, and the following chapters contain only a very small amount of what is to be found in those files..

I begin with my own original reports, which I have left unaltered, on two interesting people I met in São Paulo, a versatile artist and (apparently) a former prostitute from Pompeii.

# 2

## LUIZ AND CELIA

S ATURDAY, June 8th 1974. It is 6 p.m., and I am sitting at a large
table with six other people in a São Paulo Spiritist centre. The
young man directly opposite me is Luiz Antonio Gasparetto,
aged twenty-four, a social worker and psychology student who for the
past ten years or so has produced a steady stream of work in what appears to be a relatively rare field nowadays - that of psychic art. Luiz
has never sold a picture, or even tried to, and he has never learned to
draw. Those are just two of the unusual things about him.

Artists have often been known to go into a trance and produce work
unlike what they can do in their normal state - if any artist worth the
name can ever be said to be in a normal state. William Blake, for instance,
seems to have been in a trance for much of his life. Trance painting by
untrained mediums was a popular phenomenon in the nineteenth century, the work of Victorien Sardou and the Scotsman David Duguid attracting much attention. In this century we have had interesting trance
art from Augustin Lesage, a French miner, and from professionals like
Austin Spare and Ingo Swann, while in England a lady named Coral
Polge does fine pencil drawings of spirits she claims to see around her
sitters. My friends, who have heard of most of these people, assure me
that Luiz has some surprises in store for me, as indeed he has.

We sit in silence for a few minutes. On the table between Luiz and
myself is a pile of fourteen pieces of thick drawing paper, measuring 28
by 20 inches, and a new box of sixty artist's crayons of all colours. I have
already taken elementary precautions against possible fraud, holding each
sheet of paper up to the light, making sure it was blank and that there

were no concealed finished drawings in the pile. I do not feel it necessary to search the medium, since you cannot very well hide a 28 by 20-inch drawing up your sleeve.

The session begins. It is, they have told me, a regular Saturday evening session held whether there are visitors like myself present or not. The purpose of the sessions is to enable Luiz to develop his abilities under the orientation of his spirit guides. These, I am assured, include a host of discarnate artists such as Manet, Renoir, Modigliani, the Brazilian Tarsila do Amaral and many others.

The bright lights are switched off, leaving the room lit only by two weak red bulbs some twelve feet from where Luiz and I are sitting. I notice that in the red light you cannot tell one colour from another, though it is light enough to see what is going on and also to write on my notepad.

At 6.13, Luiz goes suddenly into action. Leaning his head on his left hand and turning slightly to the left, he runs the fingers of his right hand over the crayons in the box, without looking at what he is doing. With his face still covered, he attacks the paper with his right hand with such energy that the paper starts to slide around on top of the pile. I hold down the corners nearest me with two fingers. In just under three minutes, Luiz has completed a vivid portrait of a girl, his hand flying over the paper at astonishing speed As soon as he has finished and signed (from where I am it looks like 'Renoir'), the woman beside him lifts it off the pile and he starts another drawing without a moment's pause.

Very interesting, I say to myself. It cannot be easy to draw in semi-darkness even without a hand in front of your face. But it is hardly paranormal. What else can he do, I wonder?

As if reading my thoughts, Luiz embarks upon his next drawing. Taking a new chalk, he makes the outline of a face at great speed, still without looking at what he is doing, and immediately sketches in a pair of eyes at the bottom of the face. For a moment I decide he has missed out on this one, but as his hand continues to fly around the paper, jabbing at it like a high-speed boxer in a hurry to finish off his opponent, it gradually dawns on me that he is doing a portrait *upside down*, or the right way up as seen from my position.

I begin to feel quite impressed.

He draws upside down as quickly and assuredly as he does the right way up, and the new portrait is finished in a little over three minutes. Next, he takes the pile of paper and turns it sideways, picking up a chalk in each hand, and proceeds to draw two heads at once, one beside the other.

Luiz's two heads are quite different, and his two hands seem totally independent of each other, though I notice that occasionally one hand will jump across the paper to help the other with its portrait. While one hand dots in an eye, right on the spot, the other shades in a background of the other head. I would have said this performance was almost impossible, but one never really finds out what human beings can be capable of.

Luiz seems to pick up that thought as well, because for his next picture he repeats the phenomenon of drawing two heads at once. This time, however, he introduces yet another refinement: one of the heads is the right way up and the other is upside down!

I feel distinctly impressed.

As he starts his next picture, I fear Luiz has gone mad. He picks up a light-coloured crayon (it is difficult to tell what colour in the dim red light, though one can tell light from dark shades) and using the side of it he makes a huge oval blob in the middle of the paper, like a furious child just making a mess. When he is satisfied with his blob, which has used up almost the whole of the crayon, he picks up a darker one, makes a few lightning strokes on the paper, and in a matter of seconds there is an unmistakably Modigliani-like face in front of me.

To imitate a Modigliani portrait cannot be too difficult, with those oval faces and exaggeratedly long necks. Luiz promptly does it again, only this time he starts with the outline of the face and fills in the blank spaces later, using several different crayons. At this stage it occurs to me that every drawing so far has been made in a different way. We have had linear portraits drawn with great precision, another in a more impressionistic style with economy of line, and another with the strong colour areas and bold strokes of an expressionist. It seems I am being given a demonstration of every possible way of reproducing the human face on paper.

The only feature I can detect that is common to nearly all of them is a kind of aura effect around the faces. It is not an exaggerated aura, such as you find in paintings of saints, but just a faint outline following the contour of the cheek. On more than one occasion I notice that Luiz draws the outline of a face in thick strokes, then throws the chalk aside and immediately picks up another lighter one and follows the outline of the face exactly with the second chalk. The chalks, incidentally, may have begun the evening in a neat row in their box, but before long Luiz has used more than half of the sixty, and their stumps are lying all over the place. And more than once I note that he locates a colour he has already used and discarded in order to complete a certain line or shaded area.

The session ends at 7.05, by which time Luiz has produced a total of fourteen drawings, averaging just under four minutes each. Throughout the session neither he nor I have spoken a word until the start of the last picture, another of his double-portrait feats. At this point, Luiz starts to speak in a voice they told me later was that of the centre's spirit guide-in-chief, a certain Father Zabeu, who is well known in local Spiritist circles. Luiz certainly gives a fair impression of speaking in the voice of an elderly priest, and for three or four minutes there he is, drawing two portraits at once and delivering a homely little sermon at the same time. This may be possible, but normal it is not.

After the session, the lights are turned on again and Luiz looks at his evening's output, like a photographer eager to see how his film has come out. He gives no sign of having any recollection of what he has been up to for the past hour.

I am struck by the quality of the drawings. They might not pass for original Renoirs or Modiglianis, but they would decorate any home wall. They are all full-face portraits, none of them of anybody present, and each face has a lively expression and an air of serenity about it. Although done at frantic speed, they bear no resemblance to the lightning cartoons people often do in cafes and bars for tourists. They are pleasing pictures skilfully drawn in the styles of the artists whose names were signed on them.

I decide without much hesitation that Luiz should be investigated more thoroughly, and promptly make arrangements to return the following Saturday with the full IBPP research team, to which Luiz agrees at once.

The following week, Ney Prieto Peres of the IBPP shot about twenty minutes of colour film of Luiz at work, while Suzuko Hashizume tape-recorded the sound of his hand flying over the paper, and Hernani Guimarães Andrade and I took nearly 200 colour slides of the session. When we showed the film later, nobody could believe it. It looked as though it had been speeded up, like an old Keystone Cops comedy. We checked the projector and found it in perfect order. We showed other films, which appeared to be running at the right speed. I went over my original notes and found the time of each drawing matched with the film.

This was quite an interesting situation. You might suppose that if you film something apparently anomalous, you will satisfy yourself that it really happened when you see the film afterwards. But the opposite seemed to be the case here. I had watched two of Luiz's hour-long sessions and seen him produce thirty drawings and two oil paintings within a few feet of where I sat. I had ruled out all the obvious possibilities for fraud or hallucination. I had been present when the film was shot, and yet - seeing it all on film was far less convincing than seeing the real thing had been.

We talked to a number of professional artists and showed them a selection of Luiz's work. All agreed that for a man with no art training to produce pictures of such quality in a weak red light, without looking at what he was doing, drawing upside down, doing two heads at once, and firing off portraits of unseen sitters one after the other sometimes in as little as thirty seconds simply could not be done. We also agreed that it had been done. A leading Brazilian artist, teacher and critic, after studying thirty of Luiz's drawings, pointed out a few minor anatomical errors here and there, but stated very firmly that he did not think even a trained artist could produce work of such variety and skill under the conditions we described, which he later saw for himself.

There remained one other doubt to clear up: Luiz had been producing drawings for about ten years, and somebody suggested that he might have simply memorized a set of portraits to the point where he could reproduce the same ones on demand. Accordingly, we asked to look at all the drawings he had preserved, and Luiz obligingly produced a number of thick folders containing over a thousand examples of his work. Many more had been given away, but none had ever been sold. No two pictures were identical, though many could be grouped into categories that strongly recalled the work of a dozen masters from Rembrandt and Hals to Manet, Degas, Renoir and Modigliani. There were ornately dressed laughing cavaliers, more sombre faces of elderly Jews, elegant Parisiennes, shapely ballerinas, voluptuous looking models and a host of others, many unsigned.

Here indeed was the Rosemary Brown of the art world.

London housewife Rosemary Brown has baffled critics for several years by producing a stream of piano pieces in the style of several dead composers, especially Liszt. She has had little musical training, yet she has somehow written down music that is recognizably in the style of the composer who purports to have dictated it from the spirit world.

British (living) composer Humphrey Searle, a recognized authority on Liszt, has said that one of her pieces, Grübelei, is the kind of music Liszt might have written had he lived a few years longer, and that it is not a paraphrase of anything he is known to have written while alive. Mrs Brown's pieces contain faults, according to Vernon Harrison, a founder member of the Liszt Society, but they are 'too good to dismiss lightly'.[1]

So it is with Luiz Gasparetto. His drawings are there for all to see, and he is convinced that they are the work of the spirits of the artists concerned. Luiz is an intelligent, well-educated young man from a comfortable middle-class family. He has never sought publicity, nor objected to being studied by researchers. He spends much of his time working without pay at a school for retarded children, and he does intend eventually to sell his drawings to raise money for a new Spiritist centre. I am sure we shall hear more of him.

Next, let me introduce you to the lady from Pompeii.

Celia, as I shall call her here, is an attractive and vivacious lady of about fifty, though she looks fifteen years younger. Her husband Leo is a very successful construction engineer, and their daughter has married into one of Brazil's grand old families. I have known them well for more than three years, and spent many hours listening to Celia's accounts of her extraordinary life, or I should say lives.

From a very early age, it was clear that she was not like the other little girls in the small town where she was born into a wealthy and traditional Catholic family of pure Brazilian lineage. As her mother, family servant and Celia herself readily agreed, she was a little terror.

By the time she was six years old, she had developed two great passions; dancing and boys. Rather than play with her many expensive toys, she would be out in the streets with the gang, inventing contests in which the winner had to kiss her on the mouth. She would go out of her way to play off one little boy friend against another, and one of her early triumphs was a knife fight provoked in her honour. She loved every minute of it.

At the age of eight, she saw a man shot dead in front of her. She calmly gave her parents the details over dinner, putting them off their appetites while she munched a bloody underdone steak without a qualm. On another occasion, she watched impassively as a man was lynched to death with iron crowbars. Such callousness in the face of death is most untypical in Brazilian women; once, Celia was driving me across São Paulo when we passed the scene of a gruesome road accident in which a motor-cycle had been flattened by a large truck. Celia drove by without a single comment; the incident meant no more to her than a hole in the road.

Almost as soon as she was able to walk, she began to dance. Most girls at that age like dancing, but Celia really took it seriously. When her parents went out for the evening, she would make up her pugnacious little face at her mother's dressing table, drape any piece of cloth available around her skinny body, put a record on the gramophone and simply take over the whole house, dancing wildly all over the place. One night her parents brought some friends home, to find Celia swirling sensuously around the living room stark naked. They watched in amazement.

'Who taught her to move her body like that?' one asked. But nobody had taught her anything; behaving like a Spanish gypsy seemed to come naturally to her.

After lunch, she would reluctantly have to lie down in her room and rest. Yet instead of sleeping, she would often lie and stare at the white ceiling, where she would see scenes of startling eroticism. Men and women were taking part in Roman-style orgies, drinking, lying around and making love to each other, and Celia felt she was part of the action as well. One of her older boy friends had told her, when she was six, all the details of how men and women made love, and she had listened without interest. She already knew.

She had her first clear memory of another lifetime at the age of five, as she sat on the steps of the house one day and gazed into the blue sky above. Suddenly she seemed to be somewhere else, under another blue sky, and the thought of it gave her a sudden feeling of melancholy and nostalgia. Nostalgia for what, she could not yet say. From then on, throughout her life, Celia has had a series of recurrent dreams, some of which still come two or three times a year. Three of them are especially vivid, and it has often taken her all day to recover from the effects of them.

In the first, she is in a boat approaching an island, not a typical Brazilian one with sandy beaches and palm trees, but a bare slab of rock lashed by violent seas. She feels she is being taken there for some specific reason, and can see flaming torches dotted around the island.

The second recurrent dream takes place in a dark room that seems like a sort of corridor made of blocks of stone. Various men are lounging about on benches, flirting with a young girl whom Celia knows to be herself. Through a window she can see people walking about with baskets on their heads, coming back from market. Everybody is wearing tunics. At the end of the dream, she walks down a passage on the way out of what seems to be a bath house, and meets a sallow-faced old man who blocks her way. She feels a great desire to excite him sexually, and kisses him on the mouth, but is horrified to find his lips are stone cold. 'You can't do me any more harm,' the man says, 'because I have been dead for two thousand years.'

The third dream is by far the most vivid and frightening. Celia is at the window of her house, looking over the rooftops at a distant mountain.

Suddenly she gets a feeling of terror, runs out of the house, along a street, through an archway and on to a beach. Then she rushes headlong into the sea and is drowned.

In addition to these three recurrent dreams, Celia has had a number of once-only ones that she has remembered in great detail. In one, she is dancing around a camp fire and doing her best to provoke a man who eventually takes her by the waist, forces her to the ground and kills her. In another, somebody is singing a Spanish gypsy song to guitar accompaniment, while she plays a game where she has to eat a whole plate of grapes before the music stops. In another, she is simply eating a meal in a poor-looking brick house, picking up pieces of sausage with her fingers and dipping them in salt. In all these dreams, she is aware that she is a member of a tribe of Spanish gypsies, and one of its star dancers.

When Celia heard the sound of castanets for the first time, she became so excited that she followed the sound to a ballet school near her house, where she marched in and immediately started to learn Spanish dancing. Or, more accurately, she just started to do it, for she seemed to know it all and there was little her teacher could tell her. She took to the castanets like a duck to water and became the best dancer in the school.

Spanish dancing is not widely popular in Brazil, where the majority of the people are of Portuguese stock and Spanish immigrants have tended to abandon their native customs. Even traditional Portuguese folk music is rarely heard, and Spanish music almost never. Yet to Celia, flamenco dancing was the most natural thing in the world, and soon she was to become quite well known for a time as a Spanish dancer on television, convincing many of her partners that she came from Spain, although she had never been there. At least, not in this lifetime.

Girls tend to be strictly brought up in Brazil, especially in Catholic families from small towns in the interior. But Celia refused to conform to any conventions. As a child, she would peel off her clothes and jump naked into the swimming pool regardless of who might be watching. She would drink wine and beer without feeling this was in any way unusual. Early in her teens, she would go all out not only to attract men but to sleep with them, and by the time she was an adult, she was something of a nymphomaniac.

Moving to the city of São Paulo, she soon met her future husband Leo, and married him when she was twenty-four. Leo was engaged already, but Celia simply set out to push the other woman out of the way and get her man. They became a couple of young swingers, living it up all night in bars and clubs and making love to each other (which they still do at least twice a week) on all possible occasions. Eventually they had to reinforce their sex lives with pornographic films and books, of which Celia bought and read large quantities although she has scarcely ever read any other kind of book.

They even indulged in *sex à trois*, with the help of a lady friend brought in to liven up their night life.

After some years of this sort of behaviour, odd things began to happen. Doors would slam loudly in the night, lights would turn on and off, and inexplicable noises of all kinds would be heard when there was nobody else in the house.

On the advice of a close friend familiar with poltergeist phenomena, who told them that such things often happened to people who led sexually depraved lives, they decided to change their way of living and behave more normally.

Then both of them learned to their surprise that they were what are known as mediums. They went along to the São Paulo Spiritist Federation to study this strange phenomenon, and Leo soon found he had an unusual ability to transfer energy to other people through what are called mediumistic passes. Neither of them was ever what could be called the religious type, as they are not today, but in retrospect both feel that they were literally saved by their Spiritist friends from a life of total depravity and uselessness.

In 1970, Celia went abroad for the first time in her life, on a grand tour of Europe with her daughter and three close friends. They saw all the usual tourist sights, none of which made much impression on Celia. But when they took a boat to the island of Ischia, off the Italian coast, she had one of the most profound shocks of her life. There was 'her' rock, the one she had been dreaming about for forty years. It was exactly the shape it had been in her dreams, although it was now dotted with luxury villas instead of flaming torches. She had unquestionably been there before.

Then the party went to visit the ruined Roman city of Pompeii, near the volcanic Mount Vesuvius that had showered it with flaming lava in the year 79 AD. As soon as she set foot in the place, Celia led her friends on a guided tour of the well-preserved ruins, pointing out her bath house, her amphitheatre, and finally her house. To everybody's alarm (except Celia's), they learned from the real tourist guide that this had been the local brothel and was not open to visitors.

The following year, Celia came back to Pompeii with Leo and they spent more time there. She was furious to find that her house was still locked up, and only after much persuasion and bribery were they able to get inside. Celia had already described the place in detail to her husband. Upstairs there were a number of small rooms, each decorated with friezes of pornographic scenes, showing naked men and women doing things that may be new even to students of the Kama Sutra of Vatsyayana. And from the small window in her room, there was a perfectly framed view of Mount Vesuvius.

They went into the building, and there it all was, exactly as Celia had so often seen and described it. The friezes were still there, and Vesuvius was still where it always had been, neatly framed in the window of *her* room. In great excitement, Celia led her husband out of the whorehouse and showed him the route she had taken on the day the mountain had erupted. She led him along her street, the Via dell' Abbondanza, under the arch and outside the city limits.

Here, something was wrong. There was no sea in sight. The coastline was more than a mile away, and a group of archaeologists was digging in the ground near the spot where Celia recalled making her fatal dash into the waves. They went over to talk to the archaeologists, asking if they knew by any chance where the shoreline had been at the time of the destruction of Pompeii.

'Right here, Signora,' they replied.

Celia had hardly heard of Pompeii in her present life. As a child she had scarcely read any foreign history, and her film going had been restricted to the regular local fare of Tom Mix and Rin-Tin-Tin. There was no television in Brazil in those days. She had in fact always thought that her dreams were of ancient Egypt rather than Pompeii, but after her two visits to the ruined Roman seaside resort, a flood of detailed memories came back to her, and in 1973 she recorded sixteen hours of these memories on tape.

I wondered if she had ever read Bulwer-Lytton's *Last Days of Pompeii*. She had, she told me, recently picked up a copy, but had given it up half way through.

'It wasn't like that at all,' she commented. Women, she assured me, were not the meek and passive creatures depicted in Bulwer-Lytton's book. 'We used to run everything in those days!' So it does not seem likely that her memories of Pompeii were based on anything she had read.

On their way back to Brazil (after Leo had had some difficulty in dragging his wife away from Pompeii), the couple stopped off in Spain. Having identified the site of one past life, Celia was determined to locate another. She never managed to discover a particular place she recognized as easily as Pompeii or Ischia, but she felt quite at home in the dry countryside around Granada, and was flattered when a shop assistant refused to believe she was a Brazilian. *'Parece mas una española que yo!'* the woman said. ('You look more Spanish than I do!') On several other occasions she would be greeted by Spaniards with the question 'But aren't you a *mora* (gypsy)?' As far as she was concerned, of course she was. Or had been.

Readers may have concluded by now that Celia is no more than a hysterical, suggestible and altogether nutty member of the wealthy class, who has nothing better to do than dream. This would be totally wrong; it is not possible to feel that way if you knew her. She is certainly not a typical Brazilian; women of her age and social status tend to be very class conscious, and to do all they can to preserve, or at least simulate, an appearance of respectability and culture. Celia, however, could not care less about social conventions. Her high society friends regard her as a colourful eccentric, vivacious and uninhibited but never vulgar or crude.

They are impressed by her fearless character. Once, she spotted a suspicious looking prowler outside her house, and rather than call the police or her husband, she took her own revolver, stuck it in the astonished man's back and marched him over a mile to the nearest police station. Brazilian women do not normally do such things.

There is no ready explanation as to how the daughter of a rich and respectable family (her father was a senior government official) should grow into a reincarnation of a Spanish gypsy or a trollop from Pompeii, which Celia freely admits she was, in great detail. Hers is the kind of experience that seems to cross the border from the merely abnormal into the totally paranormal. She accepts reincarnation as a matter of course, though she has not the slightest interest in the religious or metaphysical aspects of this much-debated subject. As far as she is concerned, her present life is merely one stage in the long personal process of evolution through trial, error and experience. She is aware of the fact that in this lifetime she has been happily married for the first time, to a man she has known several times before. Her daughter does not resemble her in the least; she is a quiet and well-balanced young woman whose presence in the family home seems to bring her lively extrovert parents together and calm them down.

Celia is a very practical person, an efficient organizer of social and charitable functions, and the most popular teacher at the ballet school where she gives lessons in Spanish dancing. She has little interest in the paranormal as such, though she accepts the basic principles of Spiritism. She takes a realistic attitude towards her own experience, feeling that she was born this time round into a family that gave her a chance to improve on her licentious former lives, although this took some time; to make an excellent marriage and raise a daughter whose virtues are as noticeable as her own shortcomings, to do some useful social work and generally become more aware of the purpose of life, death and rebirth.

Was she really recalling one or more past lives? If her dream memories were unique, I could dismiss them as one-off fantasies possibly constructed by her subconscious mind. Yet, as I was soon to discover, they were far from unique. Hers was just one of the 71 cases in the IBPP files of what have become known as 'cases suggestive of reincarnation'. Here follows a selection from the other seventy.

# 3

## BORN AGAIN?

SILVIA was born in a São Paulo hospital at nine in the morning on March 20th, 1963. She was her mother's first child, and she spent the first day of her life in an incubator, for she had been born a blue baby a few weeks premature. Her grandmother, a trained nurse and obstetrician, looked after her while her mother recovered from her ordeal, and it was Grandma who picked up the day-old Silvia and greeted her with the words *amore mio*. She did not know at the time, nor has she known since, why she used the Italian words for 'my love' instead of the Portuguese *meu amor*. Silvia, however, smiled happily as if she understood.

When she was less than a month old, a large aeroplane flew over the house while Grandma was giving her the bottle. Silvia stopped sucking the rubber teat and looked at her grandmother in apparent terror. 'Don't be afraid, *amore mio*,' Grandma soothed her. 'It's nothing, just a plane going by. You can drink your milk!' Again, she had no idea why she used the Italian phrase Like Silvia's parents, she was Brazilian-born, and the only Italian ancestor in the family was the baby's maternal grandfather, who had died in 1954.

Although São Paulo has welcomed millions of immigrants from Italy since late in the nineteenth century, the Italian language is practically never heard there, for Italians find little difficulty in learning Portuguese. Yet before little blue-eyed Silvia was two years old, she had shown another peculiarity in addition to her inexplicable fear of aeroplanes; a fluent knowledge of Italian. When her first sister was born, Silvia greeted her as *mia sorela*, not *minha irmã*. Her mother was *mamina*

159

rather than the Portuguese *mamãe*. She would ask for her *bambola* instead of her *boneca*, or doll. One day on being woken up by *mamina* she announced that she was *felice*, a word with one more syllable than the Portuguese for happy, *feliz*. Her mother repeated this to the washerwoman that afternoon.

'But nobody here speaks Italian,' the woman replied, amused.

'*Io parlo*,' Silvia interrupted at once.

She was a talkative child, whatever her favourite language, and was quite fluent in normal Portuguese by the age of two despite her surprising Italian vocabulary. One day she was babbling away merrily to her mother, who was not paying much attention to what she was saying, until she suddenly turned and said: '...there, on the *capitolio*, isn't it, *mamina*?'

What's that?' her mother asked. All it suggested to her at the time was the Capitol building in Washington.

'It's a *monte*, of course!' Silvia replied, and subsequent reference to the dictionary showed that it was indeed the name of one of the seven hills on which Rome was built, as well as that of the temple of Jupiter that stood there.

Before she was three, Silvia came out with more unexpected words for a Brazilian-born girl of immediate Brazilian descent.

When her mother sent her on an errand with her grandfather she exclaimed '*Andiamo*' an expression quite unlike the Portuguese *vamos*, or 'let's go'. When she was playing with a ball of wool and getting it all tied in knots, she handed it to Grandma and said: 'Here, it's all *spancagliata*' This is how Grandma recorded the word at the time. It may have been an attempt at *sparpagliata*, (literally, scattered). Once, Silvia climbed into a pair of her mother's shoes and started clattering round the house. When Grandma told her to be quiet, she replied: 'Don't disturb me, I'm doing a *pestadura*. This means nothing in Portuguese, but in Italian it is literally 'hard foot' or stamping, which is indeed what she was doing. Seeing her youngest sister lying in her pram, Silvia commented on the fact that she was *losca*, or cross-eyed, the Portuguese for which is *vesgo*.

Grandma noted all these words in the special diary she had kept since the day of Silvia's birth. This was to prove of great value when IBPP researchers eventually began to study the case. For Silvia's third birthday, Grandma gave her an Italian dictionary with a specially written dedication listing fourteen words in Italian she had spoken up to then.

'I do not know what connection we had before in another incarnation,' Grandma wrote on the flyleaf of the dictionary. 'I only know that I loved you very much, as I love you now, and that we have met again, *amore mio.*' Silvia's family were all Spiritists, and accepted reincarnation as a perfectly normal event, which explains why they never scolded her for 'talking nonsense', as many parents would have done when she began to come out with apparent memories of another life, and words in a foreign language. They knew that by the age of eight or nine such memories would have faded, and Silvia would be a perfectly adjusted and happy little Brazilian girl, provided they looked after her properly.

The first sign of what some researchers now like to call extra-cerebral memory came one day when Grandma was walking Silvia around the block.

'Grandma, do you want me to tell you about my friend?' Silvia asked. 'There were two bad boys who tried to take my friend's money away, and she went after them and she hit them.'

'You liked your friend a lot, didn't you?' Grandma commented. 'Do you miss her?' Silvia lowered her head, and when she raised it again Grandma saw tears running down her cheeks.

Gradually, other scraps of information about Silvia's previous life in Rome came out, usually one at a time and in brief fragments, although both her mother and grandmother later recalled that she was always a talkative child, and much of what she said was soon forgotten.

They clearly remember many references to Silvia's special friend, and one day she came out with the name Affonsa Dinari, whose husband was called Gennaro and who used to look after Silvia and her other friends. They all seemed to live on or in the Capitol, though Silvia never made it clear whether she meant the hill or the temple.

Gennaro would bring them rice to eat, and sometimes they had macaroni with wine. The house where they lived was 'all broken' and there was no roof on the kitchen.

She remembered what had happened to some of her friends. Tita was hurt in the leg and had to be treated by a doctor from what Silvia called 'the United of States'. Then Tita went away to a hole full of earth, and they threw more earth on top of her and she never came back.

Cecilia (pronounced in the Italian manner) was very naughty and kept running away, and Silvia would have to go after her. One day another girl 'went to sleep' in a closed wooden cradle and never woke up.

Then there were the bombs. One day a few months after her third birthday, Silvia was playing in the garden when an aeroplane roared overhead. As usual Silvia showed signs of fear; when this happened while she was inside the house she would ask her mother to shut the door 'to keep it out'.

Grandma assured her that this was just a nice plane carrying people around, and it was nothing like the ones she had seen from the Capitol.

'That's right,' Silvia replied. 'There in the Capitol the planes would drop bombs this big ... and then there were a lot of pieces of metal on the ground that hurt people.' On one occasion she gave a description of a bomb as looking like a pen you write with, and bombs resembling fountain pens were known to have been dropped on Rome after the Allied occupation.

In January 1967, Silvia caught sight of a new calendar hanging on the wall (a present from a local tradesman) and pointed excitedly to the colour photograph of Rome.

'There it is!' she cried. 'That's the Capitol. That's the house I used to live in, and that's the school, and those are the rocks I used to jump about on ...'

The only caption under the picture read 'Rome, Italy,' but the scene did indeed show the temple of Jupiter, some buildings in the background, and several stumps of columns in the foreground. The word Capitol did not appear anywhere on the calendar, and Silvia was the only one who recognized the scene.

'I don't want to go back to the Capitol,' she said later. 'Now I was born here and I only want this mother, this is the one I want ...'

It was on Easter Sunday in April 1966, when Silvia was three years and one month old, that she came out with her most startling memory. Her grandfather was in the kitchen preparing lunch, when an aeroplane went overhead, producing the usual reaction of alarm on Silvia's normally happy face.

'You know, Grandma, when I was there in the Capitol, a boy came running along with a bomb in his hand, and it blew up ...' Later, she described this as one of the fountain-pen-type bombs.

'I felt something indescribable inside me,' Grandma recalled later, 'but I asked her what had happened next.'

'The bomb blew up,' Silvia went on, 'and it hurt my cousin, my friend Affonsa Dinari very much on her head, and a lot of blood came out ...' She ran her hands over her face to show how the blood had flowed.

'And what about you, darling?' Grandma asked.

'I went and hid in the corner.' She clasped her arms over her chest, imitating fear and pain.

'What then?' Grandma prompted.

'Then my friend and me, we went up and up ...'

'Up what? The stairs of the Capitol?'

'No, Grandma, we went up, high up there ...'

This was too much for Grandma. She stopped what she was doing, took Silvia in her arms, and asked, with tears in her eyes: 'And then?'

'I don't know,' Silvia replied simply. 'Then I came here.'

Tina, a lawyer with a public utility company, was born in the town of Araraquara, 175 miles from São Paulo, though still within the state of the same name. Unlike Silvia, she remembered her previous life long after her present childhood, and was able to give a detailed account of some episodes from it as late as 1970, when she was thirty years old.

It is rare for people to recall names from past lives, but Tina remembers herself as being called Alex (possibly short for Alexandra) Amadado Barralouf. Her father's name was Jean Paris Barralouf and her mother's first name was Angala. She thinks she came from Vichy, where she lived a quiet life, and remembers going shopping with her mother, who was tall, blonde and well dressed.

Her clearest memory is of being taken to Le Havre and looking at the ships tied up at the quay. She first mentioned this episode at the age of two and a half, at which age she had never seen a ship, Araraquara being 200 miles inland.

Early in life she showed a strong sense of identification with France, although she is of only Brazilian or Italian descent. She preferred French-style cooking to Italian, and learned the French language without difficulty, while showing no ability for English, the most popular second language in Brazil. She showed an early aversion to anything German.

She clearly remembers the day she was killed.

'i don't think there was anybody else at home that day, because it was I who opened the door. It must have been about ten in the morning, and the weather was cloudy. I was in the entrance hall, and I heard someone knock on the door. I opened it, and a soldier came in. He was wearing a round helmet and olive-green uniform, and carried what looked like a rifle. He pointed it at me and fired at the heart. I remember asking for water before I died, but I don't remember if they gave me any. I can see myself lying on the floor, on my back, wearing a light dress. I don't remember seeing any blood.' Ever since childhood, Tina has had a horror of weapons of any kind, and also of the sight of blood.

Shortly before her birth as Tina, she came to Araraquara in some sort of flying machine. This she first described when she was about three, and the memory has remained with her ever since. As recalled by her uncle, who was present when she first told it in detail, the story went like this: 'I was carried here from France in a strange vehicle, something like the fuselage of an aeroplane, but with no wings. It was all white inside and it floated about two metres above the ground. There were two crew members, and another passenger who got off in São Paulo.' Tina went on as far as Araraquara, where she recalled seeing the curtains of her new parents' home illuminated from inside. This, they told her, was where she was to be born again.

Tina herself takes up the story at this point: 'The people on board were wearing clothes like a doctor's or nurse's uniform. When we arrived in front of the house in Araraquara, one of the men said to me "You stay here". I didn't see how I got out, but I can remember watching the vehicle go away. It was all white, like the body of a plane without wings or wheels. It didn't make any noise. I was wearing a long white dress of light material. I still looked like a girl of fifteen. One of the crew members spoke to me, while the other up front kept his back to me all the time. He was dressed in white too. I don't remember how I got into my house; I just saw myself inside and looking around. The lights were on, and I don't remember seeing anybody there. I can clearly remember the living room, especially a curtain that divided off the dining area, where there's a folding door now. The curtain was printed in bright colours, mostly red and green with some sea-blue. I didn't feel unhappy, homesick or anything like that. I really didn't know what I was doing there, and I can't remember a thing after arriving until I was about two and a half or three years old.'

Tina's uncle recalled that the house had been entirely redecorated shortly before her birth, but that as soon as she could talk she would describe it as it had been. The bright curtains in the living room had been among the last items to be changed, after her birth, and she had made a particular fuss when they went.

Tina has two birthmarks. One is on the left side of her chest and the other is on her back. Exactly where a bullet aimed at her heart could have gone in and out ...

Karen also has a birthmark.

An observant grandmother is the reincarnation researcher's best friend. She is often in better shape than the mother when a baby is born, and Karen's had a special reason to be happy as well as observant when she was born in São Paulo in September, 1953. For little Karen was apparently her own sister, Clara.

Clara had been killed on November 5th, 1944, when the air-raid shelter in Vienna in which she was hiding had collapsed on her head after being hit by a bomb. Clara's son had been with her at the time, but had survived. Later, he testified that he had been knocked unconscious by the blast, and upon coming to his senses he had found his mother mortally wounded in two places on her head, the rest of her body being unmarked.

Shortly before Karen's birth, which was a few weeks overdue, Grandma was sitting with the family in the living room when suddenly she clearly saw Clara, standing behind the chair where her son-in-law was seated. The room was brightly lit, and Clara had turned to her sister and said: 'Don't worry about mother. Everything is going well. The baby is alive and will be born on September 11th. It will be of the female sex, and the girl is me, reincarnating as your grand-daughter.'

Nobody else saw the vision, which disappeared shortly after delivering the message, though everybody noticed Grandma's consternation and asked her what was the matter. She immediately told them what she had seen and heard, and the baby was born exactly as described; it was a girl, and her birthday was September 11th.

The birth, though late, was entirely normal, and there was no need for the use of forceps, which can cause deformities if manipulated carelessly. But the first thing Grandma noticed was the deep red birthmark on the left side of the parietal bone, and the second one on the occipital just above the neck. The marks were exactly where Clara's son had stated she had been fatally wounded. The first mark faded away before Karen was a year old, but the latter remained clearly visible under the hair on the back of her head, and showed up strongly on a colour photograph taken by IBPP investigators when she was sixteen.

Karen grew up normally, without significant memories of a past life, though she showed an unusual degree of affection for Grandma, treating her as a sister until she was about six and sometimes even sharing dreams with her.

The family that reincarnates together, one might say, stays together ...

Children's memories of past lives often begin with the spontaneous claim that something or other happened 'when I was big'.

'Daddy, you've got to treat me well,' three-year-old Marcos ordered his surprised father one day in 1969, 'because when you were little and I was big, I used to treat you very well.' Marcos was always talking about his 'other mummy' and 'other daddy'.

One day when he was five he was watching his mother prepare a chicken, and he mentioned the way his 'other' mother used to cook it. Rather than tell him to stop talking nonsense, his present mother asked for details. Like a practical Brazilian housewife, she was always glad to learn a new recipe.

'It was chicken in beer,' Marcos announced. This is known in parts of Europe, but not, as far as I know, in Brazil.

'Well,' said his mother, 'if you'll tell me how to do it, I'll cook it for you.' So the five-year-old expert gave his instructions. He told her to cut the chicken down the middle, seasoning it with the ingredients she was already preparing, then pour a bottle of beer over it and put it in the oven.

'When it's in the oven, it'll go all red,' he announced.

His mother had never heard of anyone cooking chicken this way before, but she did everything her son told her, and sure enough when it was time to take the bird out of the oven, it was indeed red all over.

'That's right!' Marcos exclaimed. '*Ai, que saudades!* That's the same smell as when my mother used to cook it!'

Marcos showed an unusual awareness of spiritual matters as well as cooking for a child of his age. He remembered his last mother sending him back to earth with the words: 'Go on, my prince, you must fight hard against the evil that exists on earth.'

'So here I am!' he added.

He also recalled his previous death. One morning at age three he woke up crying, with his hand on his chest.

'I've died! I've died!' he cried. 'I was crawling through the forest with Daddy, and a soldier came, and he shot me and hit me on the chest, and I'm dead!'

One of the most complicated cases in the IBPP reincarnation files comes from the town of Marilia, 300 miles north of São Paulo. It began when a local philanthropist, Mr Tavares, found a newly-born black baby girl abandoned on the street in front of his house. He took her into his home, adopted her and named her Celia.

Though he treated her with all the affection he showed to his already large family, Celia became ill just after her first birthday, with gastro-intestinal complications, and died at the age of one year and eight days.

Information received at the local Spiritist centre announced that Celia was to be born again, this time to a couple of close friends of the Tavares family. They already had a daughter, and when their next one duly arrived, they were surprised to find that she was considerably darker than either of them. They named her Celia.

Celia II showed immediate affection for Mr Tavares, but unfortunately that was not all she seemed to have in common with Celia I, for shortly after her first birthday, she too contracted a gastro-intestinal complication and died at the age of 14 months.

Shortly afterwards, Mr Tavares himself passed on. Almost immediately his spirit announced through a medium that a dark-complexioned baby girl just born to a third family was his own little Celia, born for the third time.

'We are doing all we can to make sure that she survives this time,' he said, adding that nothing had been communicated about this birth beforehand so that the mother of Celia II would not feel jealous.

Augusta, as 'Celia III' was named, became seriously ill at the age of only 26 days, and for four months it was a question of life or death. She pulled through, but became sick again at almost exactly the same age as Celias I and II, from an almost identical complaint. Third time lucky; Augusta survived and grew into a healthy and normal girl.

From childhood onwards she showed an unusually strong affection for the mother of Celia II, although it was some time before the information obtained from the spirit of Mr Tavares was revealed to her.

Another of the cases in the IBPP files comes from the town of Marilia, involving another family that also regularly attended Spiritist meetings.

In January 1956, Olavo Moreira was taking part in a special meeting held for the purpose of deobsession, when one of the mediums present, evidently incorporating a spirit, began to talk to him. The voice began to show signs of suffering, complaining of pains in the throat and stomach, and begging Mr Moreira for another chance to reincarnate. The communicator wanted to come back to earth but seemed unable to find a suitable vacancy.

Then, addressing Mr Moreira by name, the spirit identified itself as a son-in-law of his who had died a few years previously, committing suicide by swallowing formicide.

The spirit begged Mr Moreira for another chance and asked him to help.

As a practising Spiritist, Mr Moreira accepted the fact of reincarnation as a matter of course, but in this case he felt there must have been some slip-up on the other side, for he and his wife were both in their late forties and were not thinking of having another baby. He soon forgot the incident, and was very much surprised when, at a private session held at the end of the following month, another spirit announced that his son-in-law was indeed going to come back; into the Moreira family. The spirit added the information that Mrs Moreira was in fact already pregnant, of which neither she nor her husband was aware, and that the son-in-law intended to return as a woman.

Mrs Moreira's reaction to the story her husband told her when he came home from the session was one of mild disbelief. A few months later, however, she was indeed unmistakably pregnant, and baby Julia was duly born in October, just nine months after the original message from beyond. Julia was born in perfect health, though her parents were worried that she might have carried over some of her sufferings from her life as their son-in-law. There are several cases in the IBPP files of suicides who have come back to earth only to do it again.

Little Julia, however, got off to a good start in life. She was unusually precocious, and by the age of ten months could talk quite clearly. Her first apparent memories of a former existence came out when she was a year and a half old; much earlier than is usual.

'Listen, have I got two Mummies? That one you say is Grandma, and you how can she be your Mummy too? You and I were brother and sister before, so why do I have to call you Mummy now?'

Spiritist parents know that such questions are to be expected, and that children will gradually forget their past lives (Tina's case is very unusual) especially if they are loved and well cared for in their new ones. They also know that when a life is cut short, either by suicide or an accident, memories are likely to be clear and persistent at first.

Julia's lasted until she was four. She wanted to know why she was supposed to call her 'brothers' Francisco and Benedito 'uncle'. She could not work out how it was that she and her new mother used to play together and 'now you're my mother'. At least once a week she would come out with a recollection of her past life on the family farm over thirty years ago. She would describe the old white-painted brick house in detail, remembering each of the rooms, its fruit orchard, and the dam where the family used to go fishing.

Children ask a lot of questions, but they will accept any situation they find themselves in, however incomprehensible to them. Julia soon became adjusted to her new family, and grew up quite normally. When last contacted by the IBPP, she showed no sign of the bewilderment that had beset her up to the age of four. It is quite possible, however, that eventually she will find herself in a situation where she may be tempted to kill herself again, since recidivism seems to be common among former suicides.

According to the Spiritist doctrine, each life has a definite purpose, and we would never learn anything of use to our overall progress unless we had to face challenges we had failed to overcome in earlier lives.

The experience of several Brazilian Spiritist families has shown that talking to children about past lives does not traumatize them. Just the opposite; it acts as instant therapy and helps them adjust to their present families. Silvia, for instance, whose sad story I told at the beginning of this chapter, grew up into an exceptionally pretty, intelligent and happy girl, although her initial memories of a past life were extremely disturbing. Others, as we shall see, were not so lucky.

In 1992, a year short of his eightieth birthday, Hernani Guimarães Andrade set off on a twelve hour, five hundred mile road journey from his home in Bauru to a small town in the interior of the state of Minas Gerais on the trail of what he later told me turned out to be the best of the seventy-one Brazilian cases of the reincarnation type that have been preserved in the IBPP archive.

In many respects it was the ideal case. The chief witness, a woman who chose the pseudonym 'Marine Waterloo', was a very competent writer who had kept a careful record of the unusual sayings and actions of her son Kilden that began shortly before his third birthday. She had been raised and educated in a strictly orthodox Catholic environment, in a part of the country where Spiritism meant 'the work of the devil' and had no knowledge of or interest in the idea of rebirth. However, one of Kilden's earliest unexpected remarks gave her pause for thought.

One day, after his bath, he announced that his name was not Kilden but Alexandre, and that he was 'the priest.' His second name was indeed Alexandre, which was also the name of a young priest at Marine's convent school with whom she had shared a strong friendship, staying in touch with him after she had married and begun to raise a family. Then one day she heard on the local radio that Father Alexandre had died in 'a car accident' of which no details were given.

They were however given by young Kilden, who insisted it was not a car accident at all. He clearly recalled riding his scooter and being hit by a truck, then 'going down deep into the hole'. This prompted Marine to make enquiries as to the cause of the priest's death, and to discover from the original police report of the fatal accident that he had indeed been riding a scooter and had been hit by a truck.

When Marine came across an old postcard of her school, Kilden immediately pointed to 'his' house, where the priests had lived, and to the building that had housed the girl pupils. He correctly described several people that had been known to the priest, but about whom Marine knew nothing. As he grew up, his behaviour began to resemble that of Father Alexandre in several ways. He developed a somewhat off-beat sense of humour and fondness for practical jokes, for which the priest was notorious. He also had the habit of making up rhymes for people's names, such as 'Mrs Cléia likes *geléia* (jelly)'. The priest had the same habit.

Most compelling, however, was the account Kilden produced spontaneously of what happens after an accident. It was a sequel to his memory of 'going down the hole' and was strikingly similar to what are now known as near death experiences. Using a curious mixture of first and third person pronouns, this is how he described it:

'It's like this. The person who had the accident arrives and is put in a room full of instruments. The doctors connect them, then the equipment is connected to the head and chest, and they keep trying to save the person's life. At this moment the person flies to a corner of the ceiling, watching the doctors fight to save him. Then a big hole like a funnel appeared in the corner of the wall near me, trying to suck me...'

Marine interrupted him. 'You, or the person who had the accident?'
'Well, I think it was me,' Kilden replied. 'I saw my body and the doctors trying to save me.'
Marine asked if he had ever seen anything like that in a film or on television. He insisted he had not, and went on:

'When he was sucked through a hole into the tunnel, he saw a strong light at the end, so strong that I [sic] turned my head to one side. The light was very bright, and the hole closed behind him, near the wall. At that moment the doctors saw the screen on their machine stop. Then all the machines stopped working.'

One day, Marine woke Kilden early so that he could do his homework before going to school. He looked strangely frightened.

'Just as well you woke me up before the accident,' he said. 'I was just going to hit the truck when you woke me up.'

Andrade published his detailed account of this remarkable case together with Marine's account of her school days and friendship with Father Alexandre, and her apparent reuniting with him. It is now available in English. [1]

# 4

# OBSESSION

ONE way in which many Brazilians have come to accept reincarnation is through cases of what is generally known as obsession, the state of being subjugated to the influence of an evil or mischievous spirit. This may not in itself prove reincarnation, as fortunately it is usually only a temporary phenomenon, but it would seem to indicate survival of the spirits concerned, which is in itself an essential precondition for reincarnation. Since there is abundant evidence for obsession in poltergeist cases, as I will show, this emotive and much misunderstood subject deserves brief mention here.

In one of the chapters of *Evolution in Two Worlds*, automatically written by Chico Xavier and Waldo Vieira, spirit author André Luiz gives a lengthy and extremely technical account of what he calls spiritual vampirism, how it works and what we can do about it. He goes into far greater detail than Kardec, who regards domination or possession as a consequence of human weakness in allowing another spirit to take control, stressing that cases of epilepsy and madness are often just that and nothing to do with obsession at all. Kardec, incidentally, did not believe in the possibility of exorcism by outsiders; obsessing entities have to be driven out by the obsessed themselves, with the help of prayer. 'God helps those who help themselves, but not those who limit their action to asking for help,' he says, practical as ever.

According to André Luiz, the next world is full of naughty spirits with nothing better to do than make a nuisance of themselves. Victims of murder or persecution sometimes devote their energies to revenge, overlooking their own evolutionary obligations for the sake of getting their own back on their persecutors still on earth. He describes exactly how they do this, in language any advanced scientist might just understand; after one of his eighteen-line sentences explaining the mechanisms by which 'ovoid parasites' attack the physical body, he offers us one of his shorter paragraphs by way of a simplified summary: 'The obsessor or spiritual parasite may be compared up to a point to the *Sacculina carcini*, which, well provided with perfectly differentiated organs in the phase of free life, then takes root in the tissues of the host crustacean, losing its primitive morphological characteristics to convert itself into a parasitic cellular mass.'

It was a case of obsession that led to the conversion to Spiritism of one of the most distinguished Brazilians of the nineteenth century, the doctor and statesman Dr Adolfo Bezerra de Menezes who like so many Brazilians had Spiritism literally thrust upon him. In one of his many books, he describes how one of his sons, a medical student, suddenly appeared to go insane. He was given the best medical treatment available, but eventually several of his father's colleagues advised him that the only hope was to send the boy to an asylum.

'It was under this sad predicament of a separation more sorrowful than death,' Dr Bezerra wrote, 'that I listened to a friend who for some time had been urging me to turn to Spiritism.' He duly did so, and immediately obtained a diagnosis of obsession. The obsessing entity declared that he was punishing the boy for an injustice Dr Bezerra had done him in a previous life. There was nothing he could do to Bezerra himself because he was 'too advanced'. At his first session with mediums, the eminent doctor recalled that the spirit had mentioned private matters that he had not revealed to anybody.

The boy was eventually cured of his attacks, although it took three years and his brain was left permanently affected. His father went on to treat many similar cases, of which he described twenty-five in his books. [1]

Dr Bezerra laid down the basic rules of procedure that have been adopted by Brazil's many Spiritist-run mental homes and asylums. First, he recommended the use of hypnotism to help patients themselves diagnose their problem by identifying the obsessing entity. This can then sometimes be incorporated by the mediums and dealt with as a separate individual, the aim being to persuade it to leave the patient's body and get back to its own sphere.

Next, once the entity is identified, mediums get to work on it and explain how such wicked behaviour will only serve to hamper its own progress. They call for help from their own spirit guides to get the obsessor adjusted to his real condition and situation, and then usually concentrate their efforts on strengthening the spiritual and moral character of the patient; the stronger the latter's mind becomes, the more difficult it will be for a bad spirit to influence it.

Proof of the effectiveness of such methods, which are used all over Brazil every day, can be seen in the number of people who have sought the help of the São Paulo Spiritist Federation mediums and have subsequently offered their services there themselves. One of these has told me that she originally went to the Federation for help more than thirty years previously, at a time when she was suffering from every imaginable physical and spiritual problem. The Federation straightened her out and she had been there ever since as an unpaid volunteer, of whom there are now more than two hundred.

I once witnessed an extraordinary sight at a private session that was being held to 'deobsess' a patient. The chief medium's daughter, normally a very quiet and polite teenager, suddenly became violently incorporated, writhing in her chair, banging her head down on the table and jerking backwards until I felt she must break either her spinal column or her skull, or both. For over an hour, her father talked patiently and firmly to her without ever raising his voice, while she howled and screamed in the tones of an evil old hag, spitting startling obscenities around and generally creating a thoroughly alarming impression. How the poor girl survived I cannot imagine, yet eventually she calmed down and was her usual timid self when it was all over. 'We do this every Thursday', they told me.

Many Brazilian doctors, inspired by the example of Dr Bezerra, who died in 1900 after being president of the Brazilian Spiritist Federation (FEB) for five years, have achieved striking success in the treatment of apparent insanity along Spiritist guidelines. The best known of these was Dr Inacio Ferreira, who headed a Spiritist sanatorium in Uberaba (home town of Chico Xavier) for more than 35 years, claiming a success rate of up to 90% in cures of obsession and 50% for cases of other mental afflictions.

Educated in a Catholic school, Ferreira only became a Spiritist after graduating as a doctor of medicine, when the evidence of his own eyes convinced him that Spiritist mediums knew a thing or two about the cure of mental patients that his fellow doctors did not. In his own experience, cures rarely took as long as three months, and an interesting feature he observed is that the vast majority of patients seeking his help were non-Spiritists. 'If my hospital only treated Spiritists,' he once told an interviewer from Argentina, 'we would have to close down, because so few of them are affected!' (Two of his cases of successful cure of obsessions were in fact of Catholic priests). [2]

There are many large Spiritist hospitals in Brazil, of which the best known are those in Porto Alegre, Itapira and São Paulo. The first of these, originally built in 1925 and moved to its present site in 1941, is particularly impressive, with 600 beds and a staff of more than 200. For forty years it was directed by a former mayor of the city, Conrado Ferrari, who died in 1971. The kindly bearded face of Dr Bezerra beams down from the wall of the main reception room, which is named after him. Spiritist hospitals make full use of conventional medicine. They make it clear that, as St Paul put it, 'there is a natural body, and there is a spiritual body', and each must be treated accordingly, the former with medicine and the latter by Spiritist methods. [3]

As the healer Edivaldo told me, medicine and mediums must get together, and they have come together to form regular associations in many of Brazil's leading cities. One of the most active of these is the Rio de Janeiro Society of Medicine and Spiritism, founded in 1941 by Dr Levindo Mello, who died in 1964. Dr Mello had an experience similar to that of Dr Bezerra, when a Spiritist medium cured a patient of his in twenty minutes after he had failed to do so in four months.

In 1973, the Rio Society published evidence to suggest that they had identified a new form of disease, which they call spirit induction, and included 26 case histories ending in complete cure. A woman who had suffered blinding headaches for 29 years had been cured for seven years after the spirit that had been causing her problem had been identified and persuaded to leave her alone. A five-year-old boy had shown all the symptoms of tertian fever, a kind of malaria, since the age of a few months, though no trace of the agent that provokes this disease, *Plasmodium vivax*, could be found despite repeated tests. The boy undoubtedly had fever, but there was no organic cause. Therefore, Society doctors concluded, the cause had to be spiritual in the literal sense of the word. Making what they call a paranormal diagnosis, they found that the disease was being induced by the spirit of a gold prospector who had died of malaria in the northern Goias jungles. They treated the patient (and the spirit) accordingly and the boy was cured at once. For four years subsequently, they reported, the boy had been free of fever. Other cases, of which the Society has published full details, include the cure of a man who had been bothered for two months by an incessant cough. He was found to be suffering induction from a former tuberculosis patient.

Another man, himself a doctor, had suddenly been struck dumb, making it impossible for him to continue his work as a lecturer. He had become so depressed that he thought of committing suicide, but was cured on the spot by the 'deinduction' method and went back to work the following day.

According to the Rio doctor-Spiritists, induction by a spirit can take the form of fever, tremors, itching, burning sensations, somnolence, stammering or cacoethes (a form of nervous facial tic). But anybody showing symptoms of any disease, they say, may be suffering from spirit induction if it is found that there is no organic cause. [4]

São Paulo, it is often said, has everything if you take the trouble to look for it. It has a large and efficient Spiritist Federation, and a very active Medical Spiritist association (AMESP), and among the more unusual services this enormous city had to offer in the 1970s were those of a Catholic priest of European descent, whose work consisted largely of exorcizing evil spirits and generally fighting black magic by the use of what appear to be conventional Spiritist methods

Father Carlos, as he was known, held regular consultations in his church, welcoming members of all faiths who lined up by the hundreds to pour out their problems. He was usually booked in advance for private consultations for about six weeks. Instead of listening behind bars and handing out impositions of Hail Marys, he would roll up his sleeves and go after evil spirits in fighting mood. He would give his visitors magnetic passes according to the Spiritist book, and in extreme cases go to their homes to drive out the more obstreperous psi entities.

He was not the first Catholic priest to try and fight the less desirable manifestations of the spirit world. Indeed, one of his best-known predecessors, Father Boaventura Kloppenburg, carried out an energetic campaign for several years to wipe out Spiritism altogether.

An intelligent and basically kind-hearted man, Kloppenburg took the trouble to study his subject properly, and wrote four massive volumes on Spiritism. Unfortunately for him, just after his books were published, there was a dramatic about-face in the Vatican party line after Pope Paul VI decided in his *Africae Terrarum* (1967) that there might be some good after all in the primitive and 'non-Christian' rites. Amazing as it may seem, the church of Rome persists in regarding all forms of Spiritism as pagan, despite the fact that Kardecists acknowledge no source of inspiration other than Jesus Christ, and Kardec himself stated explicitly that Spiritism was 'Christianity restored'. Later, Kloppenburg admitted to author David St Clair that he had seen many things during his ten-year investigation of Spiritism that he was unable to explain. He added that he had 'new duties', and that they took up a great deal of his time. [5]

Father Carlos, the exorcist, is typical of a small minority of more realistic Brazilian Catholic priests, who are well aware of the existence of evil-minded spirits and try to do something about them without finding it necessary to bring down the whole structure of Spiritism in the process.

'The worst plague we have here in São Paulo is all this black magic,' Father Carlos said, revealing that a great many of those who sought his help were suffering from one of the most familiar of all paranormal phenomena; poltergeists. The São Paulo area seems to have attracted more than its fair share of these mysterious entities – the IBPP has records of no less than thirty-two of them, many of which were investigated by Andrade with his customary thoroughness.

Much debate rages in the psi research community over the question of whether poltergeists are a purely psychological phenomenon caused (nobody has yet attempted to explain how) by repressed teenagers, often around the age of puberty, or manifestations of some kind of discarnate entity or spirit. The second theory is not popular with non-Spiritists, while as far as Brazilian Spiritists are concerned it is the only one that makes any sense, and as we shall see there is a good deal of evidence to support it, including some I was able to collect myself.

So fasten your seat belts. We are about to land in the poltergeist zone.

# 5

# THE POLTERGEIST ZONE

'LUISA, THERE'S a hand on your bed!'

Lights were switched on hastily and cries of 'Who said that?' hurled in all directions. But apparently nobody had said it, although everybody in the room swore they had heard the words. Ah well, they thought, better leave a light on, just in case...

It was eleven p.m. on July 7th, 1972 in an old boarding house on Rua Agassis, just a block or two from the main banking district of São Paulo, Latin America's largest city. Seventeen young women lived there, and five of them shared the upstairs room where the mysterious voice had addressed one of them.

Half an hour later, a pan of milk took off from its position on top of a cupboard and zigzagged its way slowly to the floor, splashing drops of milk around but landing upright with most of its contents unspilt.

This was enough to give the women a thorough fright, though it was nothing compared to what was in store for them. The next day, after a bad night's sleep, four of them went to ask a local priest for help. They also bought a bottle of holy water and placed it on a chair.

The priest duly came, said prayers all over the place and blessed the frightened women. As he walked down the staircase a bottle was flung after him, smashing against the front door. He left and never came back.

Shortly afterwards, the bottle of holy water rose slowly into the air, hovered over the woman resting on the nearest bed, and spilled its entire contents over her. This seemed to be the signal for an attack on all fronts by the poltergeist, and from then on all hell broke loose.

A pan of macaroni shot out of the upstairs kitchen down into the hallway, glassware from inside a locked drawer was smashed on the marble stairs, an expensive pair of spectacles was snatched from its wearer's nose and flung on the floor, a jar of honey left a locked glass-fronted kitchen shelf (without breaking the glass) and hurled itself against the tiled wall, scattering honey and glass fragments all over the place. Even heavy objects like a clothes iron and a waste bucket were projected down the staircase.

It all went on for about three weeks, on and off; mostly on. Some of the women went to sleep with a neighbour, a bedridden lady who had heard regular screams of terror coming from the boarding house. The others huddled together in the downstairs bedrooms at night, few of them managing more than a few hours' sleep.

The ghost even began to play elaborate practical jokes. One tenant put three ten-cruzeiro banknotes in her handbag and locked the bag in her cupboard, only to find the notes missing when she took the bag out again. She found them stuffed inside a bottle rolling around the floor downstairs.

Three carloads of police searched the house from top to bottom on the track of some skilful prankster, but found nothing, and left after making some indecent suggestions to the young women and complaining that this sort of thing was out of their hands.

Two more priests were called to the house by the desperate owner, who feared he was going to lose all his tenants, but to no avail. The house soon became the talk of the neighbourhood, and several illustrated articles on the disturbances appeared in local magazines and newspapers.

Finally, as usual in Brazil on such occasions, the women (most of whom were Catholics) turned to the last resort: Spiritism. The first 'father-in-sainthood' they called in accepted an advance fee of fifty cruzeiros (then worth about ten dollars) for his services, which consisted of impaling the front door of the house with a dagger. This soon disappeared and so did he.

They had better luck with their next 'father', a young man from a nearby *candomblé* centre, who visited the house frequently for six days, announced that the damage was the work of a mischievous spirit, summoned one of his own spirit guides to help him out, planted candles and glasses of rum at strategic points around the house, and promised the women there would be no more trouble.

He was absolutely right, and the phenomena ceased as abruptly as they had begun. To make doubly sure, the young exorcist took one of the tenants, suspected as being what researchers call the 'psychokinetic agent' or epicentre, along to his premises and gave her a thorough spiritual spring-cleaning, sacrificing a goat to the spirit that had been bothering her for good measure.

And so peace returned to Rua Agassis, after IBPP researchers had taped more than six hours of testimony from 23 witnesses, and concluded that it was another case of a perturbed teenager attracting forces that were converted into what is known in the trade as RSPK or recurrent spontaneous psycho-kinesis; random physical violence.

The 24-year-old *candomblé* exorcist was happy to tell researchers how he had driven out the spirit. An *exu morcego*, he explained, was a type of pagan spirit dwelling in the shadows, probably that of a former criminal who had nothing better to do than bother people.

'Pagan spirits have to vegetate,' he explained further, 'wandering around in the darkness until they can reincarnate or just stay where they are. But I've been in the cult since I was eight years old, and I know how to deal with these situations.' He had, he said, enticed the pagan spirit out of the house by promising to sacrifice a goat for him and giving him a drink of beer. Then he had taken the spirit to the cult centre, where he promised to treat him with love and kindness, and eventually to domesticate him.

'He also deserves our respect,' he added. This may sound to some like superstitious nonsense, yet it undoubtedly worked.

Probing into the background of the case, IBPP researchers found that as so often where there is a poltergeist, there is (or was) somebody with a grudge. The owner of the boarding house had been badly hurt in a car accident some time before, and had spent six months in hospital. Assuming him to be on the point of death, another man had managed to get possession of the house, and the wife of this other man had died shortly afterwards. It was generally thought that she might have had a grudge against the original owner, who recovered, and might have caused the disturbances in revenge.

According to the dictionary, a poltergeist is a ghost that manifests itself by noises and rappings, the word coming from the German *poltern* (to make a racket) and *Geist* (ghost). To most of us, poltergeists are simply Things that Go Bump in the Night.

In Brazil, they also go bump in the daytime, and are not content with merely bumping. They throw rocks around, overturn furniture, wreck kitchens, set clothing on fire, soak rooms with water, rearrange people's personal belongings and often steal them, transport anything from babies to two-ton trucks, and generally drive a lot of peace-loving citizens out of their minds. There is also evidence that they do far worse things, seriously wounding and even killing people. They are infernal nuisances and there ought to be a law against them.

July 1972 was a vintage month for poltergeist activity in Brazil, and at one point IBPP researchers found themselves working on three cases at once; two more in addition to the one described above.

The first of these manifested itself in the town of Sorocaba, 63 miles west of São Paulo. It was an interesting case in that the poltergeist was not content with chasing a whole family out of its house, but followed it to another house and virtually wrecked the entire establishment.

It began on July 18th in the modest home of Fernando, a 48-year-old house painter, his wife Alda, and their six children. First signs of action were loud knockings, and then household objects started flying about and breaking; almost every single piece of furniture in the house being overturned, some of them more than once.

A heavy wooden shutter was wrenched off its hinges, and a bizarre touch was provided by a large motor tyre in the back yard which simply rose three feet into the air and stayed there for a few moments, long enough to scare Fernando out of his wits.

Tipped off by a local resident, four IBPP researchers rushed to the scene, arriving four days after the initial manifestation. Hernani Guimarães Andrade and two of his sons, Sergio and Ricardo, began to make a survey of the six-room premises and take photographs of pieces of smashed furniture, while Suzuko Hashizume stood at the window of the front room, tape recorder around her neck, talking to Alda and examining the broken shutter. Every member of the household was under observation by one or more of the IBPP team. Nobody was in the kitchen except the family poodle, which was asleep on the floor.

Suddenly there was a thunderous crash, followed by a sharp yelp as the little dog ran limping and whining out of the kitchen. Everybody rushed in to find a heavy wooden shelf lying on the floor well away from the wall. Twelve-year-old Yara was comforting the terrified dog, which seemed to have hurt one of its paws when the shelf fell. The researchers photographed the shelf and lifted it back to its normal position, deciding it was far too heavy for the dog to have knocked it over accidentally even if it had been awake, and waited to see if it would fall again.

The poltergeist failed to oblige, so they went on with their work. It was the first time they had recorded an unmistakable paranormal phenomenon on tape, though it was not to be the last.

There were some interesting features of the Sorocaba case. The poltergeist had begun its activity outside the house with raps, stone throwing and tyre levitation, and had then moved indoors, working its way methodically through every room in order. It had overturned every single piece of furniture in the house, wrecking some of them beyond repair. Not only that, but when the family had moved out to stay with relatives, it had followed them and done the same again. 'It looked as if a tractor had driven through the place,' a neighbour commented. When they moved back to their own home, the trouble began again, though their relatives were left in peace amid their wreckage.

At the Rua Agassis boarding house nobody had been hurt except a woman who had fallen downstairs in fright, but at Sorocaba the situation had become dangerous. Alda was hit on the head by a flying brick, and one of the girls had scalding water spilt on her face and dress as the kettle she was boiling to make coffee was wrenched from her hands.

The most impressive feat of all was the overturning of a concrete water tank, which according to Fernando normally took three men to lift. This had simply been raised from its brick support and dumped on its face in the back yard. It is an appalling thought what poltergeists could do if they felt like it, or were able to. What they do already is bad enough.

The Sorocaba case was never satisfactorily solved, as the family decided they had had enough and left town, and the IBPP lost touch with them. The researchers reckoned they had identified twelve-year-old Yara as the agent, for she had been present on all occasions where there had been violence, and on most of them she had been well in view of other members of the family. An interesting detail was that although the poltergeist seemed to have no qualms about performing in broad daylight, it would never do anything at night when lights were switched on. It was just as if it knew somebody was trying to catch it in the act.

The third poltergeist case to come to light in July 1972 was the most bizarre of all. It was also the longest lasting, for it had been going on for more than three years before word of it reached São Paulo.

Kenzo Okamoto was a Japanese immigrant farmer who lived some twelve miles from the remote town of Ponta Porã in the state of Mato Grosso, just across the frontier in Paraguay. This is a thinly populated area largely devoted to agriculture and, it is alleged, smuggling.

The trouble began when a Paraguayan peasant bought a bunch of bananas and sat down by the roadside to eat some. He ate one, and then noticed that two of his original dozen had disappeared. He ate another, and four more vanished. He decided to hide what was left of his bunch, and immediately received a hard blow on the back. This caused him to faint from shock, and when he came round he hurried off to tell his story to friends, none of whom believed him.

At about the same time, a poltergeist invaded the house of a neighbour of Okamoto's. A bed was lifted into the air at night, and occupants of the house were pushed around by an invisible force, which then proceeded to throw a number of objects out of the house. Everybody left the building in terror, except for one stout old lady of 76, who worked on Okamoto's tomato patch.

One day, she was bombarded by green tomatoes as she was working in the patch. Thinking Okamoto was playing tricks with her she threatened to call the police, but the bewildered farmer assured her he had nothing to do with it. Some days later, two of his own children received a pelting of tomatoes, ripe ones this time, which stained their clothes and caused incipient panic all round.

Next, the poltergeist moved in with the Okamoto family. Stones began to fall on the metal gas container; stones that were quite warm and dry though it was raining outside. Soon after this, a friend from São Paulo came down to visit, and on his return home he described what he had been told to one of the city's Japanese-language newspapers, which decided to send a reporter down to investigate.

Brazilian journalists are noted for their wild irresponsibility when covering stories with a paranormal aspect, with the exception of such distinguished veterans as Wallace Leal V.Rodrigues, Jorge Rizzini and Moacyr Jorge, but on this occasion the writer turned out to be as conscientious and competent as he was sceptical of anything paranormal. Sceptical to begin with, that is.

Thirty-four-year-old Kazunari Akaki went down to the Okamoto farm on July 1st and spent five days there. As soon as he arrived after the long journey, over 600 miles, he was shown into the upper room over the storeroom, connected by a narrow stairway that could only be used by one person at a time. The room contained a bicycle, two gas containers, a hand cart and a number of smaller objects that, according to Okamoto, had been transported there from down below. Akaki helped carry them down again, and then went off to town to see to his tourist visa. When he came back, everything he had moved was back in the upstairs room again. Clearly, he decided, Okamoto must be playing tricks.

Stones began to fall during dinner, but Akaki was still unimpressed. As he was getting ready to go to bed, some wrapped chocolates fell onto the floor of his bedroom. They could, he decided, have been thrown over the partition. The following day, as Mrs Okamoto was making up his bed, he heard a loud crash coming from the bedroom, and found a large truck wrench under the bed.

Akaki, the most resolute of sceptics, was still unconvinced that anything paranormal was happening. There had to be a simple explanation. Somebody had to be playing tricks. The following afternoon he was forced, at last, to think otherwise.

Returning from a drive in Okamoto's two and a half ton Toyota jeep, he left it parked outside the front door and went into the house. Immediately he got indoors, he heard a loud thud, and hurrying outside again he saw the jeep some forty yards away, with its front end resting against a wooden fence. He noted that there were no tyre marks in the soft mud in between where he had left it and where it now most undoubtedly was. Moreover, the jeep was in a position slightly up-hill from where it had been parked. Akaki had left it in gear, and if it had somehow worked itself loose it would have rolled in the opposite direction.

Akaki, now beginning to suspect that something genuinely unusual might indeed be going on, decided to make a test. Okamoto had told him that when the engine of the jeep was running, objects seemed more prone to being thrown about, so he asked the farmer to bring the jeep (undamaged except for a bent front mudguard) back to the front door and leave the engine running. He also noted that in the past, twilight had been a time for peak poltergeist activity.

Sure enough, as soon as Akaki went back into the house, some torch batteries were flung against a wall, while upstairs in his bedroom where he had been only a few minutes previously, there was a large piece of iron rail lying on the bed.

'I began to believe in the phenomena,' he noted tersely.

The piece of rail weighed 25 kilos and was nearly a metre long. Nobody could have carried it upstairs in the short time since he had been in the room before. The Paraguayan poltergeist was real.

Even by Japanese standards, Kazunari Akaki showed a high degree of imperturbability, and before he returned to São Paulo he witnessed a number of other phenomena without showing the slightest sign of alarm. A pair of tyres that had been tied to a post by a thick piece of steel cable were found in the upstairs room over the store, the cable snapped in two. Shoes appeared that had been lost days before. Clothing from a closed drawer was found hanging high in a tree as if left to dry in the sun. A bottle and a can of hair spray appeared on one of the crossbeams in the house, so high up that they could not be recovered without the use of a long ladder.

Akaki duly noted all this, photographing what he could, and on his return to São Paulo he published a series of eighteen articles in the bilingual *Jornal Paulista*, starting on July 11th and ending on September 18th, 1972. Never had a Brazilian newspaper given such detailed coverage to a case of this kind. And was more there to come. In September, word reached São Paulo (accompanied by photographs and detailed descriptions) that the poltergeist had gone a stage further. It was now setting things on fire. The first object to combust, apparently spontaneously, at the Okamoto home was a damp shirt that was hanging on the back of a chair. A large circular hole was burned in the lower part of its back by a 'fireball', that appeared from nowhere and vanished at once, after also making a mark over an inch in diameter on the family dog. The dog was asleep at the time and did not even wake up. Dogs, as I was to see for myself on another case to be described here, tend to be absolutely useless on poltergeist cases.

Next, part of the wooden partition in the bathroom was struck by what seemed to have been a ray of lightning, to judge from the burn mark nine feet long and about half an inch wide that was found there. Finally, a burn appeared on the thatched roof of a small hut near the main house, and why the whole hut did not burn down altogether remains a mystery, for no material is more inflammable than thatch.

There was even more to come from Paraguay. In May 1973 the poltergeist began to play games with the Okamotos' ten-month-old baby. On one occasion, the baby, which had been sleeping in its pram, simply vanished altogether, pram and all. After a frantic search, it was found outside the house under a tree; dry and unalarmed although it was raining at the time.

Eventually things quietened down and the Okamoto family learned to live with their unseen prankster. This case was unusual in that there was no obvious choice for an agent or epicentre. The only young girl involved was frequently away from the area when phenomena took place. These covered an unusually wide area, and no reason was ever found why anybody living or dead should want to bother the Okamoto family.

In December 1972, an exhibition of the work of the Paraguay poltergeist was held at the Brazil-Japan Cultural Alliance in São Paulo.

Many of the objects dislocated were shown, along with detailed drawings, plans of the house and numerous photographs.

Although the Rua Agassis, Sorocaba and Paraguay poltergeist cases each revealed points of interest, the classic Brazilian case remains the one that took place in the town of Suzano in 1970. This one is notable for its repeated manifestations of spontaneous combustion, and also for the quality of its evidence, for witnesses included no less a person than the local chief of police.

IBPP researchers had their share of good luck. Although the state of São Paulo is larger than the entire United Kingdom, they were able to get to distant parts of it in time to gather fresh evidence on a number of cases, especially those of poltergeist activity. Suzano is only about an hour's drive from São Paulo, and the IBPP was able to follow this case to its conclusion. On at least three occasions, phenomena took place in their presence, on two of which they were recorded on tape.

The Suzano story began with a bang.

It was just after midday on May 22nd, 1970. Nobody was in the house at the time, and fifteen-year-old Irene was washing clothes in a neighbour's house when the loud explosion was heard, coming from her home. Smoke began to seep through the tiles of the roof, and neighbours rushed in to find that fire had broken out inside a wardrobe, burning holes in several pieces of clothing.

The fire was easily put out, but at five o'clock the same afternoon bedclothes in the same room caught fire on each of the two beds. Again, there was nobody around at the time, Irene being twenty yards away outside the house. Within an hour, clothing that had been rescued from the first fire and dumped in the outside bathroom caught fire again, although it was still soaking wet.

Later that night Jeziel, the owner of the house was roused by screams and yells from the room where his four children were sleeping. A fireball, they told him, had come down and set fire to one of their mattresses. Unable to put the fire out, they dragged the mattress into the yard, where it was completely destroyed.

Ten minutes later the sofa in the living room caught fire. Water was thrown on it and the fire extinguished, but after it also had been dragged out into the yard it too caught fire again, although saturated with water, this time burning itself completely out.

At this point a police patrol happened to pass by, stopping their car to see what all the fuss was about. Once they were satisfied that nothing illegal seemed to be going on, the policemen offered to help, while one of them put through a call to headquarters to report the incident.

At the police station, the chief officer felt uncomfortable. Only a few days earlier he had received an official complaint from Jeziel that stones had been thrown through his window and even through the roof, breaking several tiles. The officer had thought little of the incidents at the time, but now he decided to have a look for himself, taking his forensic expert Natal de Lima along with him.

While waiting for their chief to arrive, one of the policemen picked up a calendar from the floor and hung it on a nail on the bedroom wall. After a few minutes it blackened and burst into flames. It was, he later testified, a bluish flame like that of a gas burner, and when he put his finger in it, he burned it as he would have done in a normal flame.

At that moment the chief arrived, and after hearing what had been going on he took a sheet of newspaper and hung it from a nail in the living-room wall. This duly caught fire right in front of his eyes, leaving a burn mark on the wall behind it, although it was damp when picked up from the floor.

The following day, another minor fire broke out in a kitchen cabinet, and five days later there were two more, one in the main bedroom (the baby's cradle, which had already been attacked) and the other in the children's room, where a bed lent by neighbours to replace the one that had been destroyed earlier also caught fire. On both these occasions nobody was in the house at the time; the children had been moved to a house nearby for their safety. This made a total of ten cases of paranormal spontaneous combustion, at least one of which had been personally witnessed by a police commissioner.

All phenomena ceased when Irene was sent away to stay with an aunt for a few days, at the suggestion of a local priest, whom the girl's mother had asked to come and exorcise the house. The priest refused to do this, so yet again the Spiritists were called in as a last resort.

Nobody concerned was prepared to give researchers much information about this episode, except that the family had contacted no less than a captain in the military police, a Spiritist, who had taken them to a centre. Here, the spirit supposed to have been provoking the trouble was identified and appeased. Again, the method seemed to work, as in the Rua Agassis case, and no more poltergeist activity was reported, although the family left Suzano shortly afterwards.

Probing into the family's history, researchers found that Irene had good reason to be highly-strung and emotionally upset. She had a very strong personality to start with, and she did not get along with her father, who often beat her. Some years previously, the father had left home to live with another woman, and to make matters worse he was unable to get regular work because of defective eyesight. Altogether, it was not the happiest of families, as so often in poltergeist cases, and it seemed likely that the sensitive and frustrated Irene was somehow providing the energy needed by the unseen home wrecker.

In February 1975 I went to Suzano to interview Natal de Lima, one of the policemen who had been at the house when the phenomena started. It is not often that poltergeist cases are witnessed by police officers, and we thought that he, the station's forensic expert, might be able to give us more precise evidence than you usually get from confused and frightened witnesses of such cases.

We were right. Natal de Lima not only remembered the events of 1970 very clearly, but told me that it had been the most memorable experience of his twenty-year career during which had witnessed a wide variety of criminal activity including several murders and suicides.

He had, as I soon found, a good eye for detail. I began by asking him about the fires he claimed to have seen breaking out.

'We were looking at the mattress,' he replied, 'and it had started to burn inside. Smoke was seeping out.'

'All over?' I asked, 'or just from one of two places?'

'No, it was coming from the middle of the mattress, slowly, just like something that's catching fire normally. But the fire came from inside. That is inexplicable by physics or chemistry or anything else.'

'Only it came from underneath', I suggested. I was quite enjoying grilling somebody who normally asks the questions.

'No,' he insisted. 'We turned the mattress over and looked. Nothing. That fire started inside the mattress. Then Jeziel said he'd cut it open as he could sew it up later. So he did, and it was burning inside.' The cotton stuffing, he added, was 'glowing like hot coals, but not producing a flame.'

Next, I asked de Lima to confirm that he had seen a stone apparently materialise inside the house. Our dialogue went like this. I began by asking, 'The stone came into the room without breaking a tile?'

'Yes.'

'But how? Through the window?'

'No, because the window was closed.'

'So it seems the stone went through the roof?'

'Yes, through the roof. I can guarantee to you that there was no possibility of that stone to appear unless somebody had come in and thrown it. But there wasn't anybody there.'

Natal de Lima described several other instances in which he had witnessed fires starting by themselves, and stones being thrown inside the house when everybody in the room was in full view. This was valuable testimony from a professional observer for two of the most controversial items in the poltergeist's repertoire.

He also confirmed to me that the troubles seemed to have ended following the intervention of a group of local Spiritists that included the Military Police officer already mentioned. According to them, the chief suspect for cause of the trouble was Jeziel's jealous ex-mistress. We were not able to follow up this lead, but we were not surprised to hear that as so often in Brazil there seemed to be a close connection between poltergeist phenomena and black magic practices. [1]

So much for haunted houses for the time being. Now the haunted car! Brasilia, showplace of some of Brazil's finest city planning and architecture, was inaugurated as the country's federal capital on April 21st, 1960, after a dream of more than a century had been made to come true by the determination and foresight of President Juscelino Kubitschek.

It is a spectacularly contemporary city, lying 3,000 feet above sea level, some 600 miles from Rio de Janeiro, on a gently sloping plateau almost entirely devoid of vegetation more than a few feet high. The whole city was built from scratch in five years, soon becoming a metropolis with a steadily growing population and not a sign of the past.

Not a visible sign, that is. For within five months of the inauguration ceremony, the city of the future had produced its first poltergeist. To be precise, it was some 22 miles from the city centre, though well within the borders of the new Federal District.

Six men and women were driving along the main road towards Belo Horizonte on the moonless night of September 18/19, 1960. The party consisted of a young couple (married that very day in the nearby town of Luisiania), the bridegroom's parents, the driver, and one of Brazil's most distinguished doctors, Dr Olavo Trindade, who attracted international attention with his discovery of new methods of treating meningitis.

The countryside around Brasilia is among the country's bleakest, with not a house and scarcely a stunted tree in sight. It was about midnight,

Dr Trindade recalls, when he and his friends were bowling along the road not far from Brasilia's Cidade Livre suburb, when the car, a Willys station wagon, began to show signs of overheating.

They stopped, finding everything in order under the bonnet. Then, all at once, stones began to be flung at them from the silent darkness around. One stone the size of a saucer landed in Dr Trindade's lap after hitting both the bride and her mother-in-law on their heads. The driver, who was outside the car, drew his gun and fired four shots without seeming to affect the mysterious bombardment in the slightest. Knowing there was a police post within two miles, the party decided to go there at once and ask for help.

Dr Trindade had managed to save two stones, which he showed to the startled policemen at the post.

One of these offered to come and examine the scene of the event, so three of the party stayed behind at the post while he climbed into the back of the car, heavily armed. Back at the original spot, Dr Trindade (who was unarmed) stayed inside the car as the others climbed out. The moment they did so, the stoning began again. The driver drew his gun and tried to fire, but found it had jammed.

A stone hit him on the arm, and another caught him on the head, drawing blood from a cut on the scalp.

Stones continued to fly from all directions, crashing against the car and occasionally against people, although the car's headlights revealed no trace of incarnate life whichever way they were turned. There seemed nothing more to be done, so they all went back to the police checkpoint for a welcome cup of coffee. While this was being brewed, a shower of gravel and sand fell on the chair where Dr Trindade had left his original pair of stones.

Back on the road, the bombardment began for the third time. Gusts of sand blew into the car's interior, although all windows were tightly closed except for a small gap in the front, while occasional metallic thuds showed that the car was still under intermittent attack. And there was worse to come. The driver had handed over the wheel to the bridegroom and was sitting in the right-hand passenger seat up front. Suddenly he let out a yell and cried that somebody was trying to open the door. Dr Trindade leaned forward and grabbed the door, helping the driver keep it in position.

'Even so,' he recalls, 'I could feel it gradually opening, by a terrible force... I gathered all my muscular strength together, and finally managed to hold it shut, and I shouted at the driver to lock the handle. But the handle unlocked itself of its own accord and the door began to open again. This happened several times.

'Once, the driver thought he saw a vague form outside the window, and aimed his gun at it, but the gun was still jammed. By this time we were all scared stiff. I thought the driver would be dragged outside if that door opened.' Dr Trindade's fingers became so sore that he could no longer hold on to the mysteriously controlled door, so he changed places with the bridegroom's father and let him take a turn at trying to keep the intruder out. The father, convinced that an evil spirit was at work, told everybody to start praying (they were all Catholics) and ask that the cause of such affliction should return to the Kingdom of Glory and leave everybody in peace.

'An awesome silence reigned,' said Dr Trindade, 'broken only by the sound of praying out loud and the stones echoing in the nocturnal solitude of the immense Goias plateau ...' The prayer seemed to have some effect, and the pressure on the door eased. It was about then that the bridegroom's father noticed that the glass had come off his wrist watch and was wedged between his fingers.

They finally reached their hotel in Cidade Livre at two o'clock in the morning. The first thing the driver did was fire his gun, finding that it worked perfectly. The honeymoon couple went off to bed, taking the damaged wrist watch with them, noticing that the metal wristband had been stretched out of its normal position. They left the watch on a table, placing the glass beside it. The following morning, the glass was back in place and the wristband had returned to its normal shape. There was no sign of even a scratch on the paintwork of the Willys station wagon.

Leaving the honeymoon couple to the peace and quiet (under normal circumstances) of the Goias plateau, Dr Trindade and his friends returned to their homes in São Paulo. At once, the conscientious doctor drew up a statement, which all four of them signed the following day.

'We never thought we would witness such unexpected events in such an undeniably evident manner,' the statement ended. 'Yet the reality of the facts imposes itself upon our former incredulity.'

A feature common to most poltergeist cases is that some specific person, often but not always a teenager, seems to be around whenever things start happening. This leads researchers to regard that person as the chief suspect, which can be very embarrassing when the case concerns a family whose confidence they may have taken great pains to win. It is not easy to have to face somebody who has invited you into their home, let you stay the night and turn the whole place upside down with your equipment, and spend hours dictating testimony into your tape recorder; only to have to tell them that you think they may be doing it all, or at least some of it, on purpose. You feel especially uncomfortable if something then happens that suggests your chief suspect is innocent. This is what happened during the first case in which I was able to meet a poltergeist in person, if that is the word. The case, which took place in the São Paulo suburb of Ipiranga, was of such bewildering complexity that I can only give a bare outline of it here.

I must confess that I had always considered poltergeists to be slightly comic. I hope neither I nor anyone else has such a thought again. A really persistent one – this one went on for more than six years - can drive an innocent family to desperation and even to attempted suicide

The Ipiranga case had quite a history. It had begun in 1968, and continued ever since then although the family had moved house no less than three times in an attempt to shake off the trouble. This seemed to show that poltergeist activity was person-directed, rather than place-directed, as in the Paraguay case. It also suggested that if fraud was at work, the family itself was unable to detect it in six years. A brief glance at the evidence also showed that any of the three women in the family could be regarded as the epicentre of the phenomena, or alternatively as the chief suspect.

The family involved consisted of a mother, her daughter Iracy, one of her two sons, and his wife Nora. Iracy, our main source of information about the case, was the family's main breadwinner. In her early twenties, attractive and intelligent, she had a well-paid job in the São Paulo office of a multinational company, and struck us as someone of strong character with a realistic approach to life, including the phenomena that had been part of her own life for nearly a quarter of it.

Her mother was a calm and amiable woman of Portuguese descent who had separated from her husband long before the troubles began. Her two brothers were, it seemed, the black sheep of the family; one was in prison (we didn't ask why) and the other was thought to be a drug dealer. We only met him once as he seemed to spend most of his time travelling, and he struck us as a very sinister individual. His wife Nora looked at first like the perfect epicentre for a poltergeist case. Like her mother-in-law she was quiet and friendly, but was also clearly in an advanced state of neurosis, perhaps because she had no children after six years of marriage, and seemed unable to hold down a regular job.

The first incident, which took place in 1968, was right out of the black magic textbook. A *despacho* (literally, dispatch or offering) of bottles, candles and cigars appeared one day in the garden of their original house, indicating that somebody was doing a *trabalho* (hex) against the family, though nobody could imagine who, or why. Then another (lit) candle appeared, this time inside the house, where it set fire to a curtain.

After this disturbing incident, Nora became violently possessed, spending days and nights in bed muttering in a strange voice and finally trying to jump out of a top floor window. She was taken to hospital, but escaped and found her way home. She was never able to explain how, and by the time we met her she could remember nothing of the whole episode, though Iracy remembered it well.

The family then moved house, but this seemed to have no effect at all on the poltergeist, which soon produced nearly every trick in its book of ways of driving people crazy. Bangs and crashes were heard at night, furniture was thrown around, clothing and bedding had caught fire or been soaked with water, or both. Objects would disappear and reappear with such regularity that it became almost a family joke. Iracy's prized collection of woolly animals was especially popular with her unseen enemy. One of them appeared on the roof of the house, another turned up in the middle of a busy street intersection outside the house, and when Iracy managed to retrieve it, with some difficulty and at the risk of being run over, she got home to find another animal missing. Looking out of the window, she saw it in the middle of the same intersection. This sort of thing happened so often that Iracy finally dumped her entire collection of animals in a river. She had come to suspect that some kind of evil was at work, and rivers are thought to be the best place to dispose of objects affected by black magic practices.

In the third house, where the family spent only one month in 1971, loud knocks were heard on the front door that they were sure could not have been made by anybody visible. Nora's husband's pyjamas caught fire while he was asleep in them, and finally the house, which was brand new, set itself on fire when there was nobody at home. Mother and Nora came back from shopping to find the house full of smoke; the fire had started in a bedroom and destroyed two wardrobes and an entire bed, mattress, wooden frame, sheets and all.

An interesting feature of paranormal spontaneous combustion (PSC) is that it comes in two forms. Sometimes it will be no more than a brief outbreak, and will put itself out without causing serious damage.

At other times it will completely destroy the object in question. The interesting feature of the former variety, which is hard to explain in terms of presently understood physics, is that objects that are highly inflammable will not burn themselves out. If some hoaxer was applying matches to items of clothing or bedclothes, these would either go up in flames at once, or in the case of some fabrics, crinkle up and melt. Like many schoolboys of my generation, I learned how to start a fire with the aid of a magnifying glass and the sun. By holding the glass still, the sun was focused on a piece of paper or whatever, which would gradually darken, then smoulder and finally burst into normal flames. It often looks as though poltergeists do something similar. PSC burn marks are often small round holes, as if made by a poker, and as often as not they remain small, as if the necessary energy was not available for them to spread and destroy the target object completely.

Such outbreaks of fire, along with just about everything else from the poltergeist's box of tricks, became far worse in the fourth home to be attacked by the Ipiranga invader. After ruining Iracy's entire wardrobe, it began to work its destructive way through the replacement items she kept having to buy. One morning, when she was in the bathroom, her handbag caught fire inside, totally destroying her paper money and documents.

Almost every day, somebody lost something or other and had to search the house for it. Kitchen knives would disappear, then turn up neatly arranged in a flower vase. Clothes and shoes would move themselves from bedroom to staircase or living room. Small objects would hide themselves under beds. Somebody's identity card vanished and turned up inside a kitchen drawer that was very hard to open. One day, bedclothes literally tied themselves in knots. Normal life became impossible, and Iracy began to feel the strain. The whole family was suffering, but she seemed to be the main target.

One day she received a phone call in her office, just after her extension had been changed, telling her that her married sister in Rio de Janeiro had been taken seriously ill. A friend offered to drive her there at once, but had a serious accident (his first ever) on his way to pick her up. Iracy and her mother finally got to Rio by bus only to find the sister alive and well and wondering what all the fuss was about. Two or three similar incidents involving phone false alarms took place, and Iracy even hired a private detective to track down the mystery caller, but without success.

Worst of all, however, were the *despachos*, which kept coming in a variety of forms. One day, four passport-sized photos of Iracy appeared on the living-room floor, folded and sewn up with thread. Each photo had been taken in a different year, and Iracy could not recall where they had been kept. Then it was the *patuás*. These are small leather pouches closed by pulling a thread around the top, popular with Brazilians for keeping things like coins or buttons in. These began to turn up all over the place, even out of doors. One made its way into Iracy's bed and was found to contain a live cockroach. Another fell out of Nora's dress in full view of her aunt (one of several relatives and friends who gave us supporting testimony on this case). When they did not contain live insects, they would contain disfigured photos of Nora's husband, or brief messages telling him that Nora was running around with another man. This she vehemently denied, and there was never any evidence that she was.

Altogether, it was clear that somebody, or something, was trying to drive the whole family out of its mind. But who? There were two possible deceased suspects: an ex-boyfriend of Iracy's who had committed suicide, and an elderly aunt who had died somewhat neglected by the rest of the family and might have borne a grudge against them for abandoning her. There was also a possible suspect from the land of the living. Iracy, we learned, had had a brief affair with a man who, unknown to her, was already married. Had his wife learned of this, she might well have gone to a *quimbanda* centre and ordered a *trabalho*. Then there was the possibility that this was case of a *trabalho* rebounding on the person who had originally ordered it, whoever that may have been.

Perhaps it was just as well that we did not know all this background until after we had been to the house and got to know the family. All we knew to begin with was that there was a poltergeist disturbance in a house in Ipiranga, and the family involved wanted help. So IBPP research director Suzuko Hashizume and I went along to see what was going on and what if anything we could do about it. We had no idea what to expect.

Suzuko decided to take the first night's vigil herself. She arrived at the modest house, a twenty minute taxi ride from her own home in the centre of São Paulo, at 9.35 on the rainy evening of October 18th, 1973. As soon as she stepped through the door, she was greeted by Iracy with the news that she had only just missed the latest happening.

'Wait a minute,' said Suzuko, 'I'll go and put my umbrella in the bathroom.' She went through the kitchen into the house's only bathroom, left her open umbrella there to drip on the floor, and hung her raincoat on the back of one of the kitchen chairs.

'Mother had just folded Antonio's bedclothes, pyjamas, sheets and blankets,' Iracy began. Antonio was her fiancé, who had taken to sleeping on the downstairs room's sofa lately at the request of the family, since Nora's husband was away and they felt safer with a man in the house.

'Then she came down to cook my dinner,' she went on, 'and suddenly we heard a noise upstairs. We went up to see what had happened, because whenever we hear a noise we always go up and see that everything is where it should be and nothing has caught fire.' She spoke in a matter-of-fact tone, as if it were quite normal for things to be out of place or to catch fire. In that house, it was.

'Well,' she continued, 'when we got upstairs, Mother asked if I had already taken Antonio's things downstairs. I said I hadn't, and she said she had left them on the clothes basket. So we started looking for them, and they turned up on the upstairs balcony. It was raining, and they were all soaking wet.' The interesting part of the story was that Nora had almost certainly been out of the house at the time the clothing was moved. She came home at 10.25 and immediately offered some of her own bedclothes to Suzuko, who had been intending to use Antonio's. The women had a cup of tea, Nora and Iracy going up to bed at eleven, while Suzuko settled down to watch TV after spreading her card alphabet on the floor in case the poltergeist would like to send a message across the ether. She sat through a film, and by 12.30 a.m. was on the verge of dropping off to sleep, for she had worked her usual full day at the office and was very tired.

At that moment, loud bangs from upstairs shook her into full wakefulness. Instantly, she switched on her recorder, only to find that it would not work. Kicking herself for not having tested it beforehand, she took it apart and found one of the batteries had been inserted back to front, a thing she could not recall ever having happened before.

Fifteen minutes later, with the recorder working normally, there were more thumps, followed at two further fifteen-minute intervals by more outbursts, including one that sounded like hand-clapping. It is normal for Brazilians to clap hands when calling on houses that have no bells, but not at that hour.

Suzuko managed to get to sleep at about 3.15, waking up three hours later when Mother began to make breakfast in the kitchen next door.

The first thing Mother found when she opened one of the kitchen cupboards was Suzuko's raincoat, neatly folded inside it. She immediately called for Suzuko to come and see, which she did, having the presence of mind to take a photograph before touching her coat. Then she went into the bathroom and found her umbrella had vanished. It turned up in the small yard outside the kitchen door, still open and surrounded by the family dog and her three little puppies, none of which had made a sound all night, even during the banging. Nothing else unusual happened, and Suzuko went straight to the office for another day's work.

That night, it was my turn. I arrived in the early evening with Hernani Guimarães Andrade and his son Sergio, and we spent some time making a detailed drawing of the whole house and yard, photographing everything that had been damaged by fire, checking the wiring and the plumbing and having a general look round. Then we sat down to wait until 12.30, to see if Suzuko's experiences would be repeated.

They were not, and Hernani and Sergio went home at 1.30, leaving me in the kitchen reading Frank Podmore on poltergeists. Podmore, one of the ace investigators of the early days of psychical research, seemed to think they were all due to hallucination or trickery. No doubt he was right, I thought, as I finally turned in on the sofa at 3 a.m. [2]

I had a few mild heart attacks when the very noisy cuckoo clock above my head chirped the half hours, which showed me how much louder ordinary noises sound at night.

It was no longer night but broad daylight, however, when Mother got up and went out for the bread and milk. This would have been about 5.15 and there were already traffic noises in the street. Just around 5.30, I decided nothing was going to happen, and drifted into that pleasant state in which you know you will drop off to sleep after all.

Then it started.

The timing was uncannily perfect. The banging had started the night before just as Suzuko was dozing off, and now the same thing had happened to me, but five hours later. Somehow, I managed to switch on my tape recorder in time to record Iracy opening her bedroom door, coming half way down the stairs and asking me if I had heard the bangs.

Had I, indeed?! They were not the kind of bangs anyone could sleep through. They had shaken the whole house. To me, they had seemed to come from the lighted passageway outside the two upstairs bedrooms, but Iracy later swore they sounded to her as if they had been made downstairs. I was unable to count them, but there must have been five or six. Iracy went back to bed and I struggled to wake up properly.

One minute later eleven deafening bangs resounded again from upstairs. They sounded like someone thumping the wooden floor with a broom handle, although nothing vibrated and they seemed to echo more than they should. I checked that the recorder was working properly and that nobody had switched the batteries round during the night. Then, three minutes later there were seven more bangs, followed almost at once by eight hand-claps, and at 5.40 no less than fifteen shattering thuds as if somebody was not sure if they had already managed to attract attention. Each set of bangs sounded slightly different, though they all came from roughly the same direction. It struck me at the time that Nora could have made them herself, and later I discovered a heavy pair of shoes under her bed.

At 6.02, Mother opened the door of Nora's room and spoke to her. She assured me later that Nora had taken a sleeping pill and had only just woken up. At once, the door was slammed violently in her face, almost hitting her. Tests I made later showed it was impossible to slam it so hard from the sitting position on the bed Nora swore she had been in at the time, and Mother agreed. If Nora was lying, this made Mother an accomplice, which I found a ridiculous hypothesis. That left only poor Iracy, and if the other two women were out to get her, why didn't they just kill her? It would have been far less trouble.

It was about then that I was reminded of the Sherlock Holmes story (*Silver Blaze*) in which Holmes draws Watson's attention to the curious incident of the dog in the night.

But, Watson had protested, the dog had done nothing. That, Holmes replied, had been the curious incident.

Here too the dogs, all four of them, had done nothing. This was very curious, since they had made a tremendous racket on my first arrival. Dogs are supposed to be sensitive to ghosts, yet this useless lot had snored through at least 45 loud noises in the early morning without making a sound. Could it be that all they had scented, seen or heard, was somebody well known to them? Somebody like Nora?

I was about to go to the bathroom when Nora came downstairs, and 1 stood aside to let her go first. She looked bleary-eyed and none too well. While she was in the bathroom, I noticed that two of the alphabet cards I had spread on the kitchen table had been moved.

The A and the C had been switched, the former being turned face down. Nora could have done it on her way to the bathroom, though Mother had been near, with her back to the table, and doubted this to be possible without her noticing.

Nora came out of the bathroom and I went in, to find my umbrella had moved from the shower rail where I had left it to a corner of the floor. Both women immediately assured me that they had not touched it. When I came back into the kitchen, two more cards, H and Y, had been turned over.

The cards were on a rather sticky oilcloth, and flipping them over as one passed was not at all easy, as I found by experiment.

We had coffee and rolls, sitting away from the table at my request. I explained to the women that one could sometimes make contact with poltergeists by talking to them, or even 'thinking to them' as Sir William Barrett had once managed to do, getting certain numbers of knocks in reply. [3]

While we were discussing this and generally moving around the kitchen, the letter D turned itself over. Had I not taken several photos of the cards I would never have noticed this, for at one point Mother opened the yard door to give the dogs their breakfast, whereupon they all rushed into the house to have a sniff at me. In the ensuing confusion, with three people trying to catch four lively dogs (Iracy was still upstairs), the letter D fell to the floor, though this might well have been done by mother dog's front paw looking for a piece of bread.

Suzuko arrived at 9 a.m. as planned. (It was Saturday.) We spent an hour recording deliberate handclaps and bangs on Nora's bedroom floor, made with a broom handle by everyone in the house in turn including ourselves. They all cooperated willingly, Nora proving by far the weakest thumper. Then we had them all do handclaps, and again Nora's were extremely feeble. Even I, an experienced concertgoer, was unable to make noises anything like as loud as those on the tape. While we were all banging away, I noticed that several objects in the living room vibrated, whereas I had noticed earlier that they had not done so when it was the poltergeist doing the banging.

We hoped that it would be possible to study our tapes to see if there was any difference in the acoustic patterns of our normal raps and those made by the poltergeist, which sounded much the same to us apart from this difference in the vibrations (or lack of them) that accompanied them. Many years later, this was finally done, with intriguing results. They may have sounded similar, but on chart paper they did not look at all similar. [4]

I went home for a good day's sleep, and Suzuko took the next night watch. She arrived at five to ten, finding Iracy and her fiancé downstairs watching TV, while Mother and Nora were already in bed. Almost at once there were four or five raps from upstairs, and Suzuko dashed up into the front bedroom, finding both women already installed in Nora's double bed (her husband was still travelling, and in fact I never met him) but still awake. This again established that if Nora was making the effects, Mother was an accomplice. There was another single outburst of raps just after 1 a.m., but otherwise it was an uneventful night, except for the fact that cards B and T were found turned over in the morning.

On my second night watch, I was given a display of furniture moving. After a quiet evening I got off to sleep at about three, and woke up just after seven as Iracy let herself out of the front door to go off to work. As soon as her friend's car had accelerated out of hearing, I heard a loud series of bumps, and a small upholstered footstool came bouncing down the stairs into the room where I was still lying on the sofa, though wide awake.

Grabbing my camera, I was fiddling with the light meter when Nora appeared on the staircase asking what had happened. I asked her not to touch the stool, and she went back into her bedroom. Had she opened the door of the back bedroom, where the stool had been kept on top of the wardrobe, the sunlight would have lit up the hall, stairs and part of the living room. That footstool had been thrown through a closed door.

Less than a minute later there was a loud crash in the yard. Mother gave a startled cry and exclaimed that it was going to be 'one of those days'. Out in the yard we found a heavy drawer full of clothes from the back bedroom had flown out of the window and landed all over the dogs; even this had not made them bark. Several other objects had ended up in the yard during the previous months, and I suppose dogs can get used to anything in time.

I managed to record this noise on tape, and going over it later I decided that for Nora to have thrown the drawer would have called for an impossible degree of speed, timing and subterfuge, for after the second crash she immediately came out of her own room again to see what was going on.

The following night, Suzuko slept in Nora's bed, at Nora's own request. There were no bumps, and the furniture stayed where it was, but in the morning, Suzuko was lying in bed wide awake when Mother came in to get something from a drawer. Suddenly, Nora's pillow shot from under her head, passed over Suzuko's, and landed on top of her tape recorder on the floor. Nora had made no movement at all, but immediately woke up and asked where her pillow was. Later, we made tests with the light foam pillow and found it could be flipped quite a distance with one hand, but not without making an easily noticeable movement.

Things quietened down after that, and the only strange occurrence for the next four nights was the appearance of a broken soapstone door-knob, which fell to the floor of the upstairs hall early one morning, only seconds after Suzuko had silently removed the thread she had fixed to Nora's bedroom door, the other end being tied to a small bell hanging down in the living room. Nobody could recall ever having seen such an object, and the knob is now in the IBPP's rapidly growing collection of poltergeist souvenirs. This includes several items of burned clothing and almost all the objects transported during the Paraguay affair, except the jeep.

On my next visit, I took a chance, and told Nora outright that I thought she was responsible for the phenomena; all of them. I did not suggest she was doing them on purpose, but that she was being controlled by a spirit and being made to do them in a state of instantaneous dissociation or trance. This was a lot of nonsense, or so I thought at the time, but it seemed the only way to make it clear that Nora was to be watched without offending her and losing the family's confidence.

Nora took the suggestion quite calmly, and Iracy agreed to keep a special eye on her whenever there was a happening in the future. Both Iracy and Mother assured me that several phenomena had taken place in the past when Nora had been out of the house, and indeed the most serious incident of all had happened when the house had been entirely empty.

This had been the outbreak of fire inside the closed wardrobe which had destroyed a great deal of Iracy's clothing, and had the family not returned in time to put it out, the whole house might well have gone up in flames.

The Thing certainly knew all the tricks. All seven of the IBPP researchers who visited the house at some time or other agreed that there was an intelligence behind it. Its sense of timing was too good to be natural. We noticed that things would usually happen just as people were dropping off to sleep or waking up. The early morning was the usual time for furniture moving, while the bumps were mostly at night and outbreaks of fire could happen at any time, day or night. According to Iracy, the usual sequence of events would be knockings followed by dislocations of objects, and finally outbreaks of fire. Sometimes there would be total peace for days or weeks on end, and then it would all start again. There seemed to be a tendency for phenomena to be more serious in cold weather, though nights are cool most of the year in São Paulo, which is about 2400 feet above sea level.

Once we were satisfied that the Ipiranga poltergeist was real, we took steps to get rid of it. This is a service not always provided by researchers, but the IBPP was an all-Spiritist affair and regarded the welfare of its subjects as part of the job. Soon after the end of our eight-night vigil, we set about assembling a team of mediums to come to the house.

This took time, and meanwhile the family, which was getting desperate, called in a local Catholic priest.

The priest was an amiable fellow who came and spent about an hour talking about football before wandering around the house and waving his arms in the air without much enthusiasm. This kept PK-15 quiet for all of three days, after which it burned one of Nora's peignoirs to ashes and set fire to the underside of the foot end of Mother's mattress for the third time and while she was asleep.

Finally, the IBPP managed to get a team including four mediums together, and a prayer session was held one evening in the kitchen. I could not help being impressed by the willingness of the mediums to come to the help of a family in distress unknown to them. All four had full-time jobs, yet gave up their evening without hesitation and, I need hardly add, without a fee. The chief medium, head of the centre frequented by many IBPP members, had a heavy cold and should have been home in bed. Nevertheless, she took charge of the meeting, saying she felt some hostile influence around but failing to incorporate it. She asked her spirit guides to help persuade it to leave, telling us that it might not leave at once, and might make one final defiant outburst before doing so.

There was total peace for two weeks after this, longer than there had been for several months, but then trouble began again. It was nothing compared to what the family had been through in the past, but this time they decided they could stand it no more, and called in the *candomblé* father-in-sainthood who appeared to have been mainly responsible for restoring peace to the Rua Agassis boarding house. This had remained quiet for fifteen months. He seemed to know what he was doing, so it seemed worth seeing if he could do whatever he did again.

The man duly arrived with his 'heavy mob' of helpers who tackle really tough cases, and for several days the family was subjected to powerful bouts of incense burning (during one of which they had to leave the house so as to be able to breathe) and assorted exhortations from the mediums. Their leader assured us that this was a particularly heavy case of black magic at work and might take some months to clear up. There was no incident for at least three months after the *candomblé* exorcism. Then, in January 1974, Iracy got married and moved out, and we heard no more from Ipiranga.

We heard plenty more, however, from elsewhere in the Poltergeist Zone.

Andrade, the Spiritist scientist; Father Carlos, the Catholic professional exorcist; and the young *candomblé* father-in-sainthood had one view in common. They were convinced that poltergeists are the result of black magic, except where the premises rather than the people are being haunted and in Brazil, it seems, it is invariably the people.

'In every single case of person-directed poltergeist activity where I have been able to study the family background,' said Andrade, 'there has been evidence that somebody in the house could be the target of revenge from a spirit. It may be a former lover who committed suicide, a jealous relation, a spiteful neighbour, or even a member of the same family bearing some trivial grudge. Any Brazilian is well aware that this country is full of backyard *terreiros* of *quimbanda* (black-magic centres), where people use spirit forces for evil purposes.

'You can use a knife to cut bread or to cut a man's throat,' he added, 'and so it is with the hidden powers of the mind; they can be turned to good or bad ends, though they remain the same powers. To produce a successful poltergeist, all you need is a group of bad spirits prepared to do your work for you, for a suitable reward, and a susceptible victim who is insufficiently developed spiritually to be able to resist. Black magic is a really serious social problem in Brazil, and we must find reliable ways of getting rid of it.'

This is a view not widely shared in the parapsychology community, where there much talk of 'exteriorised energy' from the subconscious mind of the epicentre, or victim. This is, of course, a hypothesis and not an explanation, and Andrade was fond of pointing out that there was a serious flaw in it. Poltergeists are capable to expending large amounts of energy, sometimes even lifting heavy weights that no normal human could lift, yet there is never any sign of energy loss among those around whom the action takes place – sometimes, we have seen, for months or even years.

While the Ipiranga case was still active, the IBPP managed to look into two other particularly sinister cases, each of which introduced a new refinement into the art of haunting. One, which took place in the suburb of Guarulhos, is one of the strangest I have ever come across, and luckily also one of the best witnessed and documented. It is described in the next chapter.

The second, in the town of Mogi das Cruzes, was nothing less than one of attempted murder. This is something poltergeists are not supposed to do, according to most authorities. Such a claim can no longer be made, for in this case not only was a house totally wrecked, but several attempts were made on the life of a baby.

After narrowly escaping death by burning more than once, the baby simply disappeared after a particularly violent outburst of poltergeist activity. Hearing stifled cries coming from a basket of dirty clothing the desperate father rushed over to find his baby entirely buried under the clothes in the process of suffocating to death. The family had to abandon the house after all the furniture had been damaged by fire and even the roof had been pounded to pieces by the furious spirit. The place looked as if a bomb had gone off inside it, and the baby, which had not yet learned even to crawl, was lucky to be alive.

Cases such as this one suggest that poltergeists can be as evil in their intentions as mortals, although fortunately for us latter they seem to need certain very precise conditions in which to carry them out.

Sometimes, however, their demands for such conditions are met, with fatal results.

# 6

# THE PSI UNDERWORLD

IN December 1965 a respectable Catholic family in the small town of Jabuticabal, 220 miles from the city of São Paulo but within the borders of the state of that name, was first visited by one of the most persistently malevolent poltergeists in history. First, pieces of brick began to fall inside the house, apparently from nowhere, although there was a pile of similar bricks out in the back yard. The family decided that someone was playing tricks with them. But nobody could suggest who, or how, and the phenomena went on for several days, until it became clear that if anybody was throwing the bits of brick, it wasn't anybody visible. So the family appealed to the local priest, who duly came and went through his traditional ritual of exorcism, with much arm-waving and prayer-intoning. The phenomena immediately became much worse.

'The gravity of any formal exorcism only excites their merriment, and they treat it as of no account,' says Allan Kardec, referring to what he calls disorderly spirits, or what we would now call poltergeists. 'The majority of them,' he goes on in his usual didactic and precise style, 'seem to have no other object than that of amusing themselves, and to be rather reckless than wicked.' Had he visited Brazil, he might have thought otherwise.

Though the Jabuticabal family had not read Kardec, they did have a neighbour, a dentist named João Volpe, who knew his Kardec very well, for he had been trained and oriented by Cairbar Schutel, one of the pioneers of the Spiritist movement in Brazil. The Catholic family turned to a Spiritist as a last resort as they so often do.

Volpe came over to his neighbours' house on December 21st. He soon decided that a quiet and pretty eleven-year old named Maria José Ferreira who was living in the house with the servants, was a natural medium and was unknowingly enabling the phenomena to take place. He immediately offered to take the girl into his own home, keep her under observation, and do what he could to treat the problem. For a few days all was quiet, but then stones began to fly around the Volpe house whenever Maria José was around. The bombardment became so intense that Volpe was finally able to count a total of 312 stones of all shapes and sizes, one weighing no less than 3.7 kilos.

Then the disorderly spirits began to throw eggs around. They became so fond of this that before long it was impossible to keep an egg intact in the house. One day, a dozen eggs were placed on the egg rack inside the refrigerator. Out in the yard, Volpe's granddaughter was feeding the chickens, when she suddenly noticed three eggs underneath one of them. This would be quite normal, except that it was a cock and not a hen, as were all the others she was feeding at the time. Back in the kitchen, it was found that there were only nine eggs in the fridge, although nobody had opened the door.

Stones kept on falling at all hours. One Sunday the Volpes went to lunch with their next-door neighbours. During the meal, a stone descended from the ceiling and split into two about four feet from the ground, the two parts proceeding in different directions as they fell to the floor. One of the women present immediately picked up the two pieces of stone and noticed that they fitted together like pieces of a three-dimensional jigsaw puzzle. Moreover, they seemed to snap together as if magnetically attracted to each other. The stone was passed around the table, and everybody noticed the strange magnetic effect, which soon weakened and disappeared.

Next door, at the Volpes' home, Maria José was getting quite accustomed to the behaviour of her unseen playmates. She found that she only had to ask them for a flower, a piece of candy or some other small object, and hey presto, it would appear at her feet. On one occasion, a stone appeared out of the air, tapped three people gently on their heads, and fell to the floor. All three people concerned stated that it was as if they had been struck by a 'ball of compressed air' rather than a stone.

This is an interesting observation. Stones thrown by poltergeists rarely hit people directly. (On rare cases where physical harm has been reported, I would like to make sure the blow was not a result of a stone rebounding off a wall or other surface.) Some think that the human bio-magnetic field acts as a sort of defence barrier against missiles from hyperspace, while others assume that the poltergeist doesn't really want to hurt anybody, but just to attract attention the way bad-tempered children do, by flinging anything within reach as far as possible. The latter hypothesis was popular in Kardec's time, but I prefer the former.

When a poltergeist really loses its temper - watch out. For a few days, nothing serious happened to or around Maria José. João Volpe gave her special treatment in his private study, where on two occasions stones appeared in the presence of him and a doctor colleague. One landed with considerable force on a writing desk, shattering its glass cover. Phenomena also took place in the open air; on one occasion as Volpe and a friend were walking along the street with Maria José, the girl suddenly mentioned that she would like a little brooch for herself, whereupon one fell at her feet. Shortly afterwards, Maria José was pelted with sugar-apple fruits while she was out in the yard. The fruit had been inside a bag in the house. Then stones would fall onto her plate while she was trying to eat her meals. The spirits still retained a certain sense of humour: Maria José was trying to pick a guava from a tree in the garden, but found she could not reach it. So she asked Mrs Volpe to pick it for her, and as she stretched out her hand, the guava simply vanished.

Then one day all hell was let loose, and for almost three weeks a succession of plates, glasses and even heavy flower vases was flung about the house in all directions, until the Volpes had no unbroken crockery left at all. Invisible hands began to slap Maria José on the face or the bottom, leaving clearly visible bruises. The spirits began to bite her all over her body. They threw chairs at her, and even a large sofa. A gas cylinder was wrenched away from the wall and hurled in her direction. Pictures jumped off walls and flew from one room to another. On one occasion, two witnesses actually saw a glass dish from the kitchen and a mirror from the bedroom cross in mid air before heading for bedroom and kitchen respectively.

Attempts were made to suffocate Maria José by forcing cups or glasses over her mouth and nose while she was asleep. There are indications that they also tried to violate her, though the poor eleven-year-old's descriptions of such attempts were none too precise. Next, about forty days after the initial outburst of brick-throwing, they began to attack her with needles.

It was always her left heel. Needles would simply appear thrust deep into the girl's tender flesh, even while she slept with her shoes and

socks on, and sometimes even while she was out walking. On one occasion, no less than fifty-five needles had to be extracted at the same
time. When her heel was bandaged, the bandages would be wrenched
off without the knots being untied.

On March 14th 1966 Maria José caught fire. She was eating her
lunch at school when her clothing suddenly began to smoulder from a
round burn that had appeared as if from a cigar-butt. The same afternoon, the Volpes' bedroom burst into spontaneous combustion, and
while João Volpe was ripping the bedclothes off the burning mattress,
he burned his hand quite badly on the pillow, which had caught fire
inside (as was reported at Suzano) without his noticing.

Maria José stayed with the long-suffering Volpes for about a year.
The phenomena eased off somewhat, but never stopped altogether for
long. Finally, Volpe took her to Chico Xavier's Spiritist centre in Uberaba, which serves as a kind of final court of appeal for really tough cases
involving spirit possession. In front of Chico, Brazil's most respected
and trustworthy medium, the obsessor came through and announced:
'She was a witch. A lot of people suffered and I died because of her.
Now we are making her suffer too.'

The Volpe's home circle gave the girl all the intensive treatment they
could, with special prayers and appeals for help from their spirit guides
in addition to repeated magnetic passes over her body. They managed
to do away with the really serious attacks, such as those with needles,
but the spirits refused to stop throwing things around, especially fruit
and vegetables. They had come to stay.

Maria José's life came to an unexpected and tragic end.

When she was thirteen, she went back to live with her mother, and
one day in 1970 she was found dead. She had apparently committed
suicide by taking formicide mixed with a soft drink, dying almost at
once. The psi underworld had finally claimed her. [1]

I took the file back to the IBPP office, where I found research director Suzuko Hashizume and secretary Virginia Bressan at work putting
a new file together in their usual neat and thorough way, with tran-
scripts of taped interviews, press clippings, background material and
investigators' field reports.

Hernani Guimarães Andrade was drafting a letter to his French colleague Emile Tizané, a retired police officer who had spent much of his
life investigating poltergeist phenomena in France.

'Well,' he asked me, 'what did you think of the Jabuticabal case?'

'Very interesting,' I replied. 'But why do these things only seem to happen to uneducated teenagers in remote rural areas? Haven't we got any good black magic going on here in São Paulo?'

Hernani opened a drawer of his file cabinet. 'Here,' he said, 'take a look at this one. It's still being investigated - and the person concerned lives just around the corner.' Now, from the researcher's point of view, who would be the ideal witness for a case of black magic? A Roman Catholic would be preferable to a Spiritist, since the latter would be predisposed to believe in it. A trained psychologist would be even better, somebody with such qualifications ought to be able to find rational explanations for the phenomena, or at least would try to find them.

I read through the file and decided it was too good to be true. Then I made arrangements to meet the person involved, and I soon decided it could be true. The young woman, whom I will call Marcia, struck me as a sensible and well-balanced person. With her Catholic upbringing and master's degree in psychology, she did not seem a likely candidate for a black magic curse. However...

At the end of May 1973, when she was twenty-eight, Marcia went for an outing with her aunt Elma during which they went for a stroll along one of the many beaches that make up the 'Brazilian Riviera' either side of the port-city of Santos. As they walked along the edge of the calm ocean, Marcia caught sight of something lying in the sand, just beyond the reach of the waves. It was a small plaster statue of a woman, about six inches high, and most of its paint had been washed off by the waves that must have lapped around it at high tide. Marcia thought it would make a nice ornament for the apartment in São Paulo she shared with another young single woman. She stooped to pick it up.

'Better leave it where it is,' Elma warned. She recognized it as a statue of the sea goddess Yemanjá. It was a long time from August 15th or New Year's Eve, Yemanjá's two traditional feast days, but somebody had evidently been making a private offering to her out of season. The statue was her property, like the white flowers that would have been thrown into the sea along with a request of some kind.

Catholic psychology teachers have no time for superstition. 'How can a statue do any harm?' Marcia said, as she picked it up. Elma said nothing. She was not a Spiritist or an *umbandista*, but she had heard about people who interfered with those ceremonies ...

Marcia took the statue of Yemanjá back to her apartment. Although the sea had washed most of the paint off, it still had one blue eye, a skin-coloured area around the lower right jawbone and neck area, and smaller patches on each arm and on the back at about the level of the right lung. It made an attractive ornament. She propped it on the mantelpiece and promptly forgot about it.

A few days later she was violently sick with food poisoning after eating a piece of chocolate. This had never happened before, although chocolate was a normal part of her diet. Hardly had she recovered from the initial effects of the poisoning, when she began to lose weight rapidly and feel generally run down. She became pale, her skin taking on a greenish-yellow tinge. She began to lose her memory and to find difficulty in relating to her work, surroundings, and friends. Her colleagues at the faculty where she taught asked what was wrong, but Marcia said it was just the after-effects of food poisoning and would soon pass.

Then she had a haemoptysis; spitting blood from the lungs or bronchial tubes. She went to a local clinic for X-rays and a thorough check-up. The first X-ray, taken on July 4th 1973, showed a patch in the right lung that could mean tuberculosis. She was given a Mantoux test for allergic reaction to the TB bacillus and a sputum test which came out positive, meaning that she did indeed have a form of TB. Nothing paranormal about that, but what was rather unusual was that within five weeks she was pronounced free of the disease, which usually takes a year or longer to treat and can often be fatal.

The doctor told her to have a good rest, and Marcia went to stay with her parents in the small town 300 miles from São Paulo of which her father had once been mayor. The little statue of Yemanjá stayed on the mantelpiece of her apartment.

A few days after her return from a two-month stay in her peaceful hometown, Marcia's pressure cooker blew up in her face, showering her with boiling beans and water. She suffered second-degree burns on both arms and on the right side of her face and neck. She was rushed to a first-aid post for treatment, and spent the next few days resting at home.

Then the gas oven exploded. There were three people in the kitchen at the time, when a sheet of flame shot out of the lower part of the stove, which was unlit, directly towards Marcia, as if it were trying to reach her. Marcia immediately fetched a plumber who took the stove apart and could find no explanation for the incident, in which the door of the oven had been blown open suddenly, although the spring-hinge was new and strong. Marcia decided to trade it in for a new one, just in case…

A few days later, a friend visiting São Paulo from her home town told her that at about the very moment her pressure cooker had exploded, her photograph had jumped off the wall of her parents' home. There had been no wind, the string had not broken, and the nail had not fallen out of the wall. The photograph had simply jumped to the floor.

Every good psychologist knows that coincidences will happen, but to Marcia there were getting to be too many of them. A friend mentioned that her statue of Yemanjá might have something to do with them.

'Nonsense,' she replied. 'How can a statue do anything?' She gave her friend a lecture on the principles of behaviourist psychology, in which she had been trained and taken her master's degree, and which she now taught at a university faculty in São Paulo.

'Behaviour is something that depends on external forces,' she explained. 'I can only evaluate what I can really see. Any interior, or non-observable event is not relevant. There cannot be any relation between a statue and a burn or a dose of TB.' The textbook phrases came tumbling out. Behaviourism, the school of psychology founded by J. B. Watson, reduces a human being to a mere object situated between a stimulus and a response. It explains such crucial life situations as whether or not a woman accepts an invitation to lunch, but it does not explain the appearance of a Michelangelo. Arthur Koestler, in *The Ghost in the Machine,* calls it 'flat-earth psychology'. The behaviourist B. F. Skinner has made the earth-shattering discovery that the mind does not exist and suggests that so-called mental events should be ignored or rejected.

Still on her best behaviourism, Marcia decided that her TB had been brought on by her lack of resistance after the period of food poisoning. The pressure cooker explosion was bad luck, the oven incident was just another incident. These things happen.

They went on happening. While Marcia and her flat-mate were crossing the busy street outside their apartment building, the flat-mate dropped the car keys. As Marcia bent to pick them up, the lights changed and cars roared past her on both sides as if on the first lap of a Grand Prix, missing her by inches. As she crouched on the road, she had a sudden impulse to commit suicide by flinging herself in front of a car, but she managed to fight it off and eventually reached the safety of the island in the middle of the road.

Some time later, as she was opening the window of her 15th-floor apartment, she again felt an impulse to kill herself. 'It was like a voice inside me saying "go on, throw yourself out",' she told me. Again, she was able to resist; one wonders whether some cases of suicide are the results of such impulses felt by people without the self-control to ward them off.

Marcia eventually did what Brazilians tend to do in the situation she was in. Casting aside her Catholic upbringing and her behaviourist education, she headed for the nearest *Umbanda* centre. As it happened, her flat-mate knew a good one.

What finally made up her mind to take this drastic step was the strange experiences she began to have at night. She had never had sleeping problems before; her busy schedule and the racket of São Paulo, one of the world's noisiest cities, usually made her drop off as soon as her head hit the pillow. But now it was different. She would feel strange sensations around her that kept her awake all night. Her bedroom would be full of - the only word she could find was 'presences'. She felt herself being touched all over the body, and one night came the ultimate horror, the phenomenon known to occultists as incubus.

The dictionary says this is an evil spirit that descends on sleeping women and has sexual intercourse with them. The dictionary may be right.

Understandably, it took some time and much tact to get the details, which Marcia only gave when we had convinced her that the IBPP never reveals the true identities of its sources without their consent.

To a suggestible and frustrated single woman, an ordinary erotic dream could easily be mistaken for an incubus. Marcia, however, is neither suggestible nor frustrated, and old enough to know the difference between an erotic dream and something else. It is slightly unusual for an attractive and intelligent woman in her late twenties to remain unmarried in Brazil, but Marcia was one of the new generation of *brasileiras* who were reacting against centuries of male domination and making careers for themselves in many professions.

She gave us a straightforward account of the facts. She had, she said, felt the sensation of complete coitus. She had felt the weight of a body on top of hers, and the 'presence of a male organ', in her own words, inside her. She had never been able to identify the face of this entity, but could clearly recall her efforts to push him away. The experience had taken place for several nights in succession, and had only ceased after she had been treated by a Spiritist from her home town who had unexpectedly turned up one day when she was staying with her parents and told her she needed help.

The director of the *Umbanda* centre in São Paulo listened to Marcia's story and immediately told her that hers was a straightforward case of a *trabalho* (hex) being put to work on her, in revenge for her unlawful removal of the statue. (At the insistence of her flat-mate, Marcia had mentioned the statue episode and brought it along to the centre).

It was only at that point that Marcia realized that she had been afflicted in some or other parts of her body that corresponded to the remaining patches of paint on the image of *Yemanjá*. The burn marks on her arms, face and neck matched closely; the patch on the back was just about where her first X-ray (which I examined and showed to a radiologist who knew nothing of her case) revealed a lesion in her right lung. True, the statue still had a piercing blue eye, and Marcia would rather not think about what that might have led to.

The *Umbanda* medium told her to take the statue back at once to the spot on the beach where she had found it. This she did at the first possible opportunity, and after two months of treatment at the centre her problems went away and her life returned to normal.

Recalling her three months of torment almost a year later, she took a very matter-of-fact approach to the whole business. Previously, she told me, she would not have been able to accept the fact that observable events could be caused by the mere presence of a small plaster statue. Now, she was prepared to admit that they could. It was as simple as that. Marcia is no longer the behaviourist psychology teacher she was, though it must be said that her rational attitude while the phenomena were taking place may well have saved her from a much worse fate.

Moral: Be careful what you pick up on Brazilian beaches.

My second close encounter with a poltergeist took place on September 24th 1974, in a rural area near the small town of Carapicuiba, half an hour by train from São Paulo. I read about it in one of São Paulo's more sensationalist newspapers, and thought it sounded worth checking out. The paper did not give an address but did mention that the local police had been called in to investigate repeated outbreaks of stone-throwing that had been causing damage to roofs and a good deal alarm to the people who lived under them. So I headed for the police station, where I was lucky to find the officer who had been sent to the scene, and was able to tell me how to get there. 'This case sounds more like your job than ours,' he told me when I had explained what our institute was and what we did.

I had difficulty in finding the house, since I only had the street name and not the house number, but posing as a roof repairer I made some enquiries along the way and found that nobody had heard anything about a roof being damaged, even as it turned out the people living nearest to the houses affected. Finally I came to an isolated group of six small houses near the end of the built-up part of the road, on the edge of open countryside. They all showed clear signs of having been pelted with stones and bits of brick. Several thick roof tiles were broken, some were missing, and some clean new ones had obviously been fitted recently as replacements.

The house nearest the road (which was completely deserted except for a dog or two) had a large concrete block on the roof, which had shattered three tiles. A woman was washing clothes in the next door yard, and as I arrived, and before I had even had time to introduce myself, she pointed to the block and told me it had fallen at that very moment, or certainly less than a few minutes previously. A promising start to the case, I thought, and wondered if there was more to come.

As I soon found, there was.

There was a pile of similar concrete blocks near the road, and the only position anybody human could have thrown it from was on the road along which I had been walking for more than five minutes, meeting nobody on it at all. It was a sparsely populated area on the side of a hill, and you could see for several hundred yards in all directions. The older children were all in school a mile away, and after we had recovered the block I asked the largest child around to see how far she could throw it. She couldn't even lift it. I calculated that to throw it from the pile by the road, some thirty feet, would have needed great strength, not to mention a motive.

The bombardment, according to the newspaper report, had been going on almost daily for more than three weeks. The six families involved agreed that nobody visible could have kept it up that long without being caught, especially as the police had been out and searched the area and the residents themselves had mounted a kind of makeshift home-guard system, keeping watch in all directions.

Less than ten minutes after my arrival, as I was standing talking to two of the women on the open ground between their houses, I had a closer encounter than I hope to have ever again. It was so sudden that it was a few moments before I realised what had happened. A hail of stones or pieces of brick had fallen at terrific speed out of a cloudless blue sky, rebounding off the roof of one house on to another at a lower level. I cannot say how many stones there were; I had the impression that they had fallen all around me, and I clearly saw a small puff of tile dust as a projectile struck the roof directly in my line of vision about ten feet from where I was standing. A small piece of broken tile landed at the feet of the woman I was talking to. I picked it up at once; it showed signs of having been recently broken. Whatever had broken that tile would easily have done the same to our skulls.

The two women and I scanned the area, and decided that the nearest house in the line the bombardment appeared to have come from was too far away to be a normal source. It was a good hundred yards up the hill on the other side of the road, and there was no sign of life anywhere near it.

This incident was enough to satisfy me that something inexplicable was going on, and I promised to come back with as many of my IBPP colleagues as I could round up as soon as I could. So a day or two later a carload of us containing Hernani Guimarães Andrade, Suzuko Hashizume, Carmen Marinho and me arrived, with our cameras and tape recorders, ready to collect what testimony we could, and we were able to meet and question all six women from the houses affected.

They were all thoroughly bewildered and frightened by the bombardments. Nobody had been hit directly, though one had been struck on the leg by a stone that had rebounded off the ground. One couple had been inside their house by the open door when a stone had whizzed past their noses as they faced each other a few feet apart.

One house, we discovered, seemed to have been attacked more than any of the other five. There were still more than twenty pieces of broken brick and tile on the roof. Would there, we asked, be a teenage girl living there? Sure enough, there would, and she was fetched out to say hullo to us. She was a plump and amiable girl, belonging to a family of Protestants who had no time for the spirits, and there seemed to be no reason why anybody would want to attack her.

Indeed, after careful and tactful questioning from Hernani, who had a remarkable ability to inspire trust in people of all ages and social backgrounds, we could find no evidence that anybody, living or dead, had any reason to terrorise this group of what seemed to be completely normal, honest and decent people. We asked them to get in touch if the trouble continued, which they promised to do but never did, so we concluded that this was one of those cases that just end themselves without any help from anybody.

Another short-lived case turned up just down the road from where I was living in São Paulo in 1974. It involved a very respectable and apparently happy Catholic family with two lively teenage boys. One of them was walking upstairs one evening when he saw an arm disappear into a bedroom. He was alarmed, thinking it must be a burglar, and even more alarmed when the whole house had been searched and everybody realized it could not have been anybody incarnate. The boy stuck to his story after prolonged interrogation from both his parents and myself.

There had been phenomena typical of poltergeist activity, I was told. A mirror had fallen from a wall, a light bulb had left its socket and fallen to the floor at an angle of about 45 degrees, a stiff tap had turned itself on within earshot of the whole family, a heavy door had opened just before somebody reached for the handle, and a table lamp had had a sudden fit of the shivers in a draughtless room. But on the whole this was rather a half-hearted poltergeist, and I managed to find possible normal explanations for some of these incidents, but not that of the boy's vision of a human arm. This had seriously upset him for a week, and nothing could shake his story. He saw a human arm, period. As at Carapicuiba, I asked the family to let me know of any further incidents, which they never did, so I wrote this off as another of those 'come and go' cases.

Sightings of disembodied limbs are rare in poltergeist cases, but they were a regular feature of one of the most unusual of the many cases investigated by the IBPP. It was especially unusual even by Brazilian standards, and any account of it could easily be mistaken for the scenario of a very low-grade horror film. For the limbs repeatedly seen by several witnesses were definitely not human.

While I was busy on the Ipiranga case described in the previous chapter, Hernani was equally busy with a new case that had come to light in the suburb of Guarulhos. He showed me some photographs he had taken on his first visit to the house affected. They were of chairs and sofas that had been slashed as if by a knife. They looked familiar to me.

'That's the work of a coati,' I said. A coati (*Nasua rufa*) is a Brazilian relative of the North American raccoon, notable for its alarmingly long claws, which it likes to keep sharp by scratching anything scratchable in sight, such as your favourite armchair or sofa. They can be domesticated, up to a point, if you don't mind having your furniture destroyed. A neighbour of mine in Rio de Janeiro had managed to tame one, and had plenty of scratched furniture as a result. The marks on her sofa looked exactly like those in the photos from Guarulhos.

As I learned more about the case, it became clear that this was no ordinary poltergeist, or indeed any ordinary coati. Nor was the family affected typical. Marcos, a successful builder, and his wife Noemia were evangelical Christians, as were his parents Pedro and Judite who lived next door. There was no obvious candidate for an epicentre who could be held responsible for the activity. The oldest child was only four.

Several members of the family concerned described having seen the slashes being produced. And that was not all they reported. Pedro gave a very precise description of what he saw:

'It was like a vision, but I was wide awake with my eyes open and I saw the hand and arm of an animal, a very big and strong one. Very sharp claws 14 to 15 centimetres long, curved, black and shiny. Short red fur, like a cougar's. If I could draw, I could draw the hand perfectly, but I can't.'

In the house next door, Noemia also had an alarming vision:

'I was doing some sewing on the machine when I felt a shiver, and I looked round and saw the cuts appear on the mattress, and an animal that looked like a gorilla. It gave me goose bumps and I felt awful.' She was telling a neighbour about this a day or two later, and then the neighbour saw a hand as well and fainted on the spot.

Then money started to go missing, as did two door keys, and stones began to fall on the roof, a regular part of the Brazilian poltergeist repertoire. Then the physical attacks began. One night at around 3 a.m. Marcos woke up suddenly finding that he had a cut on his arm, which was beginning to bleed. Noemia also woke up in time to catch a glimpse of some kind of animal beside the bed, but could not describe it in any detail. Then she was also scratched on the face, and the little daughter of a visitor had quite a nasty cut on her leg. Pedro next door was also cut on his face. Before long, the invisible beast was cutting everything in sight, sheets, blankets, clothing and even a pair of sandals and a wallet, as well as people. It also began to smash things and to start fires. It seemed about to embark on the entire repertoire of poltergeist trickery.

Moving house was no help. Marcos got a big plumbing job in the nearby town of Taubaté and rented a temporary house there, sending Noemia to stay with relatives while he was away. In his new house, two of his Bibles were slashed to pieces, and money kept disappearing. It usually came back, often turning up in the most unlikely places such as under a mattress. On one occasion he actually saw a bundle of notes drop on to the bed. Some plates that had gone missing in Guarulhos were found under the bed in Taubaté. A fire broke out inside his bag of tools. His wallet was found hanging from the ceiling light, well out of reach from the floor. And so on.

Marcos then built himself a new house, and it was not long before the poltergeist moved in along with Noemia and her two daughters, now aged four and two. It all began again – fires, stones, cuts and scratches, money disappearing and alarming signs that the two little girls were suffering incipient obsession, though fortunately only briefly. Marcos repeatedly held prayer sessions in the house, but as he noted rather sadly, this only seemed to make things worse.

Then there was a rather disturbing incident. One day, while Noemia was alone in the house, two women turned up out of the blue, asking if they could use the toilet and if they could have a glass of water. One of them, she noticed, was carrying a plastic bag with some candles and cuttings of rosemary in it.

One of the mysterious visitors said they had been sent to bless the house because something was not right. They refused to say who had sent them, and seemed determined to get inside the house. Noemia managed to get rid of them, but they said they would be back.

A couple of weeks later they were back, again when Noemia was on her own. One of them produced a piece of cake, saying she had brought it for her and the children. Noemia declined the offer, and once again refused to allow the uninvited women into the house. They had arrived by car, and she noticed that they had parked too far away for her to read the number plate. Soon after they left, she found a couple of her kitchen knives under bed, placed in the form of a cross.

Marcos did not like the sound of all this, and began to suspect that somebody was doing a *trabalho* against him, although he could not think who would want to do such a thing. So once again he appealed to his church for help, and another prayer meeting was held in his house, which seemed to have some effect.

Hernani took a special interest in this case and spent a great deal of time on it, visiting the family seven times and recording several hours of interviews with Marcos, Noemia and Pedro. His final report ran to 76 pages, making this one of the most thoroughly investigated cases of its type on record. While it was going on, he managed to fit in another investigation of a case alarmingly similar to the Guarulhos one.

This took place in the home of a Protestant family in the Vila Libanesa district of São Paulo, where two eleven-year olds described being scratched by what they could only call 'a hairy animal with huge claws'. There were also numerous instances of inexplicable outbreaks of fire.

In 1984, eight years after his sixth visit to Guarulhos, Hernani went back to see how things were. It was now more than ten years since the trouble had started in 1973, and it seemed that they had finally ended after a service conducted by members of the Assembly of God church, apart from one or two brief outbreaks of small object movements and money disappearances, and a vision of what Noemia took to be Satan, in the form of a hideously deformed human being who luckily did not reappear.

Marcos told Hernani that he was sure somebody had cursed him, and the only possible suspects seemed to be two of his former girl friends, the mother of one of whom was suspected to be involved in some kind of magic practices.

And so yet again we find evidence that poltergeist phenomena are linked to the vengeful intentions of departed earthbound spirits. This is the interpretation that Brazilian Spiritists would prefer. Yet it does not account for the fact that poltergeist cases in other countries – and they have been recorded all over the world for centuries – do not as a rule show signs of the same linkage. In the case with which I am most familiar, which took place in the north London suburb of Enfield in 1977-78, my colleague Maurice Grosse and I never came across any indication that anybody, living or dead, had any motive for making the lives of the family affected a bewildering misery, although many of the phenomena we observed and recorded at Enfield were much the same as those I had come across in Brazil. Why this should be is a question best left to anthropologists, and it is not one I can answer here.[2]

Indeed, there is little we can say about poltergeists except that the effects attributed to them are real. I did not hallucinate that shower of stones at Carapicuiba, or the loud bangs I recorded at Ipiranga, or the heavy armchair at Enfield that slid along the floor and flipped over backwards in front of my eyes.

These things do happen, and pretending they don't merely postpones investigation. Not only do they happen, but they represent a challenge by providing clear evidence that there is more to physical reality than is dreamed of by most professors of physics, with one or two honourable exceptions, and they remind us that there is still plenty we do not know about the world (or worlds?) we live in.

Researching this extended reality is not easy, as Macbeth found when he was trying to get some hard evidence for that 'unknown power' out of those prophetic witches, as I mentioned in my Introduction. On the whole though, I think I can claim that I was a good deal more fortunate than he was. I may never have seen a flying cow, but I saw quite enough of unknown powers in action to know that exist. And that, for me, is reason enough to 'seek to know more'.

# POSTSCRIPT

## IN MEMORIAM, 2011

I N 1974, when I began to write the original edition of this book, I hoped I was making a modest contribution to the history of psychical research by recording the achievements of the IBPP – the small group of enthusiastic and unfunded amateurs headed by Hernani Guimarães Andrade who, in little more than a decade, had laid the foundations for what he intended to be a permanent institute that was to do for Brazil what the Society for Psychical Research had done for Britain: establish psychical research as a valid and strictly scientific field of enquiry.

Yet it was not to be. Whereas the SPR has survived and is still going strong 130 years after its foundation, the IBPP was wound up in 1982 after less than twenty years of existence, and thirty years later there was no sign of any successor. So I find myself unwillingly writing an epitaph for that small band of explorers who showed how much evidence for the anomalous side of human experience there is to be found if anyone takes the trouble to look for it.

Was it worth it? Speaking for myself, very much so. Despite worldwide interest in such mysterious subjects as poltergeists, mediumship, psychic surgery and reincarnation, relatively little effort has been made outside a handful of countries to collect first-hand evidence for them and preserve that evidence for posterity. It has been done most successfully in Britain, Germany, France, Italy and the USA, yet in many parts of the world such work has barely begun. Brazilians may be surprised to know that the IBPP archive, modest as it may be when compared to that of the SPR, was able in a relatively short time to become one of the half dozen or so largest in the world. I am very pleased to have been able to contribute to it. [1]

It would be unfair to claim that psi research in Brazil ground to a permanent halt in 1982. The fact that the Parapsychological Association chose to hold its 2011 convention in the southern Brazilian city of Curitiba is a sign that Brazil is well established as a member of this international community. The PA has members from thirty-six countries, the Brazilian contingent being the sixth largest after those of the five countries mentioned above. At the 2010 convention, Brazilian delegates gave talks on Kardec and the development of Spiritism, and on the neuroimagery of the mediumistic trance, one of the speakers being Dr Julio Peres, whose parents Ney and Maria Julia were founder members of the IBPP.

There has also been some progress in the study of psychic surgeons, of which Brazil has produced several more in addition to those I have described. The best known of these were Edson Queiroz, who was somewhat unusual in that he was a fully qualified doctor, whose highly unorthodox surgical techniques were observed and well described by anthropologist Sidney M. Greenfield of the University of Wisconsin, who managed to follow up some of the operations he witnessed; and João Teixeira de Faria, better known as João de Deus (John of God), whose career has been documented by Australian visitor Robert Pellegrino-Estrich. [2,3]

Among the few Brazilians who have managed to witness psychic surgery and report on it in detail are São Paulo psychologist Margarida de Carvalho and a team headed by psychiatrist Alexander Moreira-Almeida of the University of Juiz de Fora which included veteran American parapsychologist Stanley Krippner. The authors make it fairly clear that they are only scratching the surface of the wealth of medical mystery yet to be uncovered in the world of the Brazilian psychic surgeon. [4,5]

An impressive public demonstration of psychic surgery was given by Edson Queiroz at the 'Psi Tage' conference in Basle, Switzerland, in 1986 when he performed three operations in a well lit hall in front of several hundred spectators. All of them involved cutting of the skin with what looked like an ordinary surgical scalpel, with no kind of anaesthesia or sterilisation, less bleeding than one would expect, and all three patients clearly remaining fully conscious throughout. Five weeks later, the doctor who had supplied the patients testified that there had been no complications or side effects. It was too soon to claim permanent cures, yet in the case of the man who had had a lipoma removed from his arm, it was quite clear that it wasn't there any longer. There could be no question, at least on this occasion, of any of the sleight of hand tricks allegedly (and in some cases undeniably) performed by less reputable surgeons. To ascribe all psychic surgery to trickery, as some diehard sceptics continue to do, is an allegation that is becoming increasingly hard to support, especially in view of the abundance of video recorded evidence such as that of Sidney Greenfield, with its close-ups of knives slicing through unanaesthetised skin and even an electric saw cutting through bones. [6]

In this book I have concentrated on the fieldwork, yet I should not give the impression that the IBPP neglected the theoretical side of the coin. Hernani's extensive writings on his theories of spirit and matter and how they interact, and his laboratory experiments deserve a book to themselves, by somebody better qualified for the task than I am.

To give some idea of Hernani's views of the nature of the composition and workings of the 'psi' world. I would like him to have the last word here, hoping that my translation does it justice. It is adapted from his first book, *The Corpuscular Theory of the Spirit* (1958) published five years before the formation of the IBPP, in which he argued convincingly that if there were such a thing as a psi or 'spirit' world, as his extensive field research was to suggest, it must have some kind of structure and it must obey laws just as our familiar physical world does. He also put forward the idea that living beings are influenced by the past history of their species, an idea similar in many respects to that of 'formative causation' proposed entirely independently some twenty years later by Rupert Sheldrake. [7]

# APPENDIX

# PSI MATTER

## HERNANI GUIMARÃES ANDRADE

I T has often been observed that the phenomenon of life seems to disobey the Second Law of Thermodynamics, which states that energy may only be transferred in one direction (from hot to cold or from an upper to a lower level), and that our physical universe shows a constant tendency towards entropy or disorganization. It is in effect running down like a clock of which the key has been lost. (This law was, of course, never intended to apply to 'open systems' or 'living matter', and is mentioned here only for purposes of analogy.)

This universe of ours seems to have begun as a huge agglomeration of particles in a state of intense movement, containing zones of considerable energetic imbalance. Some of these still exist today, for some parts of the universe are much hotter than others. Physical matter has transformed itself by natural laws into ever more stable structures, as it has come into contact with lower temperatures and caused all of our various chemical compounds to come into existence - always by a process of energetic degradation. When we come across organic molecule formations that show a high degree of energy accumulation, we have to assume that there must be an energy source capable of form¬ing them, such as ultra-violet rays or a state of high temperature or pressure.

Yet, in the face of this state of steadily advancing chaos, with all forms of energy doomed to disperse in a downward direction, we have the fact of life. This behaves in just the opposite manner, like a swimmer making good progress against a strong current. Rather than tending towards total entropy, life heads resolutely in the other direction - towards coherence, harmony and evolution. Life is negative entropy indeed.

Purely materialistic attempts to explain *the origin of life* collapse before the inexorable principle of increasing entropy. Materialists have to face the fact that there is a highly intelligent organizing principle at work in the protoplasm of living beings, which they cannot reasonably explain as being due to chance, or to the dialectical evolution of matter. In an influential textbook, The Origin of Life, A. I. Oparin has suggested that the life-principle is merely the product of natural selection at molecular level in the formation of colloidal aggregates, or coacervates. But if this were true, an extremely fortunate form of chance would have to intervene, leading towards an organization able to replicate itself indefinitely (until 'told' to stop) and set up a harmonious interdependence among its component parts. To ascribe the phenomenon of life to chance plus natural selection seems as unreasonable as to ascribe it to the mysterious properties of solar energy. Both these factors undoubtedly play an important part, but neither provides a full explanation.

The phenomenon of life has been with us for rather less than half the period of time that has elapsed since our Earth took its present shape. How life appeared, organized itself, and overcame all the many obstacles found in its path towards evolution in such a short time, is very hard to explain along purely materialistic lines, especially in our century when serious doubts have arisen as to exactly what 'matter' is in the first place.

It is not so much the high energy constitution and the astonishing asymmetry to be found in living matter that surprises us, as the perfection of organization that we can see in it, in which the aim of every separate function can immediately be identified. Living matter has an amazing ability to make use of every resource, every natural law, and every quality of substance, in order to carry out what appears to be a gigantic master plan, of which we are only able to perceive a few isolated details. Everything in the behaviour of living matter suggests the manifestation of *something that seeks and thinks* - in fact something that behaves intelligently, which inorganic matter does not.

Life creates order out of chaos, and there is no satisfactory materialistic explanation as to why this should be so. This fact becomes much less mysterious, however, if we admit the possible existence of an actual non-material component (the *psi component*) that guides living molecules along their predestined path.

Most biological phenomena take place thanks to the specific properties of protoplasm (which literally means 'the first mould'), the substance fundamental to all organized living beings. This is the level at which we find the three basic characteristics of living matter in operation: vitality, perception and intelligence. At this level, we also find these three factors associating themselves into a permanent state of coexistence.

How can we ascribe to physical matter the faculty of suddenly embarking upon a movement towards increasing organization (in defiance of the Second Law of Thermodynamics) only after reaching an advanced stage of molecular complexity? We know that proteins and nucleic acids form themselves according to natural laws and events. But what known law or event can explain the behaviour of these substances at the point where they reveal rudiments of intelligence, social collectivism, and discernment between what is useful for their growth and what is not?

We can provide a chemical explanation for the way a large organic molecule assimilates a substance that helps it to self-reproduce, and eventually to produce a whole colony of molecules. But the enigma remains: how do these molecules reach a state of association, after a certain number of attempts, that human social organizations are often unable to achieve even after considerable planning, experiment and thought?

We will make no progress towards an understanding of life unless we admit that an *extra-material principle* takes part in the process of forming living substance, a principle endowed with the same faculties that are reflected in the conduct of adult human beings. It is not being suggested that this principle intervenes ostensibly in the operation of the natural laws that govern physical matter, or that it replaces or contradicts such laws. It makes use of them, imposing an orientation and a determinism of its own, under which the laws of chance give way to the action of an intelligent will.

This principle, the *psi factor*, manifests itself as a source of order out of chaos; a plan of action with well-defined aims. We can go even further and suppose (without disappearing altogether into a cloud of metaphysical speculation) that the whole history of life on earth is only part of a long-term plan drawn up with a specific objective in view. What this objective may be, and who or what has it in view, are speculations better left for the time being to philosophers, theologians and mystics.

Two important features of living matter are the large size of its component molecules, and the constant presence in its composition of a high proportion of such low-weight elements as hydrogen, carbon, oxygen and nitrogen. The molecule is a homogenous whole, within which the different energetic levels of its component atoms combine harmoniously, by the process known in chemistry as valence.

The molecule is formed by what may seem to be blind natural forces, but once formed it adopts a distinctly intelligent course. As it moves around in its protoplasmic jelly, looking for the chemicals it needs in order to grow, it is already behaving, in embryonic form, much in the same way its end product will behave. Every reaction of its infinitesimal intelligence is a forerunner of the structural behaviour of the future organized and completed being. The autocatalysis of molecular substance is the first instance of the domination of matter by a living will, the start of a process that is to culminate in the desire to reproduce the species through the act of sexual love.

To explain the phenomenon of interaction between matter and the psi function or component, we must take some liberties with traditional concepts of physics, even those of modern physics with all its ambiguities and uncertainties. To summarise briefly:

The psi atom, the fundamental constituent of psi matter, consists of three principal particles: the *bion*, *intelecton* and *percepton*. These are (respectively) negatively, positively and neutrally charged as are the electron, proton and neutron of physical matter. Each contains a quantum (respectively) of vitality, intelligence and perception-memory.

The natural habitat of psi matter is a hyperspace of at least five dimensions, four of space and one of time. Psi matter interacts with physical matter on our plane by means of fields; the electromagnetic properties of physical matter and the *biomagnetic fields* of psi matter.

Psi matter is molecular in structure. Just as material atoms have affinities among themselves, enabling them to unite and form molecules, so do simple psi-atoms have the ability to originate combinations, or psi molecules. These are organized in a manner analogous to that of physical molecules, and from such organizations emerge the bodies of the psi world, including the *biological organizing models*. These originate in the biological process through the interaction of psi molecules with the organic molecules that enter into the composition of living tissue.

A biological organizing model (BOM) is formed by a succession of reincarnatory stages in a continuous process of evolution, or enlargement of its hyperform. A biological being is the result of a harmonious conjugation of physical and psi factors; the former contributing the phenomena of auto-catalysis, chemical selection and combination, enzymatic action, electrical and other processes governed by physical laws. The latter registers and preserves biological experience in its space-time structure, impressing its individuality on the living being and helping it to evolve by means of a rapid recapitulation of its entire experience.

Psi matter interacts with physical matter by a process of field attraction. Under the influence of a sufficiently intense field, the trajectory of the bions of the psi atom undergoes an alteration, which leads to a partial loss of the four-dimensional form of the bionic layers. In this way, the psi atom acquires a form that is intermediary between three and four dimensions. In the same way, its properties are altered, to assume the qualities of both the psi and the physical atom. This partial loss of one dimension causes the appearance of a field generated by the spins and orbits of the bion. (This is the biomagnetic field, or BMF mentioned above.) Once operating in our three-dimensional space, the psi atom behaves much like a physical one, except that it is never wholly in three dimensions. Its bions and nuclei are only partially deformed, and the field origin¬ating from the spins of its bions will vary in proportion to the extent of this partial deformation.

The mutual influence between electro- and biomagnetic fields in the neighbourhood of physical matter will lead to constant deformations in the bionic layers of psi atoms, leading to their frequent magnetic polarization. The greater or lesser number of bions in the layers around psi elements will determine their greater or lesser susceptibility to magnetic polarization.

Both bion and electron are energetic charges that can originate a magnetic field. Both are also susceptible to alterations in their kinetic state whenever they are in the presence of a variable magnetic field. In such a situation, an electron will immediately change its orbit and start to move in a direction almost perpendicular to that of the field which has disturbed it. Just as a physical atom sets up a magnetic field of its own when it is submitted to the action of a magnetic field, so does a psi atom, when it is close to physical matter. Its bions suffer the influence of the three-dimensional field, altering their orbits accordingly in order to become partially operative in three-dimensional space.

When a psi atom becomes thus polarized, a biomagnetic field is set up, and the psi atom becomes operative as an intermediary between psi and physical matter, enabling the formation of bodies that show properties common to either type of matter. This is not to suggest that full interaction of physical and psi worlds is always possible. The most likely *plug-in* stage is that of the living molecule, which is a very large object compared to a single atom. This is the point of departure for the process of individual organic growth, so it seems the logical stage for the plugging-in of the psi factor.

The term *plug-in* is used deliberately. The psi-factor does not interpenetrate physical matter, strictly speaking. It merely exercises an influence over it by means of the interaction of the respective fields. Such interaction is not always total. Plug and socket must fit each other, as in the case of household appliances. Let us examine four possible situations:

First, we have the case where a physical molecule is much smaller than a psi-atom, and gives off a low-intensity magnetic field. In this case, the molecule will exercise a barely perceptible influence on the psi-element, and the physical substance involved can hardly be said to be 'animated'. Molecules of low atomic weight come into this category, such as those of hydrogen and oxygen. Nevertheless, the weak action of the field set up by these molecules will serve to attract a certain number of psi atoms, to form a kind of layer of psi matter superimposed on the physical space occupied by the object in question. This layer is what is known as an aura, possessed by inanimate as well as animate objects.

In the second case, we have molecules of small volume but with a more intense field, such as those of mineral salts, copper, lead, and other minerals of high atomic weight These molecules, though small in volume, are made up of heavy atoms, and so have larger molecular weight, so the concentration of material mass in a small space will set up a stronger magnetic field. As in the first case above, polarization of psi atoms by such molecules as these is imperfect and unstable, and consequently there is again no 'animation'.

In the third case, we have molecules that are larger than the psi atom they attract. Here, there will be considerable action on the part of the molecule over the psi atom, but the latter will not be able to respond with equal intensity. Molecules such as those of haemoglobin and haemocyanin probably come under this category. They can be said to be animated up to a point, but their psi component is too small to exercise any detectable influence over them.

Finally, we have the case of a molecule and a psi atom of practically the same volume. Here we will have maximum interaction between the fields attached to each, with the psi component exercising its full influence on the molecule of physical matter, giving rise to an animated being of full autonomy and stability - a *biomolecule*, the basic unit of biological growth and the building block of living creatures.

As soon as the biomolecule comes into existence, it is guided along its evolutionary path by its psi component, the BOM, which carries in its perceptons a miniaturized memory-record of all previous processes of growth and association. The BOM directs the biomolecule into chains of nucleic acids and proteins, in an elementary lesson in social organization, with the DNA chain carrying the purely physical characteristics of its ancestors (condensed in the genes) along a sort of transspatial cable of information. The self-reproduction of the DNA chain and the synthesis of proteins through various catalysts lead to the first experience of cell division and multiplication. Next, the information contained in the particles of the psi atom causes embryonic organisms to develop cells that will eventually grow into organs needed to carry out the essential functions of the living species concerned.

This process takes place over and over again, with physical matter always obeying the same immutable laws, but with the psi factor constantly evolving, as it acquires new experience in its successive associations with physical matter. The history of evolution is the history of the progress of the psi factor. Physical matter does not evolve at all; what evolves is the psi matter that interacts with it and guides it. All forms of inorganic matter, and some rudimentary forms of organic matter, are much the same today as they always have been. Higher species of living beings, including *Homo sapiens*, are not.

The original biomolecules must have been formed at points along the chains of polypeptides that floated around on the waters, colliding with each other to form occasional spirals or skeins. As their joint material mass increased, they were able to attract and hold more and more complex psi elements through their biomagnetic fields, until the time came when a group of psi elements large enough to survive the process known as physical death was evolved. As millions and millions of rudimentary living beings were formed and destroyed on the stage of earthly life, long before recorded history, the psi-elements gradually grew into com¬pound formations that were finally able to animate what we would now recognize as a plant, an animal, or - much later - a human being.

Natural selection and the fight for survival undoubtedly guided all early forms of life, as they still do to some extent, enabling the psi component to guide them through the early stages of evolution. We have literally had to learn and remember everything from scratch. Prehistoric biological organizations must have originated from combinations of proteins and nucleic acids, thereby forming nucleoproteins similar to our modern bacteriophages and viruses. Later, these learned to form themselves into associations, governed by the laws regarding colloids and coacervates, until they reached the stage of plasmatic organization of living matter.

Much has been achieved in the history of biological evolution, though there is still much more to be achieved. The time will come when psi matter no longer has any need for association with physical matter in order to evolve, and the human race will be transformed, like chrysalis into butterfly, into something else. Perhaps some human races have already undergone such a process.

Faced with any stimulus, an inanimate object invariably responds with a reaction based on inertia, impeding the action of the force brought to bear on it. This can be demonstrated by striking a brick wall with your bare fist. But a living being reacts otherwise. It uses intelligence in order to avoid a source of aggression, or at least to neutralize its effects.

If we saw an inanimate object behaving like a living being - if, for instance a tennis ball we were trying to serve repeatedly kept jumping out of the way of our racket and refusing to be served, we would have to assume that there was some intelligence attached to the tennis ball.

Tennis balls do not behave in this way, though they sometimes seem to, but something similar does happen every time the presence of polarized psi elements causes bits of physical matter to behave intelligently and overcome their natural inertia. Any mechanical stimulus applied to a biomolecule will provoke an immediate reflex in the psi element attached to it, and the latter will register the stimulus and react intelligently. Such a reaction will lead to an alteration of the orbits of the bions around their psi nuclei, which in turn will react by modifying the magnetic moment of rotation that relates them to the movement of the bions. These tiny alterations, added together, lead to rudimentary bionic currents that reveal themselves by almost imperceptible contractile reactions; the foundations of the characteristics of motility and irritability peculiar to protoplasm.

Originally surrounded by liquids, forming colloids and coacervates, and submitted to stimuli and movements of all kinds, biomolecules gradually stop being pushed around by the laws of chance, thanks to the infinitesimal intelligences that animate them. They become organized, contrary to the natural tendency of matter. They accumulate experience in their perception-memory banks, applying their elementary knowledge in their struggle to survive in hostile surroundings. They associate with each other through mutual interest, and progressively impress the physical matter that constitutes them with the characteristics of an organized being.

Behind all living matter there is a psi component, stimu¬lated and affected by all the various problems that arise from the experience of association with physical matter, known in the case of humans as incarnation. Physical matter itself is inert and passive, eternally subjected to the whims of blind chance, unable to accumulate experience as it is pushed or pulled from one composition to another. It is the psi component that moves steadily forward, unable to stagnate or mark time as it helps build increasingly complex organizations. The inexorable tendency towards total entropy, ultimate symmetry and maximum disorganization gives way to the organizing power of the psi factor, and its irresistible ascending dynamism. Instead of regressing to probable states as determined by the laws of thermodynamics, organic matter moves on to achieve the plasmatic state of living substance.

The psi factor has learned to play with nature's dice. It has taken advantage of the rules of nature's games in order to conquer life through its power of ideoplasty, or the shaping of ideas.

This ideoplastic ability takes two forms; one in the evolution of species and the other in the evolution of an individual human being. In the first case, it works towards the introduction of a systematic tendency towards progress for all living beings considered as a whole. It is the fundamental cause of the apparent purposefulness of evolution, under which living beings seem to be equipped in advance with organs, before they can be expected to know what to do with them, a fact that in itself points to the weakness of natural selection as a theory to account for the *whole* phenomenon of evolution, as Alfred Russel Wallace, one of its original proponents, himself admitted.

In the second case, the psi factor with its ideoplastic action plays the part of an *organizing model* for every cell, from the first division to the stage of adulthood of the being concerned. While the genes inside the chromosomes are at work inducing the *physical* characteristics of the future adult being and helping build its body, the psi factor is building up the mind, the component that is always to be in charge of its human complex.

Let us imagine that a man with no knowledge of electronics whatsoever is listening to his radio set one day, when it suddenly stops working for no apparent reason. If he is unable to call for expert assistance, what can the man do? He can start to dismantle the set, perhaps hitting it a few times in the fervent hope that it will start to work again as inexplicably as it stopped. Eventually, faced with a bewildering organization of valves, condensers, transformers, wires or printed circuits, he will conclude that this apparatus, which normally brings him the voices of the world at the touch of a button, has been planned and put together by people who knew what they were doing. He can shake or hit his radio as long as he likes, but it will probably not work again until it has been examined and repaired by somebody who knows how these things are made.

So it is with the human body, the most complicated machine there is. Our eyes are television receivers, our ears are sonic transformers, our brains are computers, our lungs are bellows, our hearts are hydraulic pumps, our nerves are telegraph cables, and so on. Did all this evolve by chance, or was it designed and created as radio sets are?

It is not being suggested here that the traditional sciences of genetics and embryology are in any way at fault; merely that they are not yet complete. A geneticist or an embryologist is in the position of somebody solving a crossword puzzle unaware of the obvious fact that somebody set the puzzle in the first place, and that the solution already exists. We can enjoy doing crossword puzzles without knowing anything about who set them, but we need to know far more than we do at present about the source of logical will that first set the puzzle of life. Putting the pieces in place is not enough; we need to know how and above all why the puzzle was first set.

It is quite possible that science will soon produce living beings in the laboratory by artificial methods. This will no doubt be hailed as a great achievement, and Nobel prizes will probably be awarded on the strength of it. But it will be worth remembering that this memorable feat was first achieved by nature millions of years ago, without the aid of human intelligences, Nobel prize winners, research grants, or the availability of any desired equipment and raw material to order. How is nature supposed to have managed this feat unaided?

It is suggested here that there must be something interacting with all matter that is directly and solely responsible for the whole overall phenomenon of life and evolution. This is something of which we are all unconsciously aware, though we tend either to ignore its existence, or to classify it under the imprecise word *spirit*, the metaphysical and religious connotations of which have led to its rejection by science.

It is further suggested here that this 'something' is not an abstract concept, but a real substance with a composition of its own analogous to that of physical matter.

It is hoped that the psi matter hypothesis, outlined in brief here, will enable future researchers in many fields to take a new approach towards the solving of what still remains the greatest mystery in our mysterious universe – life.

# LIST OF
# REFERENCES

J/P(A)SPR 3 JOURNAL/PROCEEDINGS OF THE
(AMERICAN) SOCIETY FOR PSYCHICAL RESEARCH.

## INTRODUCTION

1   McGregor, Pedro, *Moon and Two Mountains*. London: Souvenir Press, 1966
    St Clair, David, *Drum and Candle*. Garden City N.Y.: Doubleday, 1971
    Gray, Isa, *From Materialisation to Healing*. London: Regency Press, 1972
    Dooley, Anne. *Every Wall a Door*. London: Abelard-Schuman, 1973
    Fuller, John G., Arigo: *Surgeon of the Rusty Knife*. London: Granada, 1975

2   Kardec, Allan, *The Spirits' Book*. Tr. Anna Blackwell. São Paulo: LAKE, 1972

3   Playfair, Guy Lyon, *Chico Xavier. Medium of the Century*. London: Roundtable, 2010

4   Andrade, Hernani Guimarães. *Science and Spirit*. London: Roundtable, 2010

## PART ONE

### Chapter One: PEIXOTINHO

1 Medhurst, R.G. (ed.) *Crookes and the Spirit World*. London: Souvenir Press, 1972

2 Ranieri, Rafael Americo, *Materializações Luminosas*. São Paulo: LAKE, 1955

3 Lodge, Sir Oliver, PSPR 17 (43) 1902, p.45

4 Romanelli, Rubens, Interview, IBPP, São Paulo, 1972

5 Barrett, Sir William, PSPR 31 (79) 1920, p.28

6 ----------------------- PSPR 34 (92) 1924, p.292

7 Boechat, Newton, Interview, IBPP, São Paulo, 1971

8 Beloff, John and Playfair, Guy Lyon, JSPR 59 (832) 1993, pp.204-6


### Chapter Two: MIRABELLI!!

1 De Goes, Eurico, *Prodigios de Biopsiquica Obtidos com o Medium Mirabelli*. São Paulo: Cupolo, 1937

2 May C.Walker, JASPR March 1934, pp.74-8

3 E.J.Dingwall, JSPR June 1961, pp.80-2

4 Medhurst, R.G. (ed.) *Crookes and the Spirit World*. London: Souvenir Press, 1966

5,6 T. Besterman, JSPR December 1935, pp.141-53
E.J.Dingwall, JSPR January 1936, p. 170

7 E. Feilding et al. PSPR 23 (59), 1909, pp.309-569

8 Murphy, G. and Ballou, R, (eds.) *William James and Psychical Research*. New York: Viking, 1960, ch.7

9 Besterman, T. Letter to the author, November 7, 1973

10 Driesch, H. Letter to W.H.Salter, November 28, 1928, SPR archive.

11 Imbassahy, Carlos, *O Espiritismo à Luz dos Fatos*. Rio de Janeiro, FEB, 1935

12  G.L.Playfair, JSPR January 1992, pp.201-3; G. Stein, *Fate*, March 1991, pp.86-95

G.L.Playfair and G.Stein, JSPR October 1992, pp.407-9

## Chapter Three: OTÍLIA DIOGO

1  *Edição Extra*, São Paulo, October 25th, 1963

2  *O Cruzeiro*, Rio de Janeiro, January 18th, February 1st, 8th, 15th, 1964
   *ibid.* October 27th, 1970

3  *ibid.* October 27th, 1970

4  *ibid.* December 29th, 1970

5  Aksakov, A. *Animismus und Spiritismus*, Leipzig, 1890

6  Jorge, Moacyr, *Arigó, a Verdade que Abalou o Brasil*. São Paulo: Edicel, 1964, pp.183-200

## *PART TWO*

## Chapter One: PSYCHIC SURGERY

1,2  Sherman, Harold, Wonder Healers of the Philippines. London: Psychic Press, 1966
    Fuller, John G., Arigó: Surgeon of the Rusty Knife. London: Granada, 1975

3  Playfair, Guy Lyon, If This Be Magic. 2nd ed., Guildford: White Crow Books, 2011

## Chapter Two: ARIGÓ

1  Pires, J. Herculano, *Arigó: Vida, Mediunidade e Martirio*. São Paulo: Edicel, 1970

2  Comenale, Reinaldo, *Zé Arigó, a Oitava Maravilha*. Boa Imagem, Belo Horizonte, 1969

3  *Revista International de Espiritismo*. Matão, September, 1972, p.324

4 Rose, Louis, *Faith Healing*. Gollancz, London, 1968

5 Pires, op. cit.

6 Fuller, John G., *Arigo: Surgeon of the Rusty Knife*. London: Granada, 1975, p.188 and letter to author, January 3rd, 1974. See also: *Psychic*. San Francisco, October, 1973 (Puharich)

### Chapter Three: ANTONIO SALES

1 *O Cruzeiro*. Rio de Janeiro, December 1st, 8th, 15th, 22nd, 1971

### Chapter Four: LOURIVAL DE FREITAS

1 Dooley, Anne, *Every Wall a Door*. London: Abelard-Schuman, 1973, chs. 6-11

## PART THREE

### Chapter 1: THE IBPP

1 Andrade, Hernani Guimarães, *Science and Spirit*. London: Roundtable, 2010, pp.77-134

### Chapter Two: LUIZ AND CELIA

1 Letter, JSPR March 1972, pp.51-2

### Chapter Three: BORN AGAIN?

1 Andrade, Hernani Guimarães, *Reborn for Love*. London: Roundtable, 2010

### Chapter Four: OBSESSION

1 Bezerra de Menezes, A. A Loucura sob Novo Prisma. Rio de Janeiro: FEB, 1946

2   Interview, *Conocimiento de la Nueva Era*. Buenos Aires, April/June 1964, pp.96-100

3   1 Corinthians 15, verse 44

4   *Mundo Espírita*, Curitiba, November 30th, 1973

5   St.Clair, David. *Drum and Candle*. Garden City: Doubleday, 1971, pp.218-27


## Chapter Five: THE POLTERGEIST ZONE

1   Andrade, Hernani Guimarães, *Science and Spirit*. London: Roundtable, 2010, pp.15-76

2   F. Podmore, PSPR 30, June 1896, pp.45-115

3   W.F.Barrett, PSPR 64, August 1911, pp. 377-412

4   B. Colvin, JSPR April 2010, pp. 85-6


## Chapter Six: THE PSI UNDERWORLD

1   Report by João Volpe for the IBPP Archive. All other cases mentioned in this and the previous chapter are from original reports now in the IBPP archive.

2   Playfair, Guy Lyon, *This House is Haunted*. 3rd ed. Guildford: White Crow Books, 2011


## POSTSCRIPT. In Memoriam 2011

1   The archive, now in São Paulo, can be seen by arrangement with Suzuko Hashizume (florliz@uol.com.br).

2,3   Greenfield, Sidney M. *Spirits with Scalpels*. Walnut Creek, CA: Left Coast Press, 2008
Pellegrino-Estrich, Robert, *The Miracle Man. The Life Story of João de Deus*. Author, 2001

4,5   Carvalho, Margarida de, JSPR January 1995, pp. 161-7 and JSPR October 1996, pp.243-50

Moreira-Almeida, Alexander et al. *Journal of Shamanic Practice* 2 (1), 21-31, 2009

6   Educational Communications Dept., University of Wisconsin (Milwaukee).

7   Sheldrake, Rupert, *A New Science of Life*. London: Blond & Briggs, 1981

# INDEX

# Paperbacks also available from
# White Crow Books

Leo Tolstoy—*My Religion: What I Believe*
ISBN 978-1-907355-23-3

Leo Tolstoy—*On Life*
ISBN 978-1-907355-91-2

Leo Tolstoy—*Twenty-three Tales*
ISBN 978-1-907355-29-5

Leo Tolstoy—*What is Religion and other writings*
ISBN 978-1-907355-28-8

Leo Tolstoy—*Work While Ye Have the Light*
ISBN 978-1-907355-26-4

Leo Tolstoy with Simon Parke—*Conversations with Tolstoy*
ISBN 978-1-907355-25-7

Vincent Van Gogh with Simon Parke—*Conversations with Van Gogh*
ISBN 978-1-907355-95-0

Howard Williams with an Introduction by Leo Tolstoy—*The Ethics of Diet: An Anthology of Vegetarian Thought*
ISBN 978-1-907355-21-9

Allan Kardec—*The Spirits Book*
ISBN 978-1-907355-98-1

Wolfgang Amadeus Mozart with Simon Parke—*Conversations with Mozart*
ISBN 978-1-907661-38-9

Jesus of Nazareth with Simon Parke—*Conversations with Jesus of Nazareth*
ISBN 978-1-907661-41-9

Thomas à Kempis with Simon Parke—*The Imitation of Christ*
ISBN 978-1-907661-58-7

Emanuel Swedenborg—*Heaven and Hell*
ISBN 978-1-907661-55-6

P.D. Ouspensky—*Tertium Organum: The Third Canon of Thought*
ISBN 978-1-907661-47-1

Dwight Goddard—*A Buddhist Bible*
ISBN 978-1-907661-44-0

Leo Tolstoy—*The Death of Ivan Ilyich*
ISBN 978-1-907661-10-5

Leo Tolstoy—*Resurrection*
ISBN 978-1-907661-09-9

Michael Tymn—*The Afterlife Revealed*
ISBN 978-1-970661-90-7

Guy L. Playfair—*If This Be Magic*
ISBN 978-1-907661-84-6

Julian of Norwich with Simon Parke—*Revelations of Divine Love*
ISBN 978-1-907661-88-4

Maurice Nicoll—*The New Man*
ISBN 978-1-907661-86-0

Carl Wickland, M.D.—*Thirty Years Among the Dead*
ISBN 978-1-907661-72-3

Allan Kardec—*The Book on Mediums*
ISBN 978-1-907661-75-4

John E. Mack—*Passport to the Cosmos*
ISBN 978-1-907661-81-5

**All titles available as eBooks, and selected titles available in Hardback and Audiobook formats from www.whitecrowbooks.com**

Lightning Source UK Ltd.
Milton Keynes UK
UKOW041838131112

202156UK00001B/384/P